YO-BRK-663

Critical Essays on
American Postmodernism

CRITICAL ESSAYS
ON
AMERICAN LITERATURE

James Nagel, General Editor
University of Georgia, Athens

Critical Essays on
American Postmodernism

edited by

STANLEY TRACHTENBERG

G. K. Hall & Co. / New York
Maxwell Macmillan Canada / Toronto
Maxwell Macmillan International / New York Oxford Singapore Sydney

G. K. Hall & Co.	Maxwell Macmillan Canada, Inc.
Macmillan Publishing Company	1200 Eglinton Avenue East
866 Third Avenue	Suite 200
New York, New York 10022	Don Mills, Ontario M3C 3N1

Library of Congress Cataloging-in-Publication Data

Critical essays on American postmodernism / edited by Stanley
  Trachtenberg.
     p.   cm. — (Critical essays on American literature)
  Includes bibliographical references and index.
  ISBN 0-8161-7324-9
    1. American fiction—20th century—History and criticism.
  2. Postmodernism (Literature)—United States. I. Trachtenberg,
  Stanley. II. Series.
  PS374.P64C74 1994
  813'.54091—dc20   94-26333
                                      CIP

Printed in the United States of America

for
Jane Israel Trachtenberg and Peter Benjamin Trachtenberg

Contents

◆

General Editor's Note

◆

This series seeks to anthologize the most important criticism on a wide variety of topics and writers in American literature. Our readers will find in various volumes not only a generous selection of reprinted articles and reviews but original essays, bibliographies, manuscript sections, and other materials brought to public attention for the first time. This volume, *Critical Essays on American Postmodernism*, is the most comprehensive collection of essays ever published on this elusive movement in American letters. It contains important theoretical statements by Gerald Graff, Philip Stevick, Ihab Hassan, and Barry Chabot, discussions of genre by David Kaufmann and Ellen G. Friedman, and reprinted articles addressing individual writers by John Johnston and David Cowart. In addition to a substantial introduction by Stanley Trachtenberg, which offers the best overview available of postmodernism, there are also three original essays commissioned specifically for publication in this volume, new studies by Bob Donahoo on science fiction, Stacey Olster on Susan Sontag, and Victoria Aarons on Grace Paley. We are confident that this book will make a permanent and significant contribution to the study of American literature.

JAMES NAGEL
University of Georgia, Athens

Publisher's Note

◆

Producing a volume that contains both newly commissioned and reprinted material presents the publisher with the challenge of balancing the desire to achieve stylistic consistency with the need to preserve the integrity of works first published elsewhere. In the Critical Essays series, essays commissioned especially for a particular volume are edited to be consistent with G. K. Hall's house style; reprinted essays appear in the style in which they were first published, with only typographical errors corrected. Consequently, shifts in style from one essay to another are the result of our efforts to be faithful to each text as it was originally published.

Introduction

STANLEY TRACHTENBERG

Despite its by now widespread acceptance, writing about postmodernism has always been made difficult by a lack of agreement about what the term refers to. Is it, theorists have asked, a period, a style, a philosophy, a concept, an aura, a method, an attitude, a way of representing things or of questioning their legitimation? The term has been applied variously to a body of writing, a style of architecture, a manner of photography, to linguistic or grammatical change, to movies, television, clothing, furniture, and to social and political as well as critical theory. In short the paradigm of postmodernity can be derived from culture as well as aesthetics where writers, artists, and critics alike have come to question not only our ontological condition or even the rational process by which we attempt to apprehend it, but, as though it were an entity independent of its origins, the condition of art itself.

Perhaps because of this breadth of reference, the term "postmodern" itself has encountered considerable resistance and been adopted only with great reluctance.[1] One of those who confesses some dissatisfaction is William Spanos, who in a widely quoted essay, questions the metaphysical Western literary tradition that the term evoked. In the early seventies Spanos helped to found *boundary 2*, "a journal of postmodern literature," with the idea of rejecting what he regarded as the hegemonic intent of Western thought and the interpretative process of causal relationships that sustained it, a process Spanos identified as characteristic of the detective story. Culminating in modernism, this tradition looked to recuperate meaning by coercing differences into an Aristotelian beginning, middle, and end. In this way it filled in the gaps between the world and our perception of it in an ordering and controlling strategy announced in T. S. Eliot's famous description of Joyce's method. In contrast, Spanos proposed a definition of postmodernism that resisted closure, that acknowledged temporal discontinuities and contingencies, and that emerged finally in the open-ended if stylized forms of the anti-novel.[2]

Perhaps the first question that arises in any definition of postmodernism is the degree to which it is continuous with if not, indeed, an extension of modernism. With significant exceptions like those of James Mellard and Barry Chabot, critical opinion has acknowledged a cultural rupture at least since the seventies that has divided the social practices no less than the aesthetic sensibility of the period from the modernism that preceded it.[3] Divided between the impulses of anarchy and order, modernism combined a sense of the autonomy of art with an avant-garde experimentalism intended to pave the way for social action. Though it hoped to unsettle bourgeois complacency by deliberately adopting a strategy of outrage or shock, modernism encouraged the artist to shore fragments of a tradition against a ruined culture seen as a wasteland. Yet, though it is to an aesthetic quality characteristic of modernist thought that Susan Sontag attributes the defining element of art, Sontag's work, as Stacey Olster shows, reveals an ambivalence about the relationship between aesthetics and ethics that finds in a constantly adaptive contextualizing of history a radicalism of style that blurs the boundaries between modernism and the postmodern.[4]

In one of the earliest appearances of the term "postmodern" in relation to American fiction, Irving Howe identified the emergence of a postwar generation that displaced the modernist avant-garde with a posture of conformity. Either in accommodation to this spirit or alienated from it, a generation of writers—Howe includes Norman Mailer, Bernard Malamud, Herbert Gold, J. D. Salinger, Nelson Algren, Wright Morris, and Saul Bellow— were unable to realize, which is to say convincingly dramatize, their subject of personal identity, often turning from direct representation to fable, prophecy, and nostalgia. "In their distance from fixed social categories," Howe concluded, "and their concerns with the metaphysical implications of that distance, these novels constitute what I would call 'post-modern' fiction."[5] Subject to a desire for immediacy, representation, in fact, tended to deny the individuality of the artist no less than the distinctiveness of the art itself. Along with a mode of irrealism, noted in pioneering works by Tony Tanner, Albert Guerard, and Robert Scholes, among others, the defining element of contemporary fiction, for Harry Levin, was a current of anti-intellectualism that contrasted with the values of intellect he saw as the triumph of modernism.[6]

After the conformity of the postwar era gave way to the political, social, and countercultural restlessness of the sixties, however, this mood in turn yielded to a more conservative nostalgia and the growing need to situate art within the public sphere, so that for most critics it was finally not possible to talk about the fiction of Barth or Barthelme or Coover or Pynchon or Sukenick or Sorrentino or Oates in the way one spoke of DeLillo or McElroy or Ozick or Paley or Carver or Beattie any more than one could speak of those writers in the way that one talks of Bellow or Updike or Hemingway or Fitzgerald or Faulkner or of those modernist writers in the way we once spoke of Dreiser or James or Twain.

In two essays that frame the 1960s and 1970s like bookends, John Barth alternately emphasized the used-upness of certain conventions of reality and the imaginative resourcefulness of writers in refashioning new ones. In the first of these essays, Barth described a literature—whose definitive spokesmen he took to be Beckett and Borges—that restored to the experiment of the modernist masters (Joyce, Proust, Kafka) a sense of narrative or mimesis by allowing art rather than nature to become the object of imitation. By having characters become readers or authors of the fictions in which they appear and so doubling or mirroring situations, Barth argues, these otherwise exhausted forms find a means to renew their possibilities.[7] A little over a decade later, Barth attempted to clarify his initial statement and account for the development of postmodern fiction. This time he cited Italo Calvino and Gabriel García Márquez as his two prime examples and described a literature that attempted to merge the qualities of disjunction, simultaneity, irrationalism, anti-illusionism, and self-reflexiveness with the more conventional narrative style of nineteenth-century realism. Still somewhat parodic in its impulse, the result was more accessible than modernism but aware of the continuing tradition of which it, no less than the realism it attempted to repudiate, was a part.[8]

Without giving a name to what he identifies as a new sensibility, Richard Wasson sees in such exemplary authors as Pynchon, Barth, Robbe-Grillet, and Iris Murdoch a literature aware of its own artificiality that serves to critique the modernist use of myth as a controlling or unifying discipline or metaphor as a means of reconciling opposites. Responsive to the contingent and accidental nature of things, these contemporaries, Wasson contends, see a world resistant to the subjectivity of hero and author and their attempts to subordinate that world to the drama of self.[9]

Writing toward the close of the sixties, Leslie Fiedler, whose earlier work told of the end of innocence, saw its nostalgic return in the postmodern mythologies of the western, science fiction, and pornography that attempted to close the gap between high and low art. Pop culture, Fiedler insisted, did not use the figures of contemporary myth—the comic book hero, the mythologized public figure—as a basis for ironic comparison; these, rather, were authentic in themselves, analogues that enacted in a contemporary setting the modernist ecstatic moment of epiphany. Fiedler described the emergence of a futurist fiction from the periphery of culture to its center, where popular forms of writing merged with more serious ones. More prophetic than allegorical, this postmodern impulse was animated by pornography and ultimately silence as a mode of protest, and, informed by new psychic possibilities often induced by hallucinatory drugs, it adopted even madness as a redemptive political principle.[10]

Just over a decade later, Andreas Huyssen similarly recognized in post-modernism an attempt to bridge the divide between high culture and mass culture that marked modernism. Huyssen distinguished the modernist insistence on the autonomy of art and its separation from the culture of everyday life from the intent of the avant-garde, which grew out of revolutionary politics and emerged in Expressionism, Dada, Russian constructivism, futurism, and surrealism. With the codification of modernism as canon, the conservative depoliticization of the avant-garde during the 1940s and 1950s led to its decline as a genuinely critical and adversary culture. In its wake, postmodernism emerged in at least two distinct phases. The challenge to the canon of high art diluted by a technological optimism that marked the 1960s, Huyssen concluded, became transformed in the 1970s and 1980s into an eclectic mode at once diverse and amorphous. Though it continues to reject the dichotomies of mass culture and high art, it explores both their contradictions and contingencies in a creative tension animated by the self-assertion of minority cultures and the decentering of traditional notions of identity.[11]

Although the idea of postmodernism has been impacted by various social and cultural theories—notably Saussurean linguistics, Lacanian psychoanalysis, and Althusserian Marxism—one of the earliest, though still useful, literary approaches is that of Ihab Hassan, who, in *The Dismemberment of Orpheus*, found postmodern forms evolving out of a literature of silence for which de Sade, Beckett, Henry Miller, and Marcel Duchamp serve as exemplary figures. In what he termed a "Postface" to the 1982 edition, Hassan extends his earlier view of the nihilist and self-transcendent accents of this movement to include a binary division that more sharply opposes postmodernism and modernism. The former was marked by purpose, design, determinacy, transcendence, and origins, the latter by play, chance, indeterminacy, immanence, and trace. Literature, Hassan contends, thus turns against itself in outrage and apocalypse, finally in an anti-literature of silence, concreteness, and self-parody.[12]

Writing in an allusive, jazzed-up style at once self-canceling and gnomic that he insists is less an attempt to imitate the fiction he discusses than to suggest its alternative voices, Hassan traces the current condition of postmodern knowledge and practices from the "cool, diffuse, avant-gardist strain" of the sixties through a reflexive, parodic metafiction to an eclecticism at the end of the seventies that emerges in a debate between aesthetic and social post-Marxist problematics. Beyond the expressed agonism of the postmodern, however, Hassan sees a posthumanism that turns sideways Irving Howe's view that modernism must always struggle but never quite triumph, ultimately struggle in order not to triumph. "The struggle," Hassan contends, "must always be double: to struggle and at the same time struggle to empty all struggle."[13]

The direction of writing seemed much different to Charles Altieri, who saw the orientation of postmodern poetry shift from the modernist tradition of symbolism with its emphasis on formalism to the acknowledgment of the ordering force of natural processes and so of presence rather than transcendence. Not deconstruction, then, but decreation along with "infinite modes of authenticity" becomes articulated in the work of such representative figures as Charles Olson, Robert Duncan, Frank O'Hara, Robert Creeley, and Denise Levertov, among others, who arrive at the reconciliation of fact and imagination through the process of rediscovering immanent values in ordinary domestic experience.[14]

Beginning as an outgrowth of modernism in the late 1940s and 1950s, a comic postmodernism, for Lance Olsen, emerges out of a suspicion of shared values and perceptions. This subversive mode grows increasingly formless through the early 1970s, Olsen contends, when it becomes remarginalized in a conservative neorealism that hesitantly attempts a reconciliation with the modernist concern for meaning and pattern.[15] The rupture more than the continuity of postmodernism with earlier historical movements is emphasized by Allen Thiher, who examines the work of such theorists as Wittgenstein, Heidegger, Saussure, and Derrida, which, he argues, helped to direct postmodern fiction away from visualization toward a hyperrealism of flat surfaces and toward the self-contained play of language that questions and portrays its own status.[16]

In what remains one of the most cogent and persuasive readings of postmodernism, Philip Stevick finds in recent fiction an extended range of fictional options that point to a sense of discontinuity with the modernist masters. Focusing on Barthelme, Brautigan, and Coover as exemplary figures, Stevick describes an interest in public rather than private experience (and a consequent turning away from epiphanic form), a normalization or taking for granted the extreme quality of everyday experience, an atemporality, a fabulist orientation, and an additive principle of composition. Though Stevick locates this new fiction within culture, he does not claim that it indicates a sharp break in historical eras but proposes more usefully to regard it in terms of a number of axioms, including its lack of engagement with or struggle against the tradition it supersedes; its assimilaton of bad art; its reluctance to indicate a scale of values (and consequent encyclopedic tendency); its depthlessness (and consequent resistance to symbolism); its lack of illusion; and its view of the act of writing as play.[17]

Largely limiting his observations to the new fiction enclosed by the seventies, Stevick subsequently deals with an expanded range of authors and approaches that, at the end of the decade, still seem to him to have invited relatively little critical attention. As part of a tendency toward accommodating antithetical elements, he finds the evolution of an anti-form centered on the principle of collage and incorporating the junk or dreck that lends a comic energy to the prose. This results in a uniquely contemporary mode of satire informed by a narrative posture of willed naïveté and mock factuality that undercuts its own fictive impulse no less than the world of experience from which it is drawn, whose reference remains indeterminate, and from which judgment is ultimately withheld.[18]

Central to any definition of postmodernism is metafiction, which acknowledges its own ontological condition as an intervention in the natural world. William Gass, who is generally credited with coining the term, argues that the novelist no longer pretends "that his business is to render the world; he knows, more often now, that his business is to *make* one, and to make one from the only medium of which he is a master—language."[19] Reflexivity is applied by Steven Connor even to criticism itself, where it is seen as the distinguishing problem of the postmodern as theory becomes involved in the very fields it attempts to theorize about. For Connor, the defining element of the postmodern lies in the "readjustment of power relations within and across cultural and critical-academic institutions."[20]

For Robert Scholes metafiction represents the loss of correspondence between the forms of fiction and traditional forms, ideas, behavior, or even essential values and the consequent inability of characters to communicate the subjective truth of their discoveries. Metafiction, he maintains, results from the struggle to arrive at those forms through which fiction reestablishes its connection to human existence and so prompts the assimilation of criticism into its own processes.[21]

Raymond Federman issues a manifesto for the nonreferential nature of fiction, whose primary purpose, he insists, is to unmask its own fictionality. Coining the term "surfiction," Federman argues that reality exists only in the language that describes it and that meaning is produced only in the process of writing and reading. Accordingly, in place of mimetic notions of syntax and even conventional typography he employs a self-reflexive process of improvisation that abandons the stable social and psychological determinants of character and replaces them with "word-beings."[22]

Metafiction is fiction not merely about the writing of fiction, for Larry McCaffery, but about the way language both creates meaning and shapes the world—itself a fiction. In its response—at once disruptive and playful—to the militant social unrest and correlative self-awareness of the times, McCaffery finds a concern for the broader fictive systems by means of which we attempt to structure a chaotic universe. Focusing on three exemplary writers—Coover, Barthelme, and Gass—McCaffery identifies familiar mythic forms and the recognition of history as artifice, along with, as in Coover's "cubist" fictions, contradictory possibilities that reveal the fictive nature both of the forms themselves and the reality they pretend to contain and so keep fluid the boundary between fantasy and reality.[23]

While McCaffery's views in many ways echo the almost neoclassical literalism of William Gass's belief that the referent of fiction exists only as an imaginative construct, Patricia Waugh contends that metafiction reflects a fundamental tension in all novels between the illusion of self-sufficiency and the exposure of that illusion. Contemporary metafiction, Waugh suggests, emerged out of a climate in which advances in technology and information theory rendered obsolete conventional literary codes. The conventional relations between fiction and reality were challenged by such devices as exaggerated structural patterning, infinite textual regression, literary parodies, temporal and spatial dislocations, and blurred boundaries of discourse (figures from one level of fictive existence entering another). In metafictional novels, the invented world addresses the conditions of its own creation where it locates the dramatic tensions once provided by the opposition to middle-class social values that modernism had long since exhausted. These self-conscious novels then are less a rejection of the novel form than a response to the sense of reality as provisional and to the acknowledgment that fiction represents the discourses of the world rather than the world itself. [24]

What technique discovers, then, is the working of artifice, so that storytelling assumes the configuration of an anatomy or Menippean satire of modernist forms if not modernist themes. The result is not fantasy but irrealism, which does not invite either analogy to the external world or belief in its own. One such writer is Grace Paley, whose stories, according to Victoria Aarons, interrogate notions of authorial ownership while extending the limits of narrative. The defining act for Paley's characters no less than her themes becomes a mode of storytelling itself in which an omniscient narrator is supplanted by a "rhetoric of voices" that inform everyday experience and extend our sense of what is real. [25]

A tireless advocate for experimental writing, Jerome Klinkowitz brings into relation the awareness of the moment and what he terms the self-apparency of fiction. Calling it "post-contemporary," Klinkowitz identifies a disruptive tendency in American fiction beginning in the late 1960s distinct from the seemingly exhausted conventions of realism still evident in such writers as Bellow or Updike as well as from the regressive parodies of Barth and Pynchon. Innovative writers such as Donald Barthelme, Ronald Sukenick, Ishmael Reed, Steve Katz, and Kurt Vonnegut among others were not content merely with linguistic play but grounded self-representation in language as an object in the world. More recently, Klinkowitz notes in such writers as Clarence Majors, Walter Abish, Stephen Dixon, and Guy Davenport the application of anti-illusionist techniques to an experimental realism that focused on the surface of the sign to accommodate the finality of life even as it attempted to resist the closure of fiction. [26]

Uncertainty about the way in which narrative creates the conditions of its verbal world, determines the conditions of its relation to reality, or establishes the existence of its own subject lies at the center of Patrick O'Donnell's illuminating study of several postmodern writers. O'Donnell examines the interpretation that takes place as an action within the text and finds in the production and reading of signs an affirmation of human experience. Characteristic of the contemporary novel, O'Donnell concludes, is the foregrounding of the tension between the reader's desire for involvement with the text and self-awareness of its fictionality, a passion for and dismissal of a meaning that does not collapse the distinction between author, text, and reader but widens the gap that separates them.[27]

An alternative postmodern direction to that of metafiction is found by Mas'ud Zavarzadeh in the nonfiction novel, which maps events and actions in the world in all their literalness and—along with what he terms "transfiction," a form that unmasks its own fictive conventions—serves as a response to the impact of technology and electronics and more generally of capitalistic development that deprives postwar American experience of a comprehensive view of itself. Zavarzadeh locates an approach to reality that rejects the interpretation of events advanced in the conventional totalizing novel in favor of a distinctive generic mode that is bireferential, responsive at once both to history and invention but abandoning conventional plot, character, or even linguistic reference that served as a liberal humanist legacy.[28]

The displacement of social and epistemological concerns by an art that marginalizes its own function is examined by Gerald Graff, who identifies two strains of this postmodern tendency, the apocalyptic and the visionary, one a literature of silence, the other a more energetic if equally empty disintegration of boundaries. Though skeptical of the romantic attempt to provide values and order to a chaotic society and consequently tending toward opacity, both of these modes, Graff argues, carried forward the romantic and modernist tradition of alienation and artistic autonomy. Grounded in the conviction that Western art, along with bourgeois capitalism, was devoted to maintaining the privilege and power of the ruling class, this postmodern acquiescence to, even celebration of, the loss of referentiality, however, projected alienation as no longer subversive but normative. As a consequence, Graff concludes, rather than a breakthrough, postmodern antirationalism proves to be reactionary, reinforcing rather than undermining the barrenness of a technocratic society.[29]

Graff's view of the solipsism of the avant-garde is challenged by Jerry Varsava, who makes the case for the mimetic function of postmodern fiction centered in reader reception. Operating from a theoretical basis in phenomenological hermeneutics indebted to Hans-Georg Gadamer, Varsava redefines the mimetic function so that the once fixed relationships between reader and the text are destabilized to reflect a sense of history. In the work of writers such as Walter Abish, Robert Coover, Peter Handke, and Gilbert Sorrentino, Varsava finds negative if entertaining paradigms of political morality, gender stereotyping, and the conditions of intertextuality that, he contends, defamiliarize our fictions while offering a social critique of the lived-in world.[30]

What some critics approach as a fundamentally epistemological crisis in the novel, for Brian McHale constitutes more an ontological dilemma in which the loss of bearings is attendant upon the uncertain connection the literary work bears to the real one. With reference to the theories of Benjamin

Hrushovski and Roman Ingarden and to Foucault's concept of heterotopias, which juxtapose worlds of incompatible structure, McHale traces the various forms of fictional foregrounding through which texts become iconic rather than symbolic, referring to what is present to the reader rather than absent. In what approaches a taxonomy of postmodern themes and techniques, he finds an overlapping if discontinuous plurality of worlds, multiple lines of narrative possibility (for which Borges 1941 story "The Garden of the Forking Paths" serves as a paradigm), emotional flattening, and defamiliarization of space, all of which underscore an ontological destabilization. Drawing upon Bakhtin's formulation of carnival, McHale further identifies the polyphonic mixing of styles that interrupt the text with inserted genres, recursive structures, and different levels of discourse that reconstitute representations of largely popular forms into a ludic intertextuality.[31]

A question that frequently distinguishes the modernist from the postmodern is that of referentiality. While modernism's view of the autonomy even of the religion of art contrasts with the attempt of postmodernism to locate art in its social context, a countercurrent denied the ability of language to locate an originating impulse in the world outside its own processes. The modernist slogan "make it new," becomes the postmodern nostalgia that hopes to make it *look* like new. Where, in a line extending from Henry James to Joyce and Eliot, modernism separated the author from the work, postmodernism finds the author trapped in the prison house of language.

This view is adopted by an influential school of American criticism identified prominently with the work of J. Hillis Miller, Paul de Man, and Geoffrey Hartman in the late sixties influenced heavily by French thought and, in particular, the deconstructive theories of Jacques Derrida.[32] In postmodern criticism, methodological approaches both informed and even displaced more thematic ones, even those devoted to political, psychological, feminist, or Third World canon revisions. The modernist revelation of technique as discovery came to yield primarily if not exclusively a good deal of technique and little discovery other than that of technique itself, though by returning critical inquiry to the job of interpretation, American deconstruction, according to Jonathan Culler, preserves a measure of continuity.[33]

There are, for Derrida, two approaches to interpretation, one of them a nostalgic attempt to determine the origin, the other an exposure of the presumed unity of a text as in fact an ungrounded structure of contradictory rhetorical strategies. Accordingly, the idea that author's intention governs a work is thrown into question. Where New Criticism argued for the autonomy of literature, deconstruction describes the coercive nature of language. Where New Criticism denied paraphrasable content, deconstruction admits only alternate readings. The idea of unity, which animated the New Criticism, becomes multivocality, the search for form gives way to the interrogation of structure. Every sign can be placed either in quotation marks or suspended tentatively in parentheses, so that, as Derrida argued, it is not that a text has no meaning but that it can be made to yield infinite interpretations or, alternately, incompatible or contradictory ones.

Derrida's insight, then, was that predicated on a system of differences, writing was not a displacement from its origins in speech but "always already" inscribed as a supplement of social discourse. Even the author's signature does not connect the utterance to its source or establish a presence at one time. For writing to be writing, Derrida states, "it must continue to 'act' and to be readable even when what is called the author of the writing no longer answers for what he has written, for what he seems to have signed, be it because of a temporary absence, because he is dead or, more generally, because he has not employed his absolutely actual and present intention or attention, the plenitude of his desire to say what he means, or in order to sustain what seems to be written 'in his name.' "[34]

The absence of a current intention or even an immediate referent Derrida designates in the term *différance*, which, indebted to the work of Ferdinand Saussure, allows a sign both to put off meaning and to depend for its signification on the difference from the object it refers to as well as from other signs. What Derrida termed the hierarchic nature of Western thought led him to identify a "logocentrism," grounded in his resistance to the Platonic notion of an ideal center or origin from which writing represents an absence or mediation. In contrast, Derrida contends that a written sign occurs not merely in the absence of both a receiver and a sender but in the anticipation or, more accurately, the delay or deferral of signification. Signifier and signified are thus linked in a chain of reference that articulates the desire for an immediate presence but that is capable of carrying only a trace that requires a supplement for completion. What is signified, then, is not an originary presence but an infinitely regressive sign, so that in what may be his most well-known pronouncement Derrida declares, *"There is nothing outside of the text."*[35]

In his celebrated essay "Structure, Sign & Play in the Discourse of the Human Sciences," initially delivered as a lecture at Johns Hopkins University in 1966, Derrida contends that texts present themselves as indeterminate—without truth or origin, reference or authorial intent—and invite interpretation as a playful activity. In contrast to interpretation that attempts to decipher a lost center of meaning, Derrida invites the reader to celebrate that loss and calls for the exercise of a free play that "tries to pass beyond man and humanism."[36]

The problem of knowledge and a dissatisfaction with history as teleology is the central concern of Jean François Lyotard in what has increasingly come to be thought of as one of the defining statements of postmodernism. For Lyotard, the status of knowledge has been altered because of changes both in the ways it is produced and in the ways it is transmitted, resulting in a crisis of legitimation. Contrasting scientific and narrative forms, he finds that from self-legitimating narrative, knowledge has become largely exteriorized, a commodity instrumental in productive power. In response to Jürgen Habermas's attack on postmodernism as a neoconservative falling away from the rational project of the Enlightenment, Lyotard proposes the nonrational as an alternate way of knowing. Postmodern narrative, Lyotard contends, adopts a more open "antimethod" or "paralogy" that limits itself to local truth and at the same time entertains alternate possibilities or instability rather than working toward closure or consensus.

The modernism of Joyce or Proust allowed for an elision of content while establishing a formal unity through the presence of a narrative consciousness; the postmodern condition, in contrast, rejects such unity and offers in its place instability, invention, difference, the parity of what can be imagined with that of what exists. As a consequence, the legitimating process becomes one of deliberately undermining the conventions of cause and effect so that multiple language games and, by extension, multiple worlds exist side by side. The essay is postmodern, Lyotard declares in a succinct formulation; the Athaeneum, with its absences that testify to a former unity, that is modern.

Lyotard's analysis thus points to the breakdown of coherent story, a phenomenon that occurs, unsurprisingly, when language concentrates on its own processes. The loss of access to the master or totalizing narratives that formerly unified culture results in the substitution of performance for verifiability. Accordingly, Lyotard argues, postmodernism no longer addresses the question of differentiation but concerns itself with "with undecidables, the limits of precise control, conflicts characterized by incomplete information, 'fracta,' catastrophes, and pragmatic paradoxes." In short, it no longer tells us about the world and our place in it. Postmodernism, he contends, is not a reaction to modernism but a condition that makes it possible by adopting the interrogation of itself that marked the abstract impulse of the avant-garde.[37]

Lyotard's argument has come under attack as itself totalizing (just as deconstruction invites deconstruction of its own statement) or, as Frederic Jameson has it, for itself serving as a "narrative of the end of narratives." Jameson finds in postmodernism a reaction to the oppositional stance of modernism that blurs the distinctions between high culture and popular art, transforming reality into images. Characterized by a fondness for pastiche, this impulse, unlike the satiric thrust of parody, is marked by a schizophrenic collapse of time into an ongoing present, a literalization of language, and a transformation of reality into images so that the subject of art becomes art itself.[38]

Defending a Marxist position against the argument that it, too, presented a totalizing and so outdated view, Jameson draws upon Ernest Mandel's *Late Capitalism* to arrive at a notion of postmodernism as a stage of multinational or consumer capitalism that employs informational technologies as products of commodity. Jameson finds a striking representation of postmodernism in John Portman's Bonaventure Hotel, an almost self-contained totality that is difficult to enter and disorienting once inside, and in the architect Frank Ghery's use of hyperspace to project lines in contradictory perspectives, lines that ultimately disappear in different directions. In contrast to the spatial form of modernism, then, Jameson sees a spatial as well as social confusion that postmodernism must depict at the same time as it suggests ways of orienting ourselves to it.[39]

The quality that authenticated the postmodern work of art, then, was that, like a laboratory experiment, it could be reproduced and consequently take its place in a prevailing system. At the same time, a movement away from the liberation of the text no less than from its autonomy toward a shared belief in referentiality is signaled by a "new historicism" that, while questioning the legitimation of a dominant cultural interpretation, returns to a decentered history where it attempts to locate meaning. Distinct from a coherent worldview that attempted to retrieve a static historical moment, New Historicism sees it as a contingent field dependent upon the play of power relations. This new historicism finds problematic the distinction between the social background and the literary foreground as well as between literature and nonliterary documentation. Expanding its range from an initial interest primarily in Renaissance studies, new historicism, as H. Aram Veeser conceives of it, regards both self and text as "mere holograms," produced at the intersection of cultural institutions and defined in relation to perceived threats by marginal ethnic groups and by authoritative discipline. Accordingly, it attempts to cross the boundaries separating various disciplines, taking account of the negotiation between historical event, cultural practice, and literary texts.[40]

In contrast to what he terms a monological vision concerned with internal coherence and consistency, the New Historicism, contends Stephen Greenblatt, perhaps its most visible spokesman, rejects the notion of literary works as a fixed set of texts set apart from all other forms of expression and informed by an organic unity. Looking at the contingent conditions under which a text was produced and the manner in which these were effaced, Greenblatt proposes to examine the text in terms of "how collective beliefs and experiences were shaped, moved from one medium to another, concentrated in manageable aesthetic form, offered for consumption."[41]

What Leslie Fiedler saw as the hopeful narrowing of the gap between cultural levels has in American postmodernism led on the one hand to the blurring of generic boundaries, modes of discourse, or even, as Jean Baudrillard would have it, the distinction between the simulation and the real or the appropriation of one artist's work by another. When, for example, Greenblatt examines a painting by Holbein, he is concerned with what it reveals about the social values and power relationships of the Renaissance. On the other hand, the postmodern resists the totalization of discourse or the identification of a master narrative; that is to say, it insists on differentiation. For the New Historicist, these incompatible theories—one Marxist in orientation, the other poststructural—neglect the contradictions of history. New Historicism, then, as Greenblatt describes it, blurs the boundaries of criticism and literature to define a range of aesthetic possibilities that are "more open to such works as fields of force, places of dissension and shifting interests, occasions for the jostling of orthodox and subversive impulses."[42]

Taking up this theme in a special issue of *boundary 2* that focuses on New Historicism in American Studies, Donald Pease, in a highly theoretic introduction, argues for resistance to a canonicity grounded in unified literary and cultural national metanarratives such as those of the American Adam, the Virgin Land, the romantic tradition, or the idea of an American Renaissance informed by the principle of democracy.[43] For David Suchoff, New Historicism challenged the posture of liberal modernism—shaped in part by the Cold War and articulated by critics such as Lionel Trilling—that informed a literature of alienation and the ahistorical novels that reinforced dominant power relations. Though like feminism, New Historicism took account of excluded areas of history, in drawing upon the Cold War American political strategy of "containment," Suchoff argues, it neglected the Frankfurt School's analysis of literature's domination by the marketplace. Consequently it failed to develop an oppositional analysis embedded within the novels it examined or to arrive at a critical theory of mass culture.[44]

A more humanistic view of postmodernism is that of Alan Wilde, who, following Merleau-Ponty, describes a mode of fiction somewhere between metafiction and realism that is aware of contingency but refuses explanations. Unlike modernism, which attempts to transform the world through the subjective consciousness, postmodernism, for Wilde, gives assent to its possibilities, however tentative and provisional. At the heart of this approach, is what Wilde terms an "anironic" vision that complements the distancing or mediate irony of satire with an attempt to make contact with the world and an acceptance of its disorder. "Modernist irony," Wilde writes, "absolute and equivocal, expresses a resolute consciousness of different and equal possibilities so ranged as to defy solution. Postmodern irony, by contrast, is suspensive," by which term Wilde means that "an indecision about the meanings or relations of things is matched by a willingness to live with uncertainty, to tolerate and, in some cases, to welcome a world seen as random and multiple, even, at times, absurd."[45]

Linda Hutcheon focuses on the politics of representation in postmodernism where she finds a tendency to problematize assumptions about closure, distance, and the autonomy of art and a correlative questioning of the binary opposition of the real and the fictive. In place of a totalizing view of historical representation, Hutcheon finds that postmodern fiction, architecture (with its reaction to the ahistorical purism of the International Style), and photography parodically subvert no less than inscribe their conventions and so paradoxically prove both complicit with and critical of mimetic representation and the idea of man as its center.[46]

The traditional binary division of realistic representation and antirealistic invention proves too restrictive as well for Susan Strehle, who rejects exclusive alternatives as an inaccurate index of postmodern fiction. Influenced by the theories of Werner Heisenberg, Strehle coins the term "actualism" to identify a new fiction that adopts the changes quantum theory and wave mechanics have caused in the way reality is viewed in the twentieth century. Addressing class movement as opposed to individual events or causes, the actualists see the world as discontinuous, statistical, or uncertain, its events intricately connected by metaphorical linkages that establish continuity in parallel rather than series and thus extend their work beyond metafictional self-reference to place themselves within a realistic tradition.[47]

Increasingly, the subversive intent of postmodernism has come to be seen as directed not so much at social institutions as at the fixed hierarchies of the text itself. Arthur Saltzman examines what he calls the anti-epiphanic mode in which "the questions we put to existence never escape the linguistic and cultural realities that shape and implicate all discourse." This anticlimactic mode, Saltzman argues, results in an opaque, self-conscious prose, limited to the conditions of meaning rather than its revelations, which expose their own artifice, destabilize perspective, and remain "primarily linguistic rather than spiritual."[48]

In his examination of four exemplary postmodern novels of the mid-seventies, John Johnston similarly identifies an epistemological crisis in which the world presents itself in a multiplicity of forces not subject to a single, defining relation or capable of representation by conventional fictive form. Reflecting a new cultural configuration, these fictions, Johnston argues, "neither privilege the individual 'knowing' subject nor see the workings of contemporary science and technology as necessarily dehumanizing" but defer or displace action in an endless present or in a layered multiplicity of events that restructure our experience so that originals are no longer privileged over copies and models come to displace reality.[49]

In contrast to the modernist attempt at formal unity, then, postmodernism operates from a local or regional rather than a comprehensive view. For postmodern writers such as Donald Barthelme, fragments become assembled into a collage in whose elusive ironies Brian McHale and Moshe Ron find a sense of form that remains qualified by a text that is about its own unknowability though not in itself unknowable.[50] Questions raised prominently in postmodern discourse also involve the possibilities not only of representation but of reproduction or literalization.

One form emerges in minimalism. Introducing a special issue of *Mississippi Review* devoted to minimalist fiction, Kim Herzinger argues that the broadly postmodern tendencies of irony, self-reflexiveness, and conspicuous structural invention give way in minimalism to a narrator who often speaks with the same voice as the characters. Behavior in minimalist fiction is seldom reduced to a single motivation based on socioeconomic status or presumed psychological or historical background or conditions. In fact, such background, Herzinger maintains, is defamiliarized by representation that, in its lack of irony, forces the reader to reevaluate conventional presumptions.[51]

Prominent among the writers generally regarded as minimalist are Raymond Carver, Ann Beattie, and Mary Robison, identified by David Leavitt as in turn having influenced a new generation which includes Amy Hempel, Elizabeth Tallent, Meg Wolitzer, Peter Cameron, and Marian Thurm. Generally limiting themselves to the form of the short story, these writers, contends Leavitt, who is perhaps the most well-known figure among them, address the concerns of family, marriage, love, and loyalty. They describe a world "in which very little can be taken for granted or counted on, where potentially disastrous change looms around every corner, and where marriages and families, rather than providing havens, are themselves the fulcrums of the most sweeping upheavals." Nontheless, Leavitt finds in the works of this generation the values of family and marriage that the younger characters cling to with a passion that seems beyond the grasp of their parents.[52] A much less sympathetic view of minimalist writers is that of Bruce Bawer, who describes them as a "literary brat pack" whose reputation is largely the result of an influential editor at a prestigious publishing house and whose similar style and thematic interests make them all but indistinguishable.[53]

In the 1980s, the paratactic style of Brett Easton Ellis, Susan Minot, David Leavitt, Bobbie Ann Mason, Frederick Barthelme, Jay McInerney, and, most importantly, Raymond Carver, emerged, for David Kaufmann, in a phenomenon of mass-marketing that recognized the insulation of a Yuppie generation from blue-collar concerns. Naturalizing the antimimetic fiction of such writers of the sixties as Donald Barthelme, the surface of the prose, Kaufmann contends, along with the humor that marks its dominant tone, makes it difficult to attribute cause and effect to anything other than chronology. This "Yuppie postmodernism" thus anesthetizes, often in nostalgia, the sorrows of others so that it becomes possible to deny their pain while legitimizing self-interest.[54]

In contrast to the minimalist attempt to deal with parts instead of with the whole has been the complex narrative structure Tom LeClair has termed the systems novel or novel of excess. Indebted to the theories of Ludwig Bertalanffy, who conceived of organisms in terms of complex loops of information, systems novels collapse the distinctions between what LeClair sees as the opposing terms of realism and postmodernism to arrive at a "postmodern naturalism" that represents the large realities of American public life. These novels of mastery, as LeClair additionally terms them, match the density of information that characterizes contemporary experience with a size and scope of their own, adopting such features as digressive structure, multilayered narrative, discontinuities and unpredictable connections, and an opacity of language, ultimately reorienting the reader to the information overload the novel engages.[55]

In the absorption of the avant-garde into mainstream culture, Richard Wolin sees the renunciation of form and so of subject in favor of an emphasis on immediacy and the substitution of reproducibility for individual vision. Following the repudiation of the romantic notion of the form-giving artist in the decline of the eighteenth-century bildungsroman, the disillusionment projected by Stendhal, and the emerging modernist interiorization of Proust and Joyce, the poststructural imagination celebrated a cataclysmic end of history. The consequent postmodern rejection of a humanist legacy of individual human worth, for Wolin, leads to a cybernetic society implicit in the oppositional impulses of the counterculture of the sixties and reconfigured in the systems theory of Niklas Luhmann in which individual autonomy is replaced by technical imperatives.[56]

Rather than confining the postmodern to a historical period, Frank Lentricchia locates it in an American tradition that blurs the boundaries of the fictive and the real, the authentic dissolving into the imagined self even as the narrative voice itself flows seamlessly into the consciousness of the characters and so prevents contact with an implied author. Yet the cultural density that prevents readers from ascribing universal causes to the immediacy of human situations, gives a uniquely contemporary slant to writers such as Don DeLillo, who, for Lentricchia, provides not only a critique of the postmodern substitution of image or textuality for identity but of the expectations—formed in part by those images—of both fiction and politics.[57]

Postmodernism may also be identified in a cluster of characteristics—including pluralism—opposed to closure, the absence or erasure of plot, indeterminacy, and parody and pastiche in place of unified or organic style. The loss of form accompanied the breakdown of generic barriers such as those that distinguish between high and low art, fiction and nonfiction. At least one of the functions of genre, conventional criticism maintains, is to tell us what we may expect. Grounded in social conditions, it provides clues about how to interpret behavior, what values to assign to particular actions. The expanded meanings of postmodernism, however, call the continuing value of genre into question. Pointing to the random or game-playing quality of some of our most crucial literature, to its performative rather than reportorial function, and to its assaults upon the recuperable function of language, Jonathan Culler suggests that works that in these ways defeat the conventional approaches to reading may require a theory indifferent to generic distinctions.[58] The blurring or combination of generic forms prompts Ralph Cohen to argue for the continuity of the modern and the postmodern, whose techniques of interruption, self-consciousness, multiple narrations, and discontinuity, he finds as well in the eighteenth-century novel. Yet Cohen defends the usefulness of genre as a way of understanding not only postmodern fiction but the forms of discursive writing that have recently evolved to comment on it.[59]

Unlike modernism, which was an attempt to make itself obscure, inaccessible, to outrage the middle class, postmodernism has no quarrel with intelligibility, though it characteristically adopts an irrealist technique. Isn't Main Street almost all right, goes the rhetorical question posed by the postmodern architect and theorist Robert Venturi.[60] Commenting on the state of American fiction in the 1970s and 1980s, Larry McCaffery takes note of a countercurrent to the political conservatism and a realistic minimalism that displaced an earlier postmodern aesthetic sensibility itself marked by willful disruption, playful experimentation, self-reflexiveness, and a foregrounding of artifice. Perhaps the most impressive aspect of this new writing, McCaffery contends, is its tendency toward radical formal innovation often in support of political engagement and, in particular, devoted to science fiction, which, he maintains, is "arguably the most significant body of work in contemporary fiction."[61]

Displacing the exploration of outer space that marked the traditional mimetic techniques of the genre, science fiction, for Bob Donahoo, has moved into the mainstream of American fiction by focusing less on science, or even, it turns out, on fiction and more on such issues as that of gender and a redefinition of what it means to be human.[62] Teresa Ebert envisions a new tradition emerging from the convergence of postmodern innovative fiction and a "metascience fiction" that abandons causality and coherent human identity in favor of fabulation and self-referentiality. This reconfiguration, Ebert contends, is most fully articulated in the fiction of Samuel Delany and is marked by a deemphasis on technology and a corresponding indeterminacy that extends the relations among words beyond those delimited by linear narrative form.[63]

One of the most prominent forms of such writing is cybernetic fiction, which for David Porush combines computer and informational systems with self-reflexive techniques that call attention to language as a soft machine with the ability to shape not only the character of society but the way it imaginatively attempts to apprehend itself. Addressing the tension between mechanism and meaning, Porush finds that unlike the literature of the nineteenth and early twentieth centuries, contemporary fiction does not so much resist or explain the metaphor of the machine as appropriate it to affirm the potential of fiction for dealing with the problem of remaining human in an uncertain and technological world.[64]

In the 1980s, a version of science fiction emerged known as cyberpunk that Frederick Jameson has called "the supreme literary expression if not of postmodernism, then of late capitalism itself."[65] According to Veronica Hollinger, cyberpunk deconstructs the distinctions between artificial and natural in reality and is at once antihumanist and engaged with historical processes. With William Gibson as, perhaps, its most prominent writer, Hollinger finds cyberpunk marked by a shift from symbol to surface that while resisting the apocalyptic thrust of dystopian science fiction has itself already fallen victim to its deconstructive impulse.[66]

Along with minimalism, maximalism or novels of excess, magic realism, metafiction, and midfiction, postmodernism has seen the emergence of feminism, of street writing, and even of a literature devoted to the Vietnam war that suggests the distinctive ways in which the era understood and responded to experience and in which that experience became itself a projection of that understanding. Starting in the mid-seventies, an alternative literary tradition or "fiction of insurgency" began to develop in the writing of Kathy Acker, Constance de Jong, Lynne Tillman, and a group of writers chiefly associated with Reese William's Tanam Press and with Anne Turyn's *Top Stories*. Located chiefly in New York, this "downtown" writing, as Robert Siegle calls it, is frequently the work of multimedia artists who contest the institutional values and the discourse systems that sustain them with a guerrilla action that destabilizes plot and character. Such subversive writing, Siegle contends, privileges marginal social groups, emphasizes issues of language and representation, appropriates images or texts, and employs nonsequential structure to celebrate a fluidity that resists totalization.[67]

Shaped by social forces such as the war in Vietnam and the unrest of the 1960s and propelled by women's rights and the black power movements it prompted, postmodernism, for Bernard Bell, pushed beyond the structuralist challenges of the fifties that viewed the meaning of literary texts as a function of language and of textual relations, and not the presumed consciousness of the writer or an objective social, historical, or psychological reality. Yet, Bell argues, though black postmodern writers adopted the techniques of fantasy, parody, irony, and burlesque, they are equally concerned with the struggle for social justice. As a result, postmodernism, for Afro-American writers, rejects Eurocentric models to explore a "double consciousness," often by employing a mode of fabulation to explore their folk tradition.[68]

In a critique that itself bears the imprint of a postmodern sensibility, Henry Louis Gates identifies a black vernacular tradition of signification that employs parody and pastiche as two of its main strategies in a metadiscourse combining an indigenous black principle with a more formal trope of literary revision. Incorporating both black and American myths, formal and informal texts, this double voice operates outside Western tradition to develop its own theory of literary discourse grounded in an emphasis on the figurative use of language.[69]

A poststructural, reader-response approach to black women writers is advanced by Deborah McDowell, who cautions against the critical tendency to "homogenize and essentialize" black women by neglecting social and material realities but who nonetheless warns against a unitary or essentialist view of black female identity and argues instead for viewing the self dialogically in relation to other texts and other "interpretative communities." Mc-Dowell's view is challenged by Michaël Awkward, who identifies a process of achieved unity in the characters of several African-American women writers and who questions whether a poststructural approach minimalizes if it does not outright eliminate the significance of racial and cultural elements and so fails to explore the blackness of black texts.[70]

Perhaps because it has struggled to find a unifying principle that seems to put it at odds with Lyotard's strictures against a master narrative, feminism has emerged less as a genre or subdivision of postmodernism than as a discipline in its own right that challenges the normative patriarchal constructions with new forms of representation. The diversity of approaches among feminist critics is, in fact, so vast, encompassing nationality (French and Anglo-American) and methodology (Marxist, semiotic, biological, deconstructionist, psychoanalytic) that a recent anthology of literary theory and criticism is titled *Feminisms*.[71]

In contrast to the modernist view of the outsider as a necessary position from which to issue a critique of the dominant materialist society, feminist writers such as Nancy Miller or Nancy Hartsock, among others, challenge the exclusion of women from power by a patriarchal society grounded in a tradition of Western humanism.[72] Similarly, in commenting on the critical invisiblity of feminist writing, Nina Baym finds the dominant model of American literature fashioned out of the literary experience of male writers, who doubted the importance of women's experience at the same time as they envisioned themselves imperiled by the popularity of women writers against which they had to struggle for recognition. Baym argues that much of conventional feminist literary theory has been based on an andocentric community of academicians and on Freudian and Lacanian misperceptions of adult woman's language developed from childhood fantasies. Accordingly, such theories constrain rather than explore the range of feminist writing and even reproduce the appropriation of women's experience by men.[73]

In a groundbreaking essay, Craig Owens contends that the issue of sexual difference has, for the most part, been excluded from the postmodern crisis of cultural authority, a crisis that attempts to determine what can be represented and what cannot. Pointing to the parallels between "feminist critique of patriarchy and the postmodern critique of representation," Owens questions the privileging of vision, which, for the modernist avant-garde, was linked to sexual domination and which implicates the artist in the attempt at mastery through representation of marginal groups. In contrast to a centered subject and the indeterminacy postmodernism invites, feminism, Owens concludes, exposes the violence implicit in the signifier and insists on recognizing differences in terms as well as identities with no fixed content.[74]

Breaking the hierarchic linear forms of patriarchal fiction becomes, for Ellen Friedman and Miriam Fuchs, a defining aspect of women's experimental writing in the twentieth century. The rupture of such conventional narrative devices as linear plot, recognizable conflict, a centralized point of view, and movement to closure constitute for Friedman and Fuchs a means by which the marginalized feminine consciousness can create an alternate fictive space resistant to the patriarchal mastery that informs Western culture. This resistance, Friedman has gone on to argue, has prompted women's narrative to turn outside the culture and peopled it with often nomadic, even anonymous, figures. The attempt by women writers to present what Lyotard has called unrepresentable, has, Friedman concludes, caused them to remain outside the canon.[75]

Elaine Showalter finds feminist criticism split between the ideological and pragmatic modes, one pluralist and revisionary, the other centered on women as writers. For the second of these modes she has coined the term "gynocriticsm" or woman-centered criticism, which draws on Gerda Lerner's study *The Majority Finds Its Past* (New York 1981) to suggest an awareness of the communality of women's interest, history, relationship, and means of expression. Showalter looks for a theoretical framework to Edwin Ardener's model of a "wild zone" outside the dominant structure that provides an alternative perspective on conventional formulations of literary periods based on writing from which women were largely excluded.[76]

Showalter's theoretical framework is questioned by Toril Moi, who argues that its structure reflects the tradition of Western humanism and the idea of the individual self that lies at its center. Moi objects in particular to Showalter's critique of Virginia Woolf's multiplicity of narrative perspectives as a denial of authentic feminine alienation (a denial in which implicit links are found to Georg Lukács's condemnation of a politically regressive modernism). In contrast, Moi finds Woolf's strategy a liberating lack of totalization that attempts to transform the symbolic patriarchal order to which Showalter's reading ultimately submits. The configuration of feminism and postmodernism is, then, as Moi notes, at least on its face made suspect by regarding feminism as just such a metanarrative as Lyotard finds no longer descriptive of a postmodern climate. Though recently Moi underscored her view of feminism in agonistic terms as a struggle against patriarchal and sexist oppression, she proposes a reconceptualization indebted more to the French emphasis on discourse derived from Derrida and elaborated by Julia Kristeva that favors the deconstruction of a binary sexual opposition while retaining a political commitment.[77]

Moi's argument takes on added meaning in the light of an approach to feminist theory Alice Jardine has called called "gynesis," which attempts to deconstruct what Jardine identifies as phallocentric discourse. Jardine finds the articulation of marginality allows feminist criticism to question conventional categories and so give new meaning to language that embodies their power relationships. Where gynocriticism hopes to recover the unique female voice at the center of feminine writing, however, gynesis adopts a postmodern emphasis on the textual construct or space, independent of authorial intention.[78]

A representative view of the question of feminism and postmodernism is advanced by Jane Flax, who associates feminist theory with the desire for freedom from such traditional forms of authority as the Enlightenment appeal to reason, the transparency of language, and the belief in an objective, reliable truth. Changes in economic, social, and political experience, Flax believes, have led to problematization of gender relations which involve questions of power and domination. In place of a universalizing explanation of gender relations, which, she maintains, is subject to the perspective of a dominant group, Flax calls for a recognition of gender as an issue of social relations that, like other forms of postmodernism, should accommodate ambivalence, ambiguity, and multiplicity.[79]

Nancy Fraser and Linda J. Nicholson attempt to reconcile the postmodern suspicion of metanarratives with the social critique afforded by feminism. Lyotard's suspicion of metanarrative does not, they contend, leave room for a paradigm of social criticism from which gender dominance, race, or class oppression can be engaged. Fraser and Nicholson argue for a comparative postmodern theory that would frame ahistorical categories of gender identity such as mothering or reproduction within a temporal narrative hospitable to a diversity of experience and interests.[80]

Most recently, the characteristics associated with postmodernism have themselves become the objects of parody in what might be regarded as a post-postmodernism. Such an attenuation is described by David Cowart as informing the recent fiction of even so definitive a postmodern figure as Thomas Pynchon, whose novel *Vineland* Cowart finds "devoted less to indeterminate 'play' than to totalizing modernist 'purpose.' " Though Cowart acknowledges such postmodern elements in the novel as a refusal to differentiate high culture from low and an insistence on surface rather than depth, he argues that it is informed by a historical consciousness that privileges even as it deconstructs several myths, employing such strategies as the attribution of moral choice in the Edenic myth of America to Eve rather than the Adamic figure.[81]

What this seemingly looped feedback suggests is that postmodernism continues to resist definition, and in particular a definition based on an oppositional relation to modernism, and that it has evolved as a critical term that finds a unifying point of reference only in its own fluidity.

Notes

1. A brief survey of negative responses can be found in Brian McHale, *Postmodernist Fiction* (New York and London: Methuen, 1987): 3–6. Even such advocates as Philip Stevick ("Scheherazade runs out of plots, goes on talking; the king, puzzled, listens: an essay on new

fiction," *TriQuarterly* 26 [Winter 1973]: 338) acknowledge the term to be annoying and unhelpful. While accurately conveying the sense of the period to be not so much that of transition as arrest, Stevick, in a more recent essay, provides a brief but comprehensive survey of both its vitality and imaginative richness. See Philip Stevick, "Literature," in *The Postmodern Moment: A Handbook of Contemporary Innovation in the Arts*, ed. Stanley Trachtenberg (Westport, Conn.: Greenwood Press, 1985), 135–56.

2. William V. Spanos, "The Detective and the Boundary: Some Notes on the Postmodern Literary Imagination," *Repetitions: The Postmodern Occasion in Literature and Culture* (Baton Rouge: Louisiana State University Press, 1987), 13–49. This is a revised and expanded version of an essay that was initially published in *boundary 2* 1 (Fall 1972): 147–68. Spanos's reservations about the term "postmodernism" may be found on pages 192–93 of *Repetitions*.

3. C. Barry Chabot, "The Problem of the Postmodern," *New Literary History* 20 (Autumn 1988): 1–20. Chabot, who regards as premature the designation of American literature as postmodern, examines such representative theorists as Ihab Hassan, Jerome Klinkowitz, and Alan Wilde, whose arguments he finds flawed by a concentration on the statements rather than the practices of the writers they discuss and by a failure to distinguish an overall definition of modernism from such constituent movements as surrealism, imagism, or vorticism. Chabot's essay is reprinted in this volume. See also James Mellard, *The Exploded Form: The Modernist Novel in America* (Urbana: University of Illinois Press, 1980). Unlike those critics who find in postmodernism a different consciousness, Mellard describes its explosion into fragmented forms as an extension of the modernist self-conscious exploration of the relation between artifice and reality. Postmodernism, in this view, signals the reconciliation of subject and object tentatively undertaken by modernism. Mellard does acknowledge that postmodernism is distinct in confronting the juncture at which the reportorial or realistic mode confronts the subjective or inventive and so brings to completion a modernist ethos while anticipating a new, naive stage of experimentation.

4. Stacey Olster, "Hebrew/Greek, Ear/Eye, Moral/Aesthetic: Susan Sontag's Bridging the 'Archaic Gap.' " This essay was written specifically for this volume and appears here for the first time with permission of the author.

5. Irving Howe, "Mass Society and Post-Modern Fiction," *A World More Attractive* (New York: Horizon, 1963): 93.

6. Tony Tanner, *City of Words: American Fiction 1950–1970* (New York: Harper & Row, 1971); Robert Scholes, *The Fabulators* (New York: Oxford University Press, 1967); Albert J. Guerard, "Notes on the Rhetoric of Anti-Realist Fiction," *Triquarterly* 30 (1974): 3–50. Harry Levin, "What Was Modernism," in *Refractions: Essays in Comparative Literature* (New York: Oxford University Press, 1966), 271–95.

7. John Barth, "The Literature of Exhaustion," *Atlantic* 220 (August 1967): 29–34.

8. John Barth, "The Literature of Replenishment," *Atlantic* 245 (January 1980): 65–71.

9. Richard Wasson, "Notes on a New Sensibility," *Partisan Review* 36 (1969): 460–77.

10. Leslie Fiedler, "Cross the Border, Close the Gap," *The Collected Essays of Leslie Fiedler*, vol. 2 (New York: Stein and Day, 1971), 461–85. Subsequently Fiedler acknowledged that the mass audience did not grow closer to the elite audience as he predicted, but rather with the death of the novel simply proliferated into competing subgenres. See his *What Was Literature?: Class Culture and Mass Society* (New York: Simon & Schuster, 1982), 80. See also Fiedler's essay "The New Mutants," *Partisan Review* 32 (Fall 1965): 505–25.

11. Andreas Huyssen, *After the Great Divide: Modernism, Mass Culture, Postmodernism* (Bloomington: Indiana University Press, 1986).

12. Ihab Hassan, "Postface," *The Dismemberment of Orpheus: Toward a Postmodern Litera-*

ture 2nd ed. (Madison: University of Wisconsin Press, 1982). The essay is reprinted in this volume.

13. Ihab Hassan, *The Postmodern Turn: Essays in Postmodern Theory and Culture* (Columbus: Ohio State University Press, 1987), 216. See also Hassan's *The Right Promethean Fire: Imagination, Science, and Cultural Change* (Urbana: University of Illinois Press, 1980), 23.

14. Charles Altieri, "From Symbolist Thought to Immanence: The Ground of Postmodern American Poetics," *boundary 2* 1 (1973): 605–41. Altieri subsequently revised his assessment of several postmodern poets while citing as a definitive element of postmodernism the writerly text, one that stressed the dichotomy between the textual and the existential and that, in fiction, emphasized the act of composition over the situation of characters. See Altieri, "Postmodernism: A Question of Definition," *Par Rapport* 2 (Summer 1989): 87–100.

15. Lance Olsen, *Circus of the Mind in Motion: Postmodernism and the Comic Vision* (Detroit: Wayne State University Press, 1990), 28–29.

16. Allen Thiher, *Words in Reflection: Modern Language Theory and Postmodern Fiction* (Chicago: University of Chicago Press, 1984).

17. Philip Stevick, "Scheherazade runs out of plots, goes on talking; the king, puzzled, listens: an essay on new fiction," *TriQuarterly* 26 (Winter 1973): 332–62. The essay is reprinted in this volume.

18. Philip Stevick, *Alternative Pleasures: Postrealist Fiction and the Tradition* (Urbana: University of Illinois Press, 1981).

19. William H. Gass, *Fiction and the Figures of Life* (New York: Vintage, 1971), 24.

20. Steven Connor, *Postmodernist Culture: An Introduction to Theories of the Contemporary* (New York: Blackwell, 1989), 12.

21. Robert Scholes, "Metafiction," *Iowa Review* 1 (Fall 1970): 100–115.

22. Raymond Federman, "Surfiction: Four Propositions in Form of an Introduction," *Surfiction: Fiction Now . . . and Tomorrow*, ed. Raymond Federman (Chicago: Swallow Press, 1975), 5–15.

23. Larry McCaffery, *The Metafictional Muse: The Works of Robert Coover, Donald Barthelme, and William H. Gass* (Pittsburgh: University of Pittsburgh Press, 1982).

24. Patricia Waugh, *Metafiction: The Theory and Practice of Self-Conscious Fiction* (London and New York: Methuen, 1984).

25. Victoria Aarons, " 'Every window is a mother's mouth': Grace Paley's Postmodern Voice." This essay was written specifically for this volume and appears here for the first time with permission of the author.

26. Jerome Klinkowitz, *Literary Disruptions: The Making of a Post-Contemporary American Fiction* (Urbana: University of Illinois Press, 1975). A revised edition of this work was published in 1980. See also Klinkowitz's more theoretical complement to the earlier literary history in *The Self-Apparent Word: Fiction as Language/Language as Fiction* (Carbondale & Edwardsville: Southern Illinois University Press, 1984).

27. Patrick O'Donnell, *Passionate Doubts: Designs of Interpretation in Contemporary American Fiction* (Iowa City: University of Iowa Press, 1986).

28. Mas'ud Zavarzadeh, *The Mythopoeic Reality: The Postwar American Nonfiction Novel* (Urbana: University of Illinois Press, 1976).

29. Gerald Graff, "The Myth of the Postmodernist Breakthrough," *TriQuarterly* 26 (Winter 1973): 383–417. This essay, slightly revised, was reprinted in Graff's *Literature Against Itself* (Chicago: University of Chicago Press, 1979) and also appears in this volume.

30. Jerry Varsava, *Contingent Meanings: Postmodern Fiction, Mimesis, and the Reader* (Tallahassee: Florida State University Press, 1990).

31. Brian McHale, *Postmodernist Fiction* (London and New York: Methuen, 1987).

32. In a critical essay-review of two volumes of deconstructive criticism—he terms it "a style of accusation"—Denis Donoghue questions whether all of the critics associated with

this school may truly belong to it. See Denis Donoghue, "Deconstructing Deconstruction," *The New York Review of Books* (12 June 1980): 37–41. The review is reprinted here. An equally skeptical, self-described common-sense approach that nonetheless rejects the idea of a single, definitive interpretation of a work is advanced by Gerald Graff in a review of the same volume, "Deconstruction as Dogma, or, 'Come Back to the Raft Ag'in, Strether Honey!'" *Georgia Review* 34 (Summer 1980): 404–21. Along with Harold Bloom, who is sometimes grouped with them, all of these critics were, at one time, associated with Yale University. In contrast to Derrida's assertion that there is nothing outside the text, however, Bloom contends, "There are no texts but only relationships between texts" (Harold Bloom, *A Map of Misreading* [New York: Oxford University Press, 1975], 3). Accordingly Bloom insists the influence of previous poems determines the form of subsequent ones, while at the same time arguing that language doesn't determine meaning, people do. Among the more perceptive studies of this school are Jonathan Culler, *On Deconstruction: Theory and Criticism After Structuralism* (Ithaca: Cornell University Press, 1982); Christopher Norris, *Deconstruction: Theory and Practice* (New York: Methuen, 1982); Vincent B. Leitch, *Deconstructive Criticism* (New York: Columbia University Press, 1983); Art Berman, *From the New Criticism to Deconstruction: The Reception of Structuralism and Post-Structuralism* (Urbana and Chicago: University of Illinois Press, 1988); and William Cain, "Deconstruction in America: The Recent Literary Criticism of J. Hillis Miller," *College English* 41 (December 1979): 367–82. A less sympathetic assessment is provided by Michael Fischer, *Does Deconstruction Make Any Difference?: Poststructuralism and the Defense of Poetry in Modern Criticism* (Bloomington: Indiana University Press, 1985).

33. Jonathan Culler, *On Deconstruction: Theory and Criticism After Structuralism* (Ithaca: Cornell University Press, 1982), 220.

34. Jacques Derrida, "Signature Event Context," *Glyph 1* (Baltimore: Johns Hopkins University Press, 1977), 181, 185–86, 192.

35. Jacques Derrida, *Of Grammatology*, trans. Gayatri Chakravorty Spivak (Baltimore: Johns Hopkins University Press, 1976), 158. Gayatri Chakravorty Spivak, "Translator's Preface," xii.

36. Jacques Derrida, *Writing and Difference*, trans. with intro. by Alan Bass (Chicago: University of Chicago Press, 1978), 292.

37. Jean-François Lyotard, *The Postmodern Condition: A Report on Knowledge*, trans. Geoff Bennington and Brian Massumi, foreword by Frederic Jameson (Minneapolis: University of Minnesota Press, 1984). See also Jürgen Habermas, "Modernity Versus Postmodernity," *New German Critique* 22 (Winter 1981): 3–14. Under the title "Modernity—An Incomplete Project," this essay was reprinted in *The Anti-Aesthetic: Essays on Postmodern Culture*, ed. Hal Foster (Port Townsend, Wash.: Bay Press, 1983), 3–15.

38. Frederic Jameson, "Postmodernism and Consumer Society," *The Anti-Aesthetic: Essays on Postmodern Culture*, ed. Hal Foster, 111–25. Jameson has been reluctant to have this essay reprinted, preferring a more extended treatment of the subject in his *Postmodernism or, The Cultural Logic of Late Capitalism* (Durham, N.C.: Duke University Press, 1991). See also Jameson's foreword to Lyotard's *The Postmodern Condition*.

39. Frederic Jameson, *Postmodernism, or The Cultural Logic of Late Capitalism* (Durham, N.C.: Duke University Press, 1991).

40. H. Aram Veeser, "Introduction," *The New Historicism*, ed. H. Aram Veeser (New York: Routledge, 1989), ix–xvi. In challenging its own totalizing narratives, Brook Thomas identifies at least two strains of new historicism, one that reconstructively attempts a more inclusive literary history, the other focusing on a new poststructural analysis of canonical models. Both, Thomas argues, are indebted to Mikhail Bakhtin's rejection of univocal histories in favor of a response to previously marginalized voices. See Brook Thomas, *The New Historicism and Other Old-Fashioned Topics* (Princeton, N.J.: Princeton University Press, 1991).

41. Stephen Greenblatt, *Shakespearean Negotiations: The Circulation of Social Energy in Renaissance England* (Berkeley: University of California Press, 1988), 5.

42. Stephen Greenblatt, *The Power of Forms in the English Renaissance* (Norman, Okla.: Pilgrim Books, 1982), 5–6. See also Greenblatt's essay "Towards a Poetics of Culture," in *The New Historicism*, ed. H. Aram Veeser, 1–14.

43. Donald E. Pease, "National Identities, Postmodern Artifacts, and Postnational Narratives," *boundary 2* 19 (Spring 1992): 1–13.

44. David Suchoff, "New Historicism and Containment: Toward a Post–Cold War Cultural Theory," *Arizona Quarterly* 48 (Spring 1992): 137–61.

45. Alan Wilde, *Horizons of Assent: Modernism, Postmodernism, and the Ironic Imagination* (Philadelphia: University of Pennsylvania Press, 1987), 44. In an important subsequent book, Wilde locates the assent to the ordinary if diminished scale of contemporary life in such writers as Barthelme, Max Apple, Thomas Berger, Stanley Elkin, and Grace Paley between metafiction and the minimalist writers he describes as a school of "catatonic" realists. Terming this largely antiformalist work midfiction, he shows it to be concerned with heterogeneity of style, absence of closure, shifting of meanings, and an insistence on returning to the world, however compromised both that return and the world itself are found to be. See Alan Wilde, *Middle Grounds: Studies in Contemporary American Fiction* (Philadelphia: University of Pennsylvania Press, 1987).

46. Linda Hutcheon, *The Politics of Postmodernism* (London and New York: Routledge, 1989).

47. Susan Strehle, *Fiction in the Quantum Universe* (Chapel Hill: University of North Carolina Press, 1992).

48. Arthur Saltzman, "Epiphany and its Discontents: Coover, Gangemi, Sorrentino, and Postmodern Revelation," *Journal of Modern Literature* 15 (Spring 1989): 497–518. See also Saltzman's *Designs of Darkness in Contemporary American Fiction* (Philadelphia: University of Pennsylvania Press, 1990).

49. John Johnston, "Representation and Multiplicity in Four Postmodern American Novels," *Texas Review* 10 (1989): 23–36. The essay is reprinted in this volume.

50. Brian McHale and Moshe Ron, "On Not-Knowing How to Read Barthelme's 'The Indian Uprising,' " *The Review of Contemporary Fiction* 11 (Summer 1991): 50–68.

51. Kim Herzinger, "Introduction: On the New Fiction," *Mississippi Review* 40/41 (Winter 1985): 7–22.

52. David Leavitt, "New Voices and Old Values," *New York Times Book Review* (12 May 1985): 1, 26–27.

53. Bruce Bawer, "The Literary Brat Pack," *Diminishing Fictions: Essays on the Modern American Novel and Its Critics* (St. Paul, Minn.: Graywolf, 1988), 314–23.

54. David Kaufmann, "Yuppie Postmodernism," *Arizona Quarterly* 47 (Summer 1991): 93–116. This essay also appears in this volume. A rejection of American postmodernism had earlier been advanced by Charles Newman, who conceived of it as parallel to economic inflation, which, in literary terms, resulted in moral indifference. See Newman's "The Post-Modern Aura: The Act of Fiction in an Age of Inflation," *Salmagundi* (Spring–Summer 1984): 3–199.

55. Tom LeClair, *The Art of Excess: Mastery in Contemporary American Fiction* (Urbana: Univesity of Illinois Press, 1989).

56. Richard Wolin, "Modernism vs. Postmodernism," *Telos* 62 (1984/85): 9–22.

57. Frank Lentricchia, "Don DeLillo," *Raritan* 8 (Spring 1989): 1–29. See also Lentricchia's introduction, "The American Writer as Bad Citizen," *Introducing Don LeLillo*, ed. Frank Lentricchia (Durham, N.C.: Duke University Press, 1991), 1–6.

58. Jonathan Culler, "Toward a Theory of Non-Genre Literature," in *Surfiction: Fiction Now . . . and Tomorrow*, ed. Raymond Federman (Chicago: Swallow Press, 1975), 255–62.

59. Ralph Cohen, "Do Postmodern Genres Exist?" in *Postmodern Genres*, ed. Marjorie Perloff (Norman: University of Oklahoma Press, 1989), 11–27.

60. Robert Venturi, *Complexity and Contradiction in Architecture* (New York: Museum of Modern Art, 1977), 104.

61. Larry McCaffery, "The Fictions of the Present," in *Columbia Literary History of the United States*, ed. Emory Elliott (New York: Columbia University Press, 1988), 1167.

62. Bob Donahoo, "Moving with the Mainstream: A View of Postmodern American Science Fiction." This essay was written specifically for this volume and appears here for the first time with permission of the author.

63. Teresa L. Ebert, "The Convergence of Postmodern Innovative Fiction and Science Fiction: An Encounter with Samuel R. Delaney's Technotopia," *Poetics Today* 1 (1980): 91–104.

64. David Porush, *The Soft Machine: Cybernetic Fiction* (New York and London: Methuen, 1985).

65. Frederic Jameson, *Postmodernism or, The Cultural Logic of Late Capitalism* (Durham, N.C.: Duke University Press, 1991), n.1, 419.

66. Veronica Hollinger, "Cybernetic Deconstructions: Cyberpunk and Postmodernism," *Storming the Reality Studio: A Casebook of Cyberpunk and Postmodern Science Fiction*, ed. Larry McCaffery (Durham, N.C.: Duke University Press, 1991), 203–218.

67. Robert Siegle, *Suburban Ambush: Downtown Writing and the Fiction of Insurgency* (Baltimore: Johns Hopkins University Press, 1989).

68. Bernard W. Bell, *The Afro-American Novel and Its Tradition* (Amherst: University of Massachusetts Press, 1987).

69. Henry Louis Gates, Jr., *The Signifying Monkey: A Theory of Afro-American Literary Criticism* (New York: Oxford University Press, 1988).

70. McDowell's essay "Boundaries: Or Distance Relations and Close Kin," along with responses by Michael Awkward and Hortense Spiller, can be found in *Afro-American Literary Study in the 1990s*, ed. Houston A. Baker, Jr., and Patricia Redmond (Chicago: University of Chicago Press, 1989), 51–77.

71. *Feminisms: An Anthology of Literary Theory and Criticism*, ed. Robyn R. Warhol and Diane Price Herndl (New Brunswick, N.J.: Rutgers University Press, 1991).

72. Nancy Miller, "The Text's Heroine: A Feminist Critic and Her Fictions," *Diacritics* 12 (Summer 1982): 48–53, repr. in *Feminist Literary Criticism*, ed. Mary Eagleton (London and New York: Longman, 1991), 61–69. Nancy Hartsock, "Re-thinking Modernism: Minority vs. Majority Theories," *Cultural Critique* 7 (1987): 187–206.

73. Nina Baym, "Melodramas of Beset Manhood: How Theories of American Fiction Exclude Women Authors," *The New Feminist Criticism: Essays on Women, Literature, and Theory*, ed. Elaine Showalter (New York: Pantheon Books, 1985): 63–80. See also Baym's essay "The Madwoman and Her Languages," in *Feminist Issues in Literary Scholarship*, ed. Shari Benstock (Bloomington and Indianapolis: Indiana University Press, 1987), 45–61; originally published in slightly altered form in *Tulsa Studies in Women's Literature* 3 (1984–85).

74. Craig Owens, "The Discourse of Others: Feminism and Postmodernism," in *The Anti-Aesthetic: Essay on Postmodern Culture*, ed. Hal Foster, 57–77. Susan Suleiman similarly points to a central linkage between an oppositional feminist politics and postmodern aesthetics (and in particular the intertextual or "carnivalized" discourse of postmodernism). Suleiman's study is devoted largely to the male orientation of such European movements as surrealism. See her *Subversive Intent: Gender, Politics, and the Avant-Garde* (Cambridge, Mass.: Harvard University Press, 1990).

75. Ellen G. Friedman and Miriam Fuchs, "Introduction," *Breaking the Sequence: Women's Experimental Fiction* (Princeton, N.J.: Princeton University Press, 1989), 4. See also Ellen G. Friedman, "Where are the Missing Contents?: (Post)modernism, Gender, and the Canon," *PMLA* 108 (March 1993): 240–52. This essay is reprinted in this volume.

76. Elaine Showalter, "Feminist Criticsm in the Wilderness," *Critical Inquiry* 8 (Winter 1981): 179–205.

77. Toril Moi, "Feminism, Postmodernism, and Style: Recent Feminist Criticism in the United States," *Cultural Critique* 9 (1988): 3–22. See also Moi's *Sexual/Textual Politics: Feminist Literary Theory* (London and New York: Methuen, 1985): 1–18.

78. Alice Jardine, *Gynesis: Configurations of Women and Modernity* (Ithaca, N.Y.: Cornell University Press, 1985).

79. Jane Flax, "Postmodernism and Gender Relations in Feminist Theory," *Signs* 12 (Summer 1987): 621–43.

80. Nancy Fraser and Linda J. Nicholson, "Social Criticism without Philosophy: An Encounter between Feminism and Postmodernism," in *Feminism/Postmodernism*, ed. Linda J. Nicholson (New York and London: Routledge, 1990), 19–38. This essay previously appeared in *Communication* 10 (1988): 345–66, and in *Theory, Culture and Society* 5 (June 1988): 373–94, among other places.

81. David Cowart, "Attenuated Postmodernism: Pynchon's *Vineland*," *Critique: Studies in Contemporary Fiction* 32 (Winter 1990): 67–76. This essay also appears in this volume.

REVIEW

Deconstructing Deconstruction

Denis Donoghue

For the past forty or fifty years, teachers of literature in American colleges and universities have acted upon a few simple assumptions, mainly derived from I.A. Richards's early books *Principles of Literary Criticism* (1924) and *Practical Criticism* (1929). The first assumption is that in reading a poem you think of the words on the page as a transcription of a voice speaking; not necessarily the poet speaking in his own person, but a hypothetical person, speaking in imagined circumstances sufficiently indicated by what he says. The second assumption is that you are interpreting the poem, trying to understand the context, the speaker's sense of it, and the cogency of that sense. The meaning of the poem is what the speaker means to say. The third assumption is that you read poems to imagine experiences you have not had, to exercise sympathy and judgment upon them, and to take part in richer communications. It follows that it is essential, in reading a poem as in taking part in a conversation, to judge the speaker's tone correctly, because tone indicates his relation both to his own feeling and to the person or persons he is addressing. These assumptions, suitably elaborated, prescribe an orthodoxy of reading.

Take, for instance, Robert Frost's poem "Acquainted with the Night," which begins

> I have been one acquainted with the night.
> I have walked out in rain—and back in rain.
> I have outwalked the furthest city light.
>
> I have looked down the saddest city lane.
> I have passed by the watchman on his beat.
> And dropped my eyes, unwilling to explain.

In an orthodox reading, you follow the speaker's feeling from first word to last. In the first line, for instance, you think of the degree of assertiveness in "I," the precise degree of knowledge claimed in "acquainted," the relation

Reprinted with permission from *New York Review of Books* 27 (12 June 1980): 37–41. Copyright 1980, Nyrev, Inc.

between the apparent precision of "acquainted" and the vagueness of its object, "the night." You gauge the tone of those repeated "I have" phrases. And so on. Reading a poem is like meeting its speaker.

These assumptions are defined and proposed in most of the textbooks that have established themselves in American courses in literature, whether survey-courses or more advanced classes in the criticism of literature. The most influential textbook is still *Understanding Poetry* (1938) by Cleanth Brooks and Robert Penn Warren, a book that begins with these sentences: "Wordsworth called the poet a man speaking to men," and "Poetry is a form of speech, written or spoken." The best motto for the orthodoxy of reading is "hearing with eyes," as in Shakespeare's Sonnet 23:

> O learn to read what silent love hath writ,
> To hear with eyes belongs to love's fine wit.

The orthodoxy has been challenged from time to time, mostly by people who feel that Richards, Brooks, Warren, and the New Critics generally have ignored the historical understanding of literature and encouraged students to raise only the questions that can be answered by pointing to a few privileged terms, notably irony, ambiguity, tension, and complexity. And it has sometimes been remarked that certain poems, such as Pound's *Cantos*, defeat the elocutionist and have to be read in some other way. But generally the orthodoxy has stood up pretty well. The vocal and acoustic character of poetry is widely accepted.

Within the past ten years or so, a new challenge has arisen. If it were to prevail, it would surround with anxiety and misgiving not only the reading of poems but the negotiation of every major theme in Western literature and philosophy. The most vigorous challenger is Jacques Derrida, and the name of the challenge is Deconstruction, a form of commentary that relies upon a diverse if selective reading of Nietzsche and Freud. Derrida reached Deconstruction mainly by an aggressive reading of Husserl and Heidegger, a discipline there is no reason to think all his followers have practiced. He does not claim that Deconstruction is in every respect a distinctive activity: how could it be, since it is mainly a commentary written in the margin of other philosophical and literary texts? And it shares some of the arguments put forward by Structuralism, even though it eventually accuses structuralists of many follies ascribed to traditional forms of thought.

What form would a deconstructive reading of Frost's poem take? I have not seen one, and it might surprise me, but if it did not surprise me it would start by suffusing the "I" of the first line with doubt; questioning its neo-Cartesian assumption, and the blatant punctuality with which it implies a speaker. It would note that the printed words are given only as script, and that the reader is urged to convert them into acoustic signs: speech is supposed to be more fully present than print. The deconstructive critic would question the apparent assumption, in the first line, that someone—the speaker—exists, and has existed even before the "I" of his self-assertion; and that this "person" guarantees the authenticity of what he says by presiding over it as a controlling consciousness.

The critic would then question the confidence with which Frost's first line begins and ends; begins, in the assertive presentation of the "I" who speaks; and ends, with the equally assertive presentation of whatever experience "the night" is supposed to denote. He would ask himself whether the apparent slide from the dogmatic "I" to the vague, third-person-pronoun "one" is an evasion making possible the more extreme evasiveness of "the night," a phrase as sonorous as it is obscure; or merely a decent confession of misgiving about the assertiveness of "I" in the first place. The critic would then go through the poem, diagnosing every example of blindness or naïveté in Frost's relation to his language; the false confidence with which he proceeds; the uncritical assumption that by miming a voice he is verifying a personality.

Deconstruction is a style of accusation. Its main charges are these. One: Western thought, whether in literature or philosophy, has been grounded upon bogus axioms of being and presence; upon being, understood as presence. Meaning has been offered by analogy with presence; the presence of an object to one's sight; the self-presence of subjectivity and consciousness, as in the speaking "I" of Frost's poem.

Two: what Derrida calls "the metaphysics of presence" has been endorsed by the presentation of meaning as speech. He calls this prison house of language "logocentrism" or "phonocentrism," and claims that it involves "the absolute proximity of voice and being, of voice and the meaning of being." The meaning of Frost's poem begins with the reader's feeling that he is in the presence of its speaker. According to Derrida, the cardinal word in Western thought is logos, taken to mean the original uttered word, identified in some theologies with the audible presence of God. The entire philosophic tradition is infatuated, Derrida alleges, with the notion of a first moment, authentic and paternal.

Three: the axiom of being as presence is mere wish-fulfillment, and those who indulge themselves in it are inauthentic; it testifies not to presence but to absence, to a desire for presence; it keeps us always turned back toward an ostensibly first moment in which we were guaranteed authenticity by the speaking voice of the Father. Reading Frost's poem by translating it into an individual voice, we are really consoling ourselves, trying to persuade ourselves that our entire lives are dialogues, continuous in some sense with the original moment in which God uttered Himself.

Four: the logos-prison has forced upon us delusions of self, personality, subjectivity, creativity, imaginative power, ego-psychology, and so forth.

Frost's poem is full of these delusions of personal grandeur: "And dropped my eyes, unwilling to explain." Five: psychological terms (such as feeling, emotion, desire, motive, drive) are misleading, they encourage us to think of them as attributes of our suffering and masterful selves; they must be replaced by linguistic terms.

So the best answer to our infatuation with voices and presences is writing—writing stripped of all delusions. Writing in this sense has given up yearning for a lost father, it knows that it is an orphan, it is merely what it is and therefore it has vetoed nostalgia, accepted its separation from any origin and settled for that separation. Deconstruction seeks, in Geoffrey Hartman's phrase, "the eclipse of voice by text." Text in that phrase means language set not to work but to play among its internal possibilities, having been released from all the old claims of meaning as voice, personal presence, and dialogue.

What Deconstruction urges is not a new system of thought but skepticism toward all the old ways, which are construed as really only one way. It proposes a certain critical position.

Deconstruction and Criticism [by Harold Bloom, Paul de Man, Jacques Derrida, Geoffrey H. Hartman, and J. Hillis Miller] is offered as a manifesto of "one of the most stimulating movements in contemporary letters." It is an odd book. The critics who have joined to produce it have only one property in common: they teach at Yale. The book has more to do with the rhetoric of power in American universities than with its ostensible subject: its evident purpose is to claim that Yale houses a major school of deconstructive criticism. But the truth is that only two of the five critics are deconstructors: Derrida and Paul de Man. J. Hillis Miller practices occasional conformity, he has written essays in the spirit and according to the letter of Deconstruction. But he seems to me still what he ever was, a phenomenologist, a critic of consciousness, his heart in the Geneva of Georges Poulet. Geoffrey Hartman is one of the most vigorous opponents of Deconstruction. His essay in the present book is a meditation on Wordsworth's poem "A Little Onward": a fine essay, indeed, but it has nothing to do with Deconstruction, and it could have been published with greater propriety in the *Review of English Studies*.

What Harold Bloom is doing in this book, I have no idea; he is not a deconstructor. A rabbi, a prophet, he would never let himself be shamed out of the language of self, presence, and voice. His essay in *Deconstruction and Criticism* rehearses his famous theory of poetry, using for his text John Ashbery's "Self-Portrait in a Convex Mirror." As always, Bloom's categories are psychological rather than linguistic, he does not claim for language anything more than an instrumental and referential function.

Derrida's essay is an account of Maurice Blanchot's fiction, *L'arrêt de mort*, concentrating on one motif, that of living and living on (*vivre; survivre*):

it has much to say about ghosts, the narrator as one who lives on, corpses embalmed, and so on. I seem to have heard parts of it in Derrida's lecture at New York University a few months ago, the most opaque and withholding lecture I have ever heard. So far as I can understand it (but that's not far), the essay is trying to dislodge from the story a language that retains an old-fashioned affection for truth and being; to dislodge it by projecting it beyond itself (*la sur-vérité*) into an empty future. In his earlier books, Derrida tried to dislodge such language by consigning it to an empty past for which the key word has always been *déjà*. Hence, in the new essay, his emphasis falls on the motif of a stairway that figures in Blanchot's fiction; there are pages upon pages of word-play on *escalier* as escalade of truth, "one truth about another, one truth *on* (top of) another, one above or below the other, each step more or less true than truth." These pages are pretty hectic, but I read them as part of the deconstructive effort to show that truth and word never coincide.

Paul de Man's essay is a study of Shelley's "The Triumph of Life"—a study in deconstruction. Most readers would probably take the poem as a vision in which Shelley sees a neo-Roman triumphal procession, with chariots, charioteers, captives, and an unnamed Shape. Shelley then speaks to Rousseau, who gives him a guided vision of Voltaire, Frederick the Great, Czar Paul of Russia, Catherine the Great, Leopold the Second, Plato, Aristotle, and Alexander the Great. Rousseau gives Shelley a vision of what we may call Ideal Beauty. I cannot report on all the various interpretations of the poem, but those I have read are compatible at least with the common sense of the poem as involving visionary meetings, partings, voices, questions, and answers.

None of this interests Paul de Man. He merely uses the poem, drags it on the wheels of his own chariot, determined to prove that poetic figures are not to be ascribed to the imagination that apparently engaged with language to produce them but rather to the arbitrariness of Language itself. The "Shape all light" encountered by Rousseau in "The Triumph of Life" is "the figure for the figurality of all signification," according to de Man. It follows, he claims, that "the figure is not naturally given or produced but that it is posited by an arbitrary act of language." By this he means:

> The positing power of language is both entirely arbitrary, in having a strength that cannot be reduced to necessity, and entirely inexorable in that there is no alternative to it. It stands beyond the polarities of chance and determination and can therefore not be part of a temporal sequence of events.

I don't understand this. De Man, implacable in denying to the poet any active power, is evidently willing to ascribe an "act" to "language"; he apparently does this merely for the satisfaction of reporting that the "acts" of language are mechanical, arbitrary, and repetitive. He will do anything, this critic, rather than read poems in terms of poets, speakers, imaginations, and languages in some sense willing to be invoked. When he adverts to rhyming words (billow, willow, pillow) in a poem, he takes the *rhyming* as primary, the meanings as secondary. Such sequences, he maintains, are generated "by random and superficial properties of the signifier rather than by the constraints of meaning." And he goes far out of his way to avoid the ordinary reader's understanding that it is a mark of the poet's skill to reconcile the constraints of meaning and the properties of the signifier; to keep his chariot going happily by driving both horses at the same speed and in the same direction.

De Man's new book *Allegories of Reading* is a study of figural language in Rousseau, Nietzsche, Rilke, and Proust. What de Man means by allegory is not as clear as it should be. Normally we think of allegory when we read such works as *The Divine Comedy* and *The Pilgrim's Progress* and sense (or know) that the narrative has another meaning or other meanings beyond the literal one. Angus Fletcher's *Allegory: The Theory of a Symbolic Mode* (1964) says of allegorical works that "as they go along they are usually saying one thing in order to mean something beyond that one thing." Allegory is a mode of writing in which one set of meanings sustains another, and the two are kept separate by being kept parallel to each other.

The common preference for symbol rather than allegory, which is found in Romantic aesthetic since the later years of the eighteenth century, is explained by this separation. Coleridge, for instance, in *The Statesman's Manual* and elsewhere, downgrades allegory as being merely "a translation of abstract notions into a picture-language, which is itself nothing but an abstraction from objects of the senses." Symbol on the other hand, as Coleridge says, "always partakes of the reality which it renders intelligible; and while it enunciates the whole, abides itself as a living part in that unity of which it is the representative." Unity of experience, as a deeply desired state, is the promise of the symbol. The symbol asserts that we may live fully in the world; we are not fated to be aliens there.

From the point of view of Deconstruction, this promise of unity—indeed the quest for unity—is yet another instance of the hated "metaphysic of presence." De Man calls it "self-mystification." In an effort to cancel the promise of unity as offered by the symbol and by the general theory of imagination, he prefers allegory:

> Whereas the symbol postulates the possibility of an identity or identification, allegory designates primarily a distance in relation to its own origin, and, renouncing the nostalgia and the desire to coincide, it establishes its language in the void of this temporal distance. In so doing, it prevents the self from an illusory identification with the non-self, which is now fully, though painfully, recognized as a non-self.

Allegory, then, holds sign and meaning to be discontinuous, just as it supposes man and the world to be strictly separate and that every attempt to blur their separateness is fraudulent.

It follows that de Man must have the same objection to metaphor that he has to symbol and imagination:

> By suggesting the potential identification of tenor and vehicle, the traditional metaphor stresses the possible recuperation of a stable meaning or set of meanings. It allows one to see language as a means towards a recovered presence that transcends language itself.

Metaphor is therefore compromised, it is a language of desire, another form of wish-fulfillment. De Man wants us to understand "the impossibility for the language of poetry to appropriate anything, be it as consciousness, as object, or as a synthesis of both."

The essay on Rilke pursues the logic of de Man's argument. Again he ascribes to "language" what ordinary readers would ascribe to Rilke. If a poem seems to denote a movement of feeling, it is merely "rhetorical agitation." If poems seem to refer to something, the something is merely virtual, it is there only for the rhymes. Themes inhabit these poems "not because they are the expression of Rilke's own lived experience (whether they are or not is irrelevant) but because their structure allows for the unfolding of his patterns of figuration."

At one point de Man examines Rilke's poem *"Ich liebe dich, du sanftestes Gesetz."* It is a difficult poem; it is hard to divine what the "gentlest law" (*"sanftestes Gesetz"*) enforces, or what the speaker's relation to God is. However, an ordinary reader would register the feeling of constraint in various forms in the first stanza, and the gradual movement to a feeling of release and freedom at the end. He would follow the speaker's voice as the several invocations lead to the change of imperatives from object to subject in the last line. He would try to interpret the poem on the assumption that it is about something rather than about nothing. He would get no help from de Man, who reduces the entire poem to euphony. The meaning of such poems "is the conquest of the technical skills which they illustrate by their acoustic success." How little "acoustic success" stands for to a deconstructor, it is unnecessary to remark.

De Man also examines Rilke's *"Am Rande der Nacht,"* but only to refute the reader's assumption that the poem has something to do with man and nature. The speaker says, among other things

> Ich bin eine Saite,
> über rauschende breite
> Resonanzen gespannt.

("I am a string strung over wide, roaring resonances.") But strings and violins do not matter, according to de Man, such references are merely ostensible: the poems "are composed of entities, objects and subjects, who themselves behave like words, which 'play' at language according to the rules of rhetoric as one plays ball according to the rules of the game." (I interrupt to remark that the ball does not play anything: the player plays the game with a ball according to rules which he knows and which the ball does not know. Left to itself, the ball would not budge.)

De Man's general argument is that ostensibly human motives are properly understood as functions of textual systems. The rhetorical mode of Rousseau's *Emile*, for instance, "produces the opposition between nature and society as a textual necessity." Vetoing the presence of the writer, de Man replaces him by an invented ghost which he inserts in a machine called grammar. Thinking of "the arbitrary power play of the signifier," he allows his mind to be driven by the metaphor of language as machine; with odd consequences for his reading of Rousseau's *Confessions*.

De Man concentrates on the episode in the second Book about Rousseau's theft of the ribbon: he steals a ribbon, tells a lie about it, and puts the blame on the servant Marion. De Man insists on reading this episode as if he were watching the repetitions of a machine. He quotes the passage in the fourth *Rêverie* where Rousseau reconsiders the theft of the ribbon, and another occasion on which he told a lie. "It is certain," Rousseau says, "that neither my judgment nor my will dictated my reply, but that it was the automatic result of my embarrassment:" "*et qu'elle fut l'effet machinal de mon embarras.*" De Man applies this *effet machinal* to the text itself, and to textuality in general.

But the matter is well enough explained by going back a few pages in the *Rêverie* to the passage where Rousseau says, "My heart followed these rules of conscience mechanically before my reason had adopted them, and the moral instinct alone made the application: "*Mon coeur suivait machinalement ces règles avant que ma raison les eût adoptées, et l'instinct moral en fit seul l'application.*" It is reasonable to translate *machinalement* as "mechanically" or "automatically," but it would not be far wrong to say "instinctively" or "spontaneously." The point is simply that Rousseau feels his conscience acted before the obligation of reason. Nothing in the passage in the *Confessions* justifies de Man's fixation upon the notion of the machine in a relentless application to the property of grammar. Besides, grammar is formal but not mechanical or automatic, it limits choice but does not prevent choice. A sufficient proof is that many different styles inhabit the same language.

But de Man can't bear to have Rousseau do what he appears to do— discuss his motives, discriminate between one force of feeling and another, account for something he has done in psychological terms. De Man wants to remove the entire discourse from Rousseau to grammar. When the question of guilt comes up, de Man says that "any guilt, including the guilty pleasure of writing the fourth *Rêverie*, can always be dismissed as the gratuitous product of a textual grammar or a radical fiction: there can never be enough guilt around to match the text-machine's infinite power to excuse." This is witty, but trivial, at best a Wildean flourish. It is always possible, de Man goes on, "to face up to any experience (to excuse any guilt), because the experience always exists simultaneously as fictional discourse and as empirical event and it is never possible to decide which one of the two possibilities is the right one." If you've ever felt guilty, the decision has been painfully easy. To remain suspended between de Man's two possibilities is a clear instance of self-mystification.

Readers of the *Confessions* think they hear someone talking about his own experience, accusing himself, justifying himself, and so forth. De Man can't bear to hear that voice, because he doesn't want to hear any voice: he wants to see a machine working without human intervention. His application of a linguistic model to all situations is pedantic. If it were enforced in practice as rigorously as he proposes, it would dismiss the questions commonly considered in morality, ethics, politics, and psychology, and treat them as purely linguistic functions. De Man draws back from that conclusion, not a moment too soon. Indeed, from time to time in *Allegories of Reading* he makes concessions which, if added together, would put in question the whole ideology of Deconstruction. I shall list them more prominently than they are listed in the book.

One: "the notion of a language entirely freed of referential constraints is properly inconceivable." When you insist upon the fallacy of reference, the insistence is referential. As de Man concedes. "The deconstruction states the fallacy of reference in a necessarily referential mode." The mode of *Allegories of Reading*, for instance, is referential. Two: de Man concedes, in his reading of Proust's novel, that as soon as you refer to the narrator, even if you reduce him to the status of a pronoun, you allow yourself to infer the intent of the subject from the structure of the predicate. The personal concession is enforced by reference to voice, even if it is only to the active or passive voice in grammar.

If you go this far, I don't see how you can prevent yourself from going further and admitting the full regalia of personal presence. De Man sometimes does this, referring with ordinary naïveté to "the essential barrenness of the self and of the world." Three: in any case, de Man is willing to allow the self to be recuperated, recovered from its dispersal in the world, if only "in the highly abstracted and generalized form of a deconstructive process of self-denial." Self-denial is just as naïve as self-delight, self-regard, self-disclosure, or any other such gesture. In de Man's terms, the self would be reinvented "at the far end of its most radical negation," no longer the dupe of its desires.

Four: de Man admits, as Derrida also does, that "deconstructive readings can point out the unwarranted identifications achieved by substitution, but they are powerless to prevent their recurrence even in their own discourse." Five: irony itself is not secure. *Allegories of Reading* ends by saying that irony, no longer a trope, is "the undoing of the deconstructive allegory of all tropological cognitions, the systematic undoing, in other words, of under-standing." No wonder Harold Bloom has referred to de Man's "serene linguis-tic nihilism."

The deconstructive reading of texts is practiced nowadays not only in seminars at Yale but in many other graduate schools. If you want a deconstructive reading of, say, *Daniel Deronda*, you can have one. But there are several problems. Deconstructive readings are written mostly for the sake of the theory they are supposed to endorse; the strings are attached before the essay is sent off to *Diacritics* or *Glyph* or *Semiotexte*. Further: nothing I have read in deconstructive criticism is likely to suppress the common desire of readers to believe that in reading a poem they are listening to someone saying something about something—whatever critical questioning they may bring to the act of listening.

No consideration of form, grammar, or structure is likely to divert an intelligent reader from the assumption that a poem consists of words spoken, hypothetically, by someone. Nor have I seen anything that seriously damages the Romantic theory of imagination as variously but on the whole consistently outlined from the late eighteenth-century German and English critics to Emerson, Stevens, Frost, and Harold Bloom; the theory by which the imagi-nation is understood as the mind in the aspect of its freedom and creativity. Genius is only an extreme degree of creative power, a degree not available, indeed, to most of us but demonstrably active in some people; in Words-worth, Beethoven, Goethe, and Baudelaire, for instance. I have not read anything in deconstructive criticism that would convince me that Words-worth's "Immortality Ode" is best read as an anonymous work of Language proceeding with mechanical and repetitive force. Deconstruction bears ap-proximately the relation to reading that Robbe-Grillet's theory bears to the writing and reading of fiction; it is cogent enough to induce an occasionally felt scruple, but not a determination to change one's ways.

Why, then, is it having a success in American universities, or at least in some of them? It can't be explained by its charm, or the pleasure it offers. What Derrida and de Man practice is merely an extreme form of skepticism: an old story, after all. Derrida's version is delivered with a certain Byronic chic. He reminds me of the Surrealists in the Thirties who, as William Empson says in a poem, enjoyed "a nightmare handy as a bike." De Man's style is a sober thing, painstaking as well as painsgiving: he seems to be the Malcontent of the movement.

Still, its success is very curious. I have only two or three thoughts on the subject. I think Deconstruction appeals to the clerisy of graduate students, who like to feel themselves superior to the laity of common readers, liberated from their shared meanings; liberated, too, from the tedious requirement of meaning as such, the official obligation to suppose that words mean something finite rather than everything or nothing. Deconstruction allows them to think of themselves as forming a cell, the nearest thing the universities can offer in the form of an avant-garde. The wretched side of this is that Deconstruction encourages them to feel superior not only to undergraduates but to the authors they are reading. There is also a suggestion of scientific method in Deconstruction which appeals to graduate students who have begun to doubt that the Humanities constitute a discipline. And there is the politics of Deconstruction: like Structuralism, it is anti-bourgeois, and particularly hostile to the ego-psychology which a bourgeois ideology is supposed to offer its members as a consolation prize.

Whatever the case may be, Deconstruction seems to be an instance of "serious folly," a phrase Shelley used in "The Triumph of Life" with something quite different in mind.

THEORY

◆

Scheherazade runs out of plots, goes on talking; the king, puzzled, listens: an essay on new fiction

PHILIP STEVICK

I

"Endings are elusive, middles are nowhere to be found, but worst of all is to begin, to begin, to begin," writes Barthelme, sympathizing with Edgar, a character with whom he shares certain problems. We all share Edgar's problems. Is it possible to begin to talk about fiction that strikes us as being in some way new or experimental without making large constructs that try to take stock of the very art of fiction itself? Indeed, of the very vitality and integrity of our time? Let us begin with no assumptions about the life of our time. The world, somebody says, is now so complicated that anything one says about it is true. As for the nature of fiction at the present time, two rather plain assumptions will suffice.

Lionel Trilling, in a recent essay in *Commentary*, has claimed that the very narrative impulse itself is exhausted, that we do not tell stories to each other any more, do not believe in stories, do not choose them as the vehicles for our deepest feelings, simply do not bother with narrative any more. Anthony Burgess, on the other hand, in his book *The Novel Now*, sets out to survey prose fiction since the great figures of the modernist period, and, although he obviously means his book to be inclusive, encyclopedic, and rather undiscriminating, it is still surprising in the sheer bulk of its subject: some two hundred writers of fiction of sufficient quality to seem to Burgess worth discussing. In fact one comes to realize that anybody with a different background, an extensive but different reading experience, and a different temperament from Burgess could easily add a hundred more writers of fiction, all of considerable seriousness and significance. Trilling's essay seems to me among the least persuasive pieces he has ever done, a last stage in Trilling's willed and rationalized withdrawal from the contemporary. That a mind so fine as Trilling's should be so repelled as he is at the narrative art of the

Reprinted from *TriQuarterly* 26 (Winter 1973): 332–62, with permission of the author. *TriQuarterly* is a publication of Northwestern University.

present time and so ingenious at explaining it away is one of the reasons that we don't understand contemporary fiction any better than we do. It is true, all the same, that Trilling's hostility to the contemporary leads him to a premise that we can adopt to a different context. Something very basic *has* changed in the primacy and centrality of the narrative motive and the narrative appeal in the last ten years. Let Trilling's essay point us toward our first assumption: that the difference between Barthelme and Katherine Mansfield, between Pynchon and Hemingway, is not a difference of historical setting, or style, or technique, or subject, or tone, or mode, although it involves all of these. The difference between the two goes to the roots of the narrative act itself, is a difference in what it means to tell. Let Burgess' inclusiveness point us toward our second assumption: that a perfectly amazing number of writers of considerable skill and utterly varied convictions about the nature of their art are flourishing at the present time, that along with some remarkably innovative fiction there are also some true and moving books being written with the technical resources of Balzac and Trollope, and that anything we say about any segment of the enormous body of contemporary fiction is bound to look partial and unjustifiably exclusive to anyone with a modest breadth of response.

The first fiction of Donald Barthelme's *City Life* begins:

> An aristocrat was riding down the street in his carriage. He ran over my father.

> After the ceremony I walked back to the city. I was trying to think of the reason my father had died. Then I remembered: he was run over by a carriage.

A short fiction by Richard Brautigan entitled *The World War I Los Angeles Airplane* begins:

> He was found lying dead near the television set on the front room floor of a small rented house in Los Angeles. My wife had gone to the store to get some ice cream. It was an early-in-the-night-just-a-few-blocks-away store. We were in an ice-cream mood. The telephone rang. It was her brother to say that her father had died that afternoon.

Robert Coover begins his fiction *A Pedestrian Accident* in this way:

> Paul stepped off the curb and got hit by a truck. He didn't know what it was that hit him at first, but now, here on his back, under the truck, there could be no doubt. Is it me? he wondered. Have I walked the earth and come here?

It is obvious at first that there are certain common characteristics of method, voice, and sensibility in the three beginnings: an extraordinary innocence, either genuine or feigned, even a kind of common prose rhythm deriving from the unwillingness to subordinate and complicate that is an attribute of that innocence, a readiness to confront certain extremities of life, in these cases pain, accident, death, and mourning, but an investing of these extremities with an odd and terribly distant artifice, a playing off of a method of wit, tough, flip, and facile, that is reminiscent of the stand-up comic ("Then I remembered. . . ." "We were in an ice-cream mood." "Is it me? he wondered.") against a personal fragility and vulnerability that is very different from the classic toughness, knowingness, and irony of the dominant modernists. It is odd how quickly these qualities of "voice" can register on us, so that we know, before the structure of the fiction begins to take shape in our minds, that we are being spoken to by an imagination post-Joycean and very much of our time, the theatricality of our three fictions being different in its tone of voice from anything we are accustomed to in Dostoevsky and Gide and Faulkner. Finally what unites the three fictions is the common presentation of the kind of event, death and violent accident, that *must* be led up to, or explained, or prepared for, or set in a context, but is, in these three cases, simply told. It is the chilling, almost pathological directness of beginning in the three fictions that is likely to seem to us most striking, for the fictions do not seem particularly "experimental," as we might use the word of other arts—their syntax is conventional and the words follow one another on the page. The beginnings seem to be as striking as they are because they are more than simply violations of conventions. They are epistemic dislocations, and the clearest analogue that I can think of is Kafka's great beginning, "As Gregor Samsa awoke one morning from a troubled dream, he found himself changed in his bed to some monstrous kind of vermin."

The differences of the three beginnings from each other are as obvious as the similarities. Barthelme exploits his fondness for the absurdities of a bookish past, the camp obliquity that corresponds, in his prose, to his use of old engravings in the texts of his more recent work. Brautigan superimposes a deliberate and affectatious naiveté upon the plausible details of California. Coover begins to play back and forth between what one does feel at moments of extreme pain and what one thinks one ought to feel, between speech which is deeply felt yet comes out as cliché and speech which is formulaic yet comes out as existential cry. It is by observing the differences between the fictions that we might assume what I believe to be true, that what we have is not a movement, not a clique, not a group, not a school, not a unified assertion of anything nor a reaction against anything, not a conspiracy. On the other hand, it is by pointing to the similarities between the fictions that we might assume what I also believe to be true, that there are indeed some shared traits among writers of non-traditional fiction, a common sense of what they are not a part of, certain shared enthusiasms, certain common characteristics of voice and technique. Both the similarities and the differences suggest why it is that we have very little critical description worth attending to that would help us make sense out of recent non-traditional fiction.

New directions in the art of the last century and a half have generally been surrounded with the appearance of social agonism (consider Spender's title *The Struggle of the Modern*, the sense at least since Wordsworth and commonplace in our time that one's own art is a counterforce, in combat with the torpor and stupidity of one's own time) and a defensive verbalism, in which the legitimacy of the new art was described in a never-ending "introduction." Every generation of poets since Wordsworth has claimed to be writing the language actually used by men, in contrast to its lumpish and stilted predecessors. Every generation of novelists has claimed to be in touch with reality in a way denied its predecessors. These defensive maneuvers loom so large that it would not be surprising to find a reader who recalled "Tradition and the Individual Talent" as clearly as *The Wasteland*, who relished Shaw's introductions rather more than the plays themselves, and who recalled that there was once such a thing as "Vorticism" without being able to name a single literary work that was in any way related to it. Of recent non-traditional fiction, however, there is not much sense of social agonism: writers like Heller, Barth, and Vonnegut are lionized. As for the manifestos, the polemical introductions, the defensive stance-taking so commonplace in the past, they are all virtually nonexistent. There has probably not been a comparable body of writing since the Romantic period in which the writers themselves have told us so little about what was wrong with their predecessors, how they hoped to improve upon them, and why we ought to be reading their works.

In the absence of tactical statements by the writers themselves, we can map out areas of coherence in literary history in a number of ways. One is by finding a commanding, charismatic figure who seems to have dominated the art of his time, allowing the figure's dominance to provide the center of that coherence. The Age of Pope is defined by defining both the nature of Pope's genius and the nature of his dominance. American tough-guy fiction is ordinarily understood by fixing Hemingway at its origins and its center. One could guess from the three passages just quoted that although the three writers might well share some affinities (for Beckett and Kafka, perhaps for Céline and Nathanael West, or among older writers for Sterne and Rabelais), they are not dominated by anybody. There is no peak to the pyramid and our search for *that* kind of coherence is pointless.

Another way of finding coherence is to discover a common ideology. The Oxford Movement is defined by what its members believed. And our habit of grouping writers according to decade or generation is based on the assumption that writers grouped in that way can be seen to cohere by reason of their shared assumptions about the nature of the world. Of our three initial examples, I am not sure what ideology means when applied to Barthelme and Coover; I think that the word may mean something when applied to

Brautigan. But in any case, if we are equipped to define literary coherence by finding a common ideology, we do seem to be out of luck here.

Still another way of defining literary coherence is to look at the aesthetic transaction itself. We have a movement, or a school, when we can point to a coherent audience or a specific group of periodicals or publishers especially receptive to a specialized kind of art. The nature of *The Yellow Book*, its contributors, and its audience all cohere as a unit. And we naturally seek to understand "Southern Agrarianism" or "The New Criticism" by understanding the journals, such as the *Sewanee* and *Kenyon Reviews*, in which those aesthetic and intellectual transactions were presented. Among our three examples, there is, again, no coherence at all. The audience for Coover does not overlap, so far as one can tell, with the audience for Brautigan, and the two are rarely published in the same places. Barthelme's case is the most peculiar of the three. *City Life* is made up of work published in *The New Yorker* and *Paris Review*; as a book, *City Life* was reviewed as an avant-garde mystification—and was offered as an alternate to the members of the Book-of-the-Month Club: I bought my copy from the revolving rack at a drugstore. In short, almost all of the equipment which we have for defining a direction in the history of an art, setting it off from what has gone before and what comes after, breaks down in the face of those writers whom we would easily call non-traditional writers of fiction, an incongruous and highly individual lot.

On the other hand, the correspondences among new writers of fiction suggest, as much as the differences between them, why it is that new fiction is so little understood. "Post-modernist" is an epithet that I, for one, find annoying and unhelpful. But it is true, all the same, that recent fiction no longer orients itself according to its own relations to the modernist masters and that this sense of discontinuity with the dominant figures of modernism is one of the few qualities that unite new fiction. (Ihab Hassan's contention that the great fountainhead of "post-modernist" fiction is *Finnegans Wake* seems to me perverse, bizarre, and unsupportable.) Yet most criticism still defines the art of our own time as being, in the case of fiction, the art of the twentieth century. A professional interest in Joyce need not be exclusive of a professional interest in Coover; but in fact the two almost always are exclusive of each other, a fact not surprising when one reflects on the gulf in time between the two, Coover being as far in time from Joyce as Joyce is from George Eliot. What recent fiction tells us on every page is that it is of another age than the modernist masters. And what we are further obliged to recognize is that our public conceptualizing has not even acknowledged the transition, much less provided the organizing devices by means of which we can make sense of it.

There was a time when the kind of public understanding that we lack was supplied by the "man of letters." But, as John Gross has magisterially demonstrated, the man of letters has fallen and figures comparable to Henley,

Saintsbury, and Middleton Murry, or more recently Edmund Wilson, are not likely to arise in our own time to mediate between new art and its anxious public in a way that those older figures did. Even if such figures did exist, they would find their function difficult to perform, since new fiction tends to mock, subvert, and preempt any traditional attempts at critical interpretation of itself. And thus recent narrative art (with the exception of "new" French fiction, which has not lacked apologetics for itself) has set about creating a new set of narrative possibilities in a time when the public for fiction does not expect or wish for anybody to seek to form its taste and instruct its response and in a time when the professional interpreters of contemporary narrative art tend to be, in fact, interpreters of modernist art, which is to say the art of the half century now past.

Finally we understand less than we should about art like that of Barthelme, Brautigan, and Coover because our modes of critical understanding are undermined by a family of metaphors to which we continue to cling with obsessive tenacity, namely the organic metaphors by which we describe the "birth," the "growth," and the "death" of fiction. Certain genres in literary history, especially the more rigid, stylized, and highly specialized ones, have been invented, have been extensively used, and have been ultimately abandoned; but such formal exhaustion has always been the result of a complex of causes involving audience, ideas, authorial motives, even the economics of publication and presentation. When we apply the organic metaphors to the flourishing and declining of literary genres, however, we pretend that no complex of causes need be found because genres, we seem to say, contain within themselves their own vitality. Furthermore, the organic metaphor is extremely tendentious. If the novel, or the short story, is, as a genre, comparable to a body, then it contains the elements of itself and is threatened by alien elements, those alien elements being, of course, prose fictions that lie eccentric to the unstated norm with which the body of fiction is identified. William Park has described the use of the organic metaphor by early historians of fiction, with all of their talk of forerunners and founders, so that by the time of Ernest Baker's *History of the English Novel* in 1924, "the growth, evolution, branches, roots, stems, and trunks occur in such profusion that we can only assume that the novel as botanical garden had been taken for granted, as indeed it still is by present-day writers, who while concerning themselves with rhetoric and 'strategy' continue to use the evolutionary metaphors."[1] As for the dying of the body of fiction, readers of the novel in the latter third of the eighteenth century, as J. M. S. Tompkins observes, thought the novel dead, its possibilities played out.[2] Which means that, if the novel has been dying for two centuries there is something wrong not with the novel but with the metaphor. For a long time serious discussion of new fiction has been hindered by the cumbersome, vacuous business of dying forms. The new fiction of the past twenty years is worth attending to on its own terms, not because it is living while something else has died.

I suggest two ways into the new fiction I describe. One is by comparison with the recent past, a piece of good fiction of not very long ago which is, most emphatically, the kind of thing which new fictions are not. The other is by something larger and riskier, an aesthetics of new fiction, set against the classic premises of prose fiction since the beginning of the novel.

II

Jean Stafford's "A Country Love Story" begins in this way:

> An antique sleigh stood in the yard, snow after snow banked up against its eroded runners. Here and there upon the bleached and splintery seat were wisps of horsehair and scraps of the black leather that had once upholstered it. It bore, with all its jovial curves, an air not so much of desuetude as of slowed-down dash, as if weary horses, unable to go another step, had at last stopped here. The sleigh had come with the house. The former owner, a gifted businesswoman from Castine who bought old houses and sold them again with all their pitfalls still intact, had said when she was showing them the place, "A picturesque detail, I think," and, waving it away, had turned to the well, which, with enthusiasm and at considerable length, she said had never gone dry. Actually, May and Daniel had found the detail more distracting than picturesque, so nearly kin was it to outdoor arts and crafts. . . .

Moving from Barthelme, Brautigan, and Coover to Jean Stafford represents no particular difference in quality. Questions of qualitative ranking tend to occupy readers and critics less than they used to; but it is clear enough that all four writers are in command of their materials and are in their quite different ways artful and sophisticated. All four works are short fiction, in which the beginnings I quote set in motion aesthetic objects which turn out to be of comparable size. The four fictions are not far from each other in time, less than twenty years. Yet the beginning of Jean Stafford's story, in comparison with the more recent fictions, reads like something from the other side of the moon. The most immediately striking differences lie in what Jean Stafford does, and the more recent writers do not do, with time and with physical objects.

"An antique sleigh," "snow after snow," "eroded runners," phrases like these from the first sentence begin to present a durational mode that is little short of obsessive, projecting us immediately into a world of waiting, expecting, contemplating, appreciating, hoping, wondering, all of those experiences in which the mind and the sensibility are deployed around the central object of their contemplation, slow change. Both objects and people bear with them the marks of their own past; everything decays and disinte-

grates; both nature and people present the appearance of cyclic or ritualisti-
cally recurring behavior. In addition, time, in such fiction, always carries
with it an implicit valuation. A character shows his age gracefully or clumsily;
the process of aging carries with it great dignity or great pathos; an aging
object carries with it a sense of decreased value, as a result of its diminished
usefulness, or a sense of enhanced value, as a result of its tasteful durability.
And so it is that we are unsure, in that first paragraph, whether the sleigh
is worn out, and should be discarded, or is an authentic antique, and should
be preserved. There is no doubt that the cyclic, ritualistic house-buying and
-selling of the "gifted businesswoman" is specious and faintly repulsive.

It need hardly be said that no one goes through life with his eye so
firmly fixed on the clock as this, saying to himself, A is older than B, but
B bears its age more gracefully than A. Such an obsession with time is a
convention which we never particularly noticed as a convention when a great
deal of fiction was written in that way. There is a perverse kind of time
sense at work in new fiction, centering especially around a fascination with
the junk of our culture, both linguistic and material. But it is in no way
comparable to the durational quality of Jean Stafford's story. If we recall the
enormous amount of critical attention given to the philosophy of Bergson
and the temporal techniques of Proust, Virginia Woolf, and Joyce, and if
we then regard the use of time in Jean Stafford's story as a stylized domestication of one of the chief modernist preoccupations, then the atemporality of
such fiction as Barthelme's, the indifference to slow change and the lack of
interest in the value-conferring process I have described all become highly
significant. The high-handed atemporality of new fiction is a remarkable
abandonment of a set of conventions and an epistemic orientation that we
had grown accustomed to thinking absolutely essential to the fictive act.

Secondly, to return to Jean Stafford's paragraph, a set of relationships
is evoked between two different modes of existence, in this case the man-
made object and the forces of the natural world, and these relationships are
played upon in a symbolistic way. The function of a sleigh is to ride on the
snow, not be covered by it. And we know, even from the first sentence,
that the presence of the sleigh, immobile and nonfunctional, will be made
into a metaphor, charged with a flexible, ironic, noncommittal value, a
metaphor for the presence of man in the world. As in the case of time, such
a man-nature dichotomy, as a center for a symbolistic charge of meaning,
is a convention, present in a large amount of modernist fiction, extended
and refined in the kind of sensibility fiction which Jean Stafford represents.
But here again it is a convention of no use to new fiction in which the made
and the born, the authentic and the schlock, the natural and the manufactured
are all taken as the given data of a difficult world which simply cannot be
divided into two halves.

Thirdly, there is, in Jean Stafford's story, the presence of the thing
itself, an object pulled out of the background and conspicuously placed before

our attention, described from a double viewpoint, near and far, given a touch of the pathetic fallacy (the sleigh has "jovial curves"), and above all invested with "taste." The sleigh, of course, is a chameleon image and is in good taste or bad according to its human context. And it is a marvelously versatile structural device, which compresses and gathers together a number of attitudes axial to the story that follows. But there is not much doubt that the image of the sleigh is more than a trope or a structural device to Jean Stafford and her readers; it is a thing, with intricacy of contour, complexity of texture, solidity, and the marks of its own past. Whatever its usefulness in the story, it is an image that issues from the imagination of a writer fascinated with the material objects of daily, sensory existence.

Such "solidity of specification," in James's phrase, is central to the purpose of the classic realistic novel. It survives, abstracted and intensified, in certain works of recent French fiction such as those of Robbe-Grillet. But again, to recall the material texture of the three beginnings, the narrator's father, in Barthelme's tale, is run over by "a carriage." The carriage is driven by "an aristocrat." Brautigan gives us something more to consider: "he" is found dead near "the television set on the front room floor. . . ." Paul, in Coover's fiction, does see and feel with painful acuity. But he is in no position to show much interest in the texture of things. Fiction of the Robbe-Grillet model has never really caught on in the United States. But allowing an affectionate interest in things to stand at the very center of one's fiction is in the Anglo-American tradition. And thus new fiction seems, at least from our sample, to have gone some distance toward disavowing the empirical solidity of classic fiction, especially the value-loaded qualities with which we invest material objects, in favor of a narrative rhythm closer to the fabulist and romantistic traditions, as nearly devoid of materiality as fiction can be and still be plausibly set in a recognizable world.

The points of contrast between Jean Stafford's story and new fiction are almost limitless. Take the phenomenal settings, for a further example, the ways in which the characters' conscious experience is controlled by the spaces in which the authors choose to present it. Jean Stafford's story begins in a front yard, but its energy and attention are directed toward a house. In due course certain exterior events will take place, but the characters' most intense emotional scenes are lived out within rooms. It is not merely a convenience of staging, to place the characters within those spaces in which they most conveniently interact. And it is not merely the realistic result of the fact that the characters, being upper middle class, do spend most of their time in rooms. There is an obsessive, house-bound quality in such fiction, reminiscent of Samuel Richardson, in which doors and windows, corridors and stairs, beds, tables, and chairs all figure heavily. Once again, it occurs to me that there was a time when it seemed to all of us that that was simply the way very much fiction was written, with characters condemned to work out their fates in studies, kitchens, and living rooms. And once again, new fiction presents a remarkable break with that convention. It is a fairly atypical beginning for Brautigan, in which rooms figure as heavily as they do. More generally, in the fiction I have been trying to describe, the physical space that encloses the consciousness of the action is undefined, nonspecific, in some vaguely hallucinatory way, or extreme, artificially constricted perhaps, or unaccountably open, or visionary, in which the contours of physical space are heavily shaped by the experiencing mind. If the action in new fiction does take place in houses, it is never for purposes of defining the "usualness" of a cast of domestic characters or for rendering the room-bound effect so useful to Jean Stafford.

Or consider matters of style. In some seemingly indefinable way, Jean Stafford's opening paragraph sounds not only characteristic of her work as a whole. It also sounds like countless other stories of about the same period. The traits of style are not really indefinable, however, are all too obvious, if anything. Take the preciousness of a phrase like "an air not so much of desuetude as of slowed-down dash." Why "desuetude"? Why not "disuse"? Consider the "as if" clause that follows. That single sentence contains the effect of two principles, one a movement toward elegance when directness would seem to interfere in the wit and flair of the phrase, second a movement toward embellishment in the interests of demonstrating an imagination expansively and leisurely at work upon its materials, comparing, supposing, qualifying, conjuring alternatives, musing. It goes without saying that the "as if" clause, as a syntactic strategy, does not exist in new fiction. The "as if" clause seems to imply that the empirical reality being described is rather bizarre, sufficiently unfamiliar so that some conjectural cause must be supplied to account whimsically for its being so bizarre. The writer of new fiction does not know why empirical reality is as bizarre as it is. He does know that the stylistic patterns which render the introspective, contemplative, domestic imagination of the fiction of the fifties are unavailable to him.

It is probably by its structure that we are best equipped to recognize the difference between fiction that seems to be classic modernist and fiction that seems to be audacious or experimental in some distinctly new way. In Jean Stafford's story, the events consist of tensions made only partly overt, harsh words, misunderstandings. Any sharply exterior events clearly exist to figure forth the moral and psychological dynamics of the characters. Ultimately the story ends with a kind of plateau of understanding toward which the rest of the fiction has worked. Epiphany is too facile and imprecise a word for what happens at the end of the story. It is a moment both of resignation and of awesome frustration in the face of the future, and any word, such as epiphany, which implies sudden insight is misleading. Still, the structure of the story is in the tradition of epiphany fiction, which is to say that it values the private and the domestic over the public and the external, that it demonstrates a belief in the possibility that an intuitive self-knowledge can cut through accumulations of social ritual and self-deception, a belief so firm that it permits the intuitive act to serve as dramatic end point and structural principle, indeed as the very moral justification for the fiction.

It takes only a sentence or two of Barthelme, Brautigan, and Coover to recognize how far they are from epiphanic form. All three tend to find more interest in the public than in the private, in the external than the internal, in the freakish and extreme than the middle range of experience. Nothing in the beginnings of the three fictions points to or seems to create the enabling conditions for the epiphanic illumination. None of the three writers seems to have much interest in such intuitive insights, perhaps not even much belief that they exist. And thus we do not need to read to the ends of the three fictions to know that their structures are antithetical to what is the most conventionalized, imitated, standardized feature of modernist fiction, especially shorter fiction, of the last generation, the epiphanic illumination, or, as in Jean Stafford, the self-generated plateau of understanding which transcends the plane of social conventionality and habitual self-deception which has made the self-understanding both possible and necessary.

As for the three examples, it is hard to say what structural principles underlie their composition. Perhaps the best way to approach the question of structure is to jettison the word structure altogether. Structure, whether we wish it to or not, carries with it connotations of economy, symmetry, accountable proportion, organic form. If pressed, most of us could apply any of those connoted values to any well-known piece of modernist fiction, certainly to Jean Stafford's story, could construct a systematic analysis by means of which every event, every image, every word could be accounted for by aesthetic principles apparently derived from the work itself. I do not think that that habit of mind is appropriate to the three examples and I do not think that that relentlessness of method will carry us very far. "We like books," says one of the characters in a well-known passage of Barthelme's *Snow White*, "that have a lot of *dreck* in them, matter which presents itself as not wholly relevant (or indeed, at all relevant) but which, carefully attended to, can supply a kind of 'sense' of what is going on. This 'sense' is not to be obtained by reading between the lines (for there is nothing there, in those white spaces) but by reading the lines themselves—looking at them and so arriving at a feeling not of satisfaction exactly, that is too much to expect, but of having read them, of having 'completed' them."

All three of our exemplary new fictions extend themselves in ways that are more additive than dramatic or progressive. In the barest and still the best definition of form, Kenneth Burke writes, "*Form* in literature is an arousing and fulfillment of desires. A work has form in so far as one part of it leads a reader to anticipate another part, to be gratified by the sequence."[3] Basically such "desires" in shorter fiction are of three kinds: problematic, psychological, and conventional. We have a problematic desire when we have a secret to be discovered during the course of the fiction, a relationship to be perceived, a motive to be revealed. When the problem is resolved our "desire" is "fulfilled." We have a psychological desire when we expect a mental process within the fiction to run its course, self-ignorance to proceed to self-knowledge, perhaps, or personal hostility to proceed to personal accommodation. When the psychological process is complete, when the character has come to know what we have expected he must know, then our "desire" is "fulfilled." We have a conventional desire when we are led to expect events, devices, and tonal manipulations typical of the genre. Jean Stafford's story is full of such conventional desires and fulfillments, the sophisticated mastery of the characters alternating with their humiliation and ineffectuality, the compassion of the author alternating with her ironic distance, the diminuendo into generalized pathos at the end, all of these being typical of the genre. In our three exemplary fictions there is no problematic desire: each begins with a death but our natural tendency to see a fictional death as a problem, to ask why, where, by whose hand, in what manner, is dissolved by the fact that in Barthelme and Brautigan we are told all that we need to know at once, in so unproblematic a way that no residue of curiosity remains, and in Coover, while the manner of death extends over the duration of the fiction, there is nothing that we might *wish* to know, as a key to understanding the death. In none of the three fictions is there any interplay between the psychological desires which the reader might project into the fiction and the fulfillment of them: the characters are constructs, types, quite deliberately devoid of much inner life. What they know they gather by bits and pieces. If they solve a problem, the solution becomes a new problem and nothing is gained. Needless to say the three fictions do not give us much in the way of conventional form. An alternative to saying that the fictions are formless, which sounds gratuitously pejorative, is to extend the idea of form, beyond the linear progression defined by Burke, toward something more mosaic, or concentric, or circular, an idea of form which is, as I suggested at the beginning of the paragraph, additive, in which the work grows by certain loosely associative principles but not with the covert purpose of arousing and fulfilling our desires at all.

The three fictions are, in different ways, variations around a thematic center. In literature an analogue is the encyclopedic passage in Rabelais, several pages of variations on the name and nature of the codpiece, for example. In experience, a loose analogy is the looking up of a word in a dictionary, finding a different word instead, becoming interested in the derivation of the second word, forgetting the word one began to look up, remembering it again, being reminded of a related word. In Brautigan's "story," each paragraph, after several introductory paragraphs, is numbered. The effect is certainly to add to the illusion of innocence, making the fiction look rather like a schoolboy's composition. But the numbering also creates a peculiar ambiguity around the form of the work. Each paragraph concerns one of the events in the life of the father mentioned in the beginning paragraph. The effect of numbering these unmodulated and disconnected "deeds" of the father is, at first, to make them seem to be about to come to an especially contrived whole, in the way in which an argument presents three points in its support, then its conclusion, or in the way in which a romance presents three adventures before certifying its hero as truly heroic. But it becomes obvious that those numbered paragraphs add up to less and less as the work proceeds. And by the time one has finished, it seems as if Brautigan's narrator has gathered random recollections, given each a number as it occurred to him, and then put them together according to the number which he had arbitrarily assigned to them. The events do, to be sure, take place in some kind of chronological order. But there is no reason why the father should have been an Idaho banker first and a parking lot attendant later. Both Coover's and Barthelme's fictions are alike in this respect: both share with Brautigan's a form in which images and events accumulate and sometimes gather great force but do not arrange themselves so as to demonstrate a theme or so as to gradually gratify the expectations and resolve the tensions generated in the beginning of the work.

It is possible, then, to disarrange prose more radically than anything in the new fiction I have been describing, as those experiments in concrete prose indicate.[4] Older explanations of avant-garde art, accounting for the work of the Italian futurists and the Dadaists as an alienated, disencumbered attempt to violate tradition, insult taste, and shock the bourgeoisie, don't have much bearing here.[5] What we do have is a body of fiction perfectly intelligible and not very shocking but strikingly different from the customary fiction of the late modernists.

III

I have kept the discussion up to this point as constricted as I have because it seems to me that some rather narrow things need to be said, about a manageable group of examples. We have now gone far enough to be able to decide what can and cannot be said, in general, theoretical, methodological ways, about recent experimental fiction.

In a finely perceptive essay in a recent *Partisan Review*,[6] Richard Wasson begins by describing the modernist imagination, which he sees as being best characterized by its use of myth without any particular belief, as an organizing structure for literary works and as "a mode of perception, even of vision, which provides the unstable subjective self with a world order that transcends individuality." Drawing primarily on Iris Murdoch, Robbe-Grillet, Pynchon, and Barth, Wasson describes the contrary position, post-modernist if one wishes, which aims its antagonism squarely at the mythic center of the modernist aesthetic. In Barth's *End of the Road*, that older mythicizing penchant is caricatured in the Mythotherapy of the Remobilization Farm in which Jacob Horner submits to his grotesque therapist. Implicitly the achieved art of Barth within his novel is the opposite of, "antidote to," says Wasson, the speciousness of myth. "Such an art," Wasson writes,

> is aware of its artificiality, its incompleteness, its partial dumbness before reality. Mythotherapy tries to force the whole world into the self and the self into the world, to make everything in the world subordinate to the drama of the self; mythoplastic art turns ironically on itself, works to recognize the separate and mysterious difference between self and other, artifice and reality.

There is nothing procrustean about Wasson's eassy. Yet it is finally too narrow either to define for us its object, recent fiction, or to lay out for us a method and a theoretical center. It is partly not Wasson's fault at all but merely the result of writing about something which is still happening; the volume of fiction in the Barth-Pynchon mode grows year by year and each year looks a little different in its totality. Certain features of Wasson's description apply to anybody who strikes us as non-traditional (his remarks on the diminishing interest in the drama of the self seem to me most durable), but if the import of Barth's *End of the Road* and the aesthetic of the end of myth are really at the center of recent fiction, it is hard to know how to account for Coover's *The Universal Baseball Association*, which is, in some legitimate sense, quite relentlessly mythic, or Gass's *Omensetter's Luck*, or Gardner's *Grendel*, which are, in ways quite different from each other, also mythic, all three of which are indisputably of the non-traditional mode we are considering. Joyce Carol Oates, in an interview, speaks of her intention to rewrite, in her own terms, a number of classic works of fiction, an enterprise rather Borgesian, very neo-modern, and quite mythic. Even Barth himself will not hold still but destroys myth with one book, only to revive it in several of the fictions of *Lost in the Funhouse*.

It is sometimes said, by Philip Roth, for example, in his essay "Writing American Fiction,"[7] that recent fiction has a bizarre, neurotic quality precisely in response to the bizarre quality of American life in the last decade. Locating the cause of the discontinuities and extremities of recent fiction in the extremities of social fact doesn't help us very much, however. Here is Roth on that set of relationships:

> The American writer in the middle of the twentieth century has his hands full in trying to understand, and then describe, and then make *credible* much of the American reality. It stupefies, it sickens, it infuriates, and finally it is even a kind of embarrassment to one's own meager imagination. The actuality is continually outdoing our talents, and the culture tosses up figures almost daily that are the envy of any novelist. Who, for example, could have invented Charles Van Doren? Roy Cohn and David Schine? Sherman Adams and Bernard Goldfine? Dwight David Eisenhower?

Those names! One realizes as the passage proceeds that the essay was written in the early sixties *about* the dear, dull fifties, and that *that* was the time of our national experience that was so bizarre that it compelled our writers to respond with ever more bizarre books.

Inevitably such arguments, Roth's or anybody else's, go in search of historical cause only to demonstrate a lack of historical perspective of astonishing dimensions. Do those who argue in this way really propose that street life in American cities is more bizarre than street life in Mayhew's Victorian London? or that public figures in Washington are more venal than the clowns who surrounded, say, the Harding administration? or that the "news" in metropolitan daily newspapers is more hysterical than it was during the lifetime of William Randolph Hearst? New fiction may be more responsive than much previous fiction to the discontinuous and surreal, the bizarre and the aberrant in current society. But it simply cannot be demonstrated that there has been some kind of quantitative increase in lunacy and that that is the cause of the newness of new fiction.

Rather than attempting to explain new fiction by social fact and rather than looking within new fiction for the indications of a new sensibility, as Wasson does, a few critics, Susan Sontag most conspicuously, attempt to define a new sensibility in world culture at large, in which some few works of recent fiction participate. "The primary feature of the new sensibility," writes Susan Sontag,

> is that its model product is not the literary work, above all, the novel. A new non-literary culture exists today, of whose very existence, not to mention significance, most literary intellectuals are entirely unaware. This new establishment includes certain painters, sculptors, social planners, film-makers, TV technicians, neurologists, musicians, electronics engineers, dancers, philosophers, and sociologists. (A few poets and prose writers can be included.)[8]

I, for one, find it difficult to take this passage seriously. There is the dipping down into various areas so as to choose, Calvinist fashion, a body of the elect. There is the calculated incongruity of the series. More than an attempt to win assent to her notion that older, compartmentalized versions of culture are now insupportable, the series is an attempt to "mau-mau," in Tom Wolfe's phrase, the literati, who have enough guilt without worrying whether we are taking with proper seriousness the TV technicians, neurologist, musicians, and electronics engineers. There is the condescension, the offensiveness of the inside-dopesterism. The passage asserts that one finds the characteristic tone of our age in a variety of "media" and hesitates to locate the dominant tone of our period in our prose fiction with the same confidence that we might once have done; with that position it is hard to quarrel. The notion, however, that prose fiction is a phenomenon on the fringes of a transformation of world consciousness and that we can only comprehend such a transformation by accepting the peripheral position of literature and attending to what the TV technicians and neurologists are trying to tell us, such a notion seems to me finally only a substitution of a very masochistic kind of polemic for the understanding that is so badly needed.

One thing that we can say about new fiction is that the range of fictional options has increased enormously in the last decade. It has occurred to me as I have been writing this essay that I have shifted in my allusions, without any feeling of constraint, between long and short fictional forms. This, in itself, is new, a tendency to be able to take short forms as seriously as one takes the novel, the result of writers like Borges, Landolfi, and a dozen others, and a tendency to be able to speak interchangeably about long and short forms as exhibits in a total range of fictional possibilities rather than stylized, circumscribed, discrete genres. Three forces have coincided to increase the range of fictional possibility in the last decade: the fatigue of the conventional modernist forms (the epiphany story, the reliance upon a heavy symbology, both public and private, to carry the import of the fiction, all of those conventions associated with interiority and the rendering of the sensibility), the influence of several individual figures, and the academic training of most writers of new fiction.

Along with the eroding of the stock of modernist forms, we have seen the vogue of Borges, the success of Gass, the transition from underground to overground of figures like Brautigan, the considerable American interest in the inimitable French *chosistes*, the conspicuousness of Mailer, the work of a considerable group of extraordinary journalists and virtuosi of the tape recorder extending from Tom Wolfe to Studs Terkel to Oscar Lewis, a collection of models remarkable for the way in which they all stretch the boundaries of fiction. In a recent issue of *TriQuarterly* a work appears entitled "Abandoned Cities" by Jack Anderson, consisting of four entries, descriptions, rather mock descriptions, of four cities. One of them is titled "Bismarck, North Dakota" and it begins in this way. "There are no suburbs. The streets stop at the wheatfields, where the iron helmets are set on black sticks to frighten off eagles. Beyond this point, the wind begins, as hard to ignore as stomachache. The townspeople fear two things always: drought and frost." Before the erosion of the modernist forms and before the interest in a dozen figures had done its work on what we thought fiction ought to be, no periodical would have known what to do with "Abandoned Cities." No readers would have known how to respond to it. And its author would not have known it could be written.

It is perhaps the academic training and associations of so many practitioners of new fiction that is most difficult to come to terms with. The old prejudices hang on and we continue to think, despite all the evidence to the contrary, that there is something about the academy that is irreconcilably opposed to the imagination of the writer, something stifling, cloying, deadening. Even those of us who are academics still take a special pleasure in the fading but still vital image of Dylan Thomas telling dirty stories to Bryn Mawr girls. I suppose, reaching into our literary past, there would have been something destructive had Dreiser or Crane or Bierce or any of the Redskins of our literary history picked up a position as a writer in residence. Yet, God knows, the lives of most of our Redskins were tortured enough and who is to say that a tenured position as professor of English and teacher of creative writing would have led them to do worse work than they did. Of our three exemplary figures, Coover has moved in and out of the academy; neither Brautigan nor Barthelme, so far as I know, has had anything to do with academic life since their emergence as writers although Brautigan is obviously more learned than he contrives to look and Barthelme is one of the most bookish authors ever to have gained prominence in the United States. A large number of writers, among the most audacious and exciting we have, do teach, Barth and Joyce Carol Oates, for example, John Hawkes, William Gass, John Gardner. Sooner or later a writer who teaches and who has a modest respect for his occupation will learn a body of other people's books, many of which are not particularly congenial to him, most of them with a kind of explicator's intensity. He will have to work his way through problems of craft that he may not feel in his own work but that other writers have felt in theirs and that his students will confront him with as genuine curiosities of their own. He will learn that our Anglo-American sense of formal possibilities is terribly limited, that the French, for example, have, for a long time, written a species of prose composition, called the *récit*, which is a most marvelously inclusive category, perfectly legitimized by French culture, in which one can make prose poems, meditations, fables, confessions, introspective interludes, an extraordinary number of things for which we have no generic home. The idea that such an involvement with the teaching of literature is somehow destructive of a writer's art seems to me preposterous. That it has made a difference with writers of new fiction, particularly in enlarging their sense of formal options, seems to me undeniable.

It is a pity that some hard questions need to be asked about the formal possibilities of prose fiction at a time when "formalism" has an increasingly bad name. It would help if someone were to do for formalism what A. O. Lovejoy once did for romanticism, that is, discriminate the several senses in which the word is used. What we do not need is criticism of new fiction as pure technique, disengaged from its cultural ambiance, "read," explicated, exhausted, like a metaphysical lyric. What we also do not need is more criticism which uses fiction as an exhibit in a historical design, new fiction being the end of something, or the beginning of something else, or an element in a cyclic movement, or evidence for the triumph of one historical principle or the defeat of another. What we do need is an aesthetic of new fiction. As a step toward that aesthetic, I propose the axioms that follow.

1. *New fiction, although aggressively non-traditional, shows less involvement*

with the tradition of prose fiction than any fiction since the beginning of the novel.
Nearly all fiction of any real quality reacts against some area of the fiction of
its past: Cervantes against romance, Fielding against early Richardson and
bad history, Thackeray against the Silver Fork School, Virginia Woolf against
the late realists, and so on. There is much in the fiction of the past which
writers of new fiction choose not to emulate. But it is extraordinary, for a
body of fiction so non-traditional, how little of traditional fiction is struggled
with, polemicized against, seriously parodied, denied, inverted, surmounted.
New fiction, more than any fiction since Cervantes, chooses self-consciously
to depart from tradition without investing that departure with any particular
urgency or without making that act of departure the starting point of the
fiction at all, in the way that such departure virtually animates the fiction of
Cervantes, Fielding, Jane Austen, Flaubert, Hemingway, and a hundred
others.

2. *New fiction is the first substantial body of fiction that self-consciously seeks
an audience that is less than universal, attempting to establish a community of
sensibility that is willfully limited.* It is the fate of the novel to be a middle-
class form and at the same time to be unaware that it *is* a middle-class form.
No classic novelist ever set out to address the members of a particular class,
or locality, or historical time. Every novelist's tacit assumption is that his
book puts us in touch with "reality," not the reality of a highly specific class,
not reality circumscribed by place and time: in that sense, every classic
novelist's work is addressed to everybody, everywhere, to his own time and
to posterity. Even those novelists who seem to us especially class-bound,
Meredith and James let us say, would never have acknowledged that the
truth of their books was specific, partial, local, and parochial. It is only the
very minor figures such as Ronald Firbank who aim at a coterie public out
of a recognition of their own exotic sensibilities. In the older neo-modern
figures such as Borges and Cortázar, Landolfi and Anderson Imbert, one has,
precisely, exotic sensibilities going in quest of other exotic sensibilities for
their readers. And in American writers like Barth, Heller, Pynchon, and
Gass one has an extension of the phenomenon, fiction which is by no means
coterie writing, precious and cynical in the manner of Firbank, but which
willingly acknowledges the partiality of its truth, the oddity of its vision,
and the limits of its audience.

3. *New fiction contains and often intensifies the tendency in most fiction of any
period to assimilate and transform the bad art of its own time.* Wellek and Warren
articulate such a principle, deriving it from the Russian formalists. They
summarize: "Shklovsky, one of the Russian formalists, holds that new art
forms are 'simply the canonization of inferior (sub-literary) genres.' Dostoevsky's novels are a series of glorified crime novels, *romans à sensation,* 'Pushkin's
lyrics come from album verses, Blok's from gipsy songs, Mayakovsky's from
funny-paper poetry.' Bertolt Brecht in German and Auden in English both
show the deliberate attempt at this transformation of popular poetry into

serious literature. This might be called the view that literature needs constantly to renew itself by 'rebarbarization.' "[9] We read Joyce, amused and entertained with the assimilation of the popular songs, headlines, religious tracts, and pornographic fiction into the texture of *Ulysses*. We may very well read new fiction, however, with dismay and irritation, because the bad art which is being assimilated is *our* bad art, what most of us have become accustomed to thinking of as a threat to the very survival of mind. Thus it is that new fiction, while extending a principle common to very much fiction, seems more audacious and abrasive than it really is, because it willingly occupies a place at what William Gass, following Barthelme, calls "the leading edge of the trash phenomenon."

4. *New fiction consolidates an attempt rare in fiction before the modern period to present elements of its texture as devoid of value; yet new fiction, in contrast to certain areas of modern fiction, seeks this value-less quality not as an act of subtraction, or dehumanization, or metaphysical mystification, not as a gesture of despair or nihilism, but as a positive act in which the joy of the observer is allowed to prevail as the primary quality of the experience.* In the fiction of Richardson the principle is most fully realized and firmly established, that the data of the fiction, its places, things, and events, are phenomena, rendered by Richardson as perceived by the characters, which means not only perceived but valued. Everything in Richardson, to put it succinctly, is worth something, to the person who sees it and reports it to us. So it has been with fiction ever since. To see, in fiction, is to rank, to prefer or to deprecate, to value. One way of attempting to break with such a compulsion to value is to experiment with point of view, as Dos Passos does, for example, in those passages of his fiction that are made to seem unselectively documentary, mechanically recorded as it were. Another way is to arrange the elements of the fiction serially or capriciously so that the mode of presentation undercuts the possibilities of conventional value, a very old technique that serves the exuberance of Rabelais, the irony of Swift, and the associative anarchy of Sterne. Beckett's fiction is the most fully realized and powerfully executed attempt in modernist literature to undercut the values implicit in syntax, conventional arrangement, and in the very act of telling, all in the service of his nihilistic vision.

In new fiction, the nihilism is still there since no structure of values has arisen to move into Beckett's vacuum. What is different is that fiction now has the luxury of taking for granted what the modernists had to demonstrate. A writer of new fiction no more needs now to strain to demonstrate the absurd than a Victorian novelist had to strain to demonstrate a Christian-capitalist ethic. A peculiarly indirect way into the value-less surface I am describing is through the description by John Barth of the substance of Smollett's *Roderick Random*.

Sailors, soldiers, fine gentlemen and ladies, whores, homosexuals, cardsharpers, fortune hunters, tradesmen of all description, clerics, fops, scholars, lunatics, highwaymen, peasants, and poets both male and female—they crowd a stage that extends from Glasgow to Guinea, from Paris to Paraguay, and among themselves perpetrate battles, debaucheries, swindles, shanghais, rescues, pranks, poems, shipwrecks, heroisms, murders, and marriages. They wail and guffaw, curse and sing, make love and foul their breeches: in short they *live*, at a clip and with a brute *joie de vivre* that our modern spirits can scarcely comprehend.

Elsewhere in the same essay, Barth summarizes the import of Smollett's novel:

> In short, *Roderick Random* is *par excellence* a novel of nonsignificant surfaces—which is not to say it's a superficial, insignificant novel, any more than the age that produced it, the age that invented the English novel, was superficial or insignificant. [10]

Compare the texture Barth finds in Smollett, the syntax of seriality, the obvious pleasure in amplitude, with a passage from a fiction by Kenneth Gangemi entitled *Olt*:

> Robert Olt walked into the department store and went directly to the TV department, where he sniffed the ozone and watched a program that showed high school kids dancing. In the jewelry department he stood in a crowd of people and watched a silversmith demonstrate the lost-wax process. In the pet department he looked at a cage of saw-whet owls and a cage of baby coatimundis. In the record department he picked up a free Köchel listing and then sat in a soundproof cubicle and listened to a new comedian. In the gourmet department he tasted a free sample of smoked sturgeon.
>
> Once he had sat in on the orientation movie shown to new salesgirls. Once he had spent two hours riding up and down the escalators on the last Saturday before Christmas. That was the Christmas they had fired their Santa Claus when a newspaper disclosed that he had been a communist.

Or compare a passage from Rudolph Wurlitzer's *Nog*:

> I ventured a peek out the door, but she had left the bedroom. I preferred to think she hadn't heard me; that, indeed, she had never heard me. I could still slip out. The terrycloth bathrobe was hanging behind the door. I put it on and turned to investigate the bathroom. It was a beautiful bathroom. There was a huge green tile tub, a new toilet and washbowl. I opened the cabinet over the washbowl. I couldn't stop looking at the objects on the top two shelves: suntan oil, Anacins, cold cream, three pink hair curlers, two yellow toothbrushes, one of which was very dirty, Dramamine pills, Itolsol eye bath, Ban, Kolex cold capsules, Ammens Medicated Powder and a small box of Benzedrine pills. I stared at each object and then went over them again.

Not all of new fiction is so gaily encyclopedic as these passages, so fascinated with variety and unordered assemblage, so determined not to confer value. But most of new fiction shares, to some degree, the spirit of those passages. It is, incidentally, the aspect of new fiction that is likely to make it most congenial to experienced readers of Joyce.

5. *New fiction presents its texture as devoid as possible of aesthetic and philosophical depth.* In some sense, nearly all writers resist assignments to them of depth. Isherwood's character George, in *A Single Man,* who teaches English, asks his class what a novel by Huxley is "about." And the narrator comments: "Nearly all of them, despite their academic training, deep, deep down still regard this *about* business as a tiresomely sophisticated game. As for the minority who have cultivated the *about* approach until it has become second nature, who dream of writing an *about* book of their own one day, on Faulkner, James, or Conrad, proving definitively that all previous *about* books on that subject are about nothing—they aren't going to say anything yet awhile." Novelists and critics as disparate as Saul Bellow, Harry Levin, and Mary McCarthy have complained of the tendency of readers to find symbols where no symbols were intended. Every novelist, out of mere self-respect, is obliged to resist the conventionalized and mechanical methods of discovering "meaning," imputing system, stating the implicit in his works. Still, no one needs to be told that modern fiction is relentlessly symbolic, enthusiastically multi-leveled, that it invites exegesis like nothing since the *Talmud.* It is the single quality that most firmly unites such otherwise quite different writers as Lawrence, Mann, Broch, Silone, Malcolm Lowry, their intention to use those techniques that permit the greatest possible resonance and amplitude of signification and that insist at every point on the existence of unstated levels of "depth" that the surface of the fiction figures forth.

The contrary principle is expressed by Wylie Sypher. In scientific observation at the present time, in contrast to classic patterns of scientific thought, "the data are the system; the matter-of-fact concreteness may or may not be explained by natural law. Accidents happen, and accidents are real." Elsewhere, he allows the principle to broaden:

Like the recent scientist, the contemporary novelist or painter detects that the ordinary, the commonplace, the superficial, the quotidian is the very mystery most inaccessible to reason and explanation and method. The immediate occasion is sufficient unto itself, and this recognition has led to a new humility, as well as a new frustration. If the significance is on the surface, then the need for depth explanation has gone, and the contingent, the everyday happening, is more authentic than the ultimate or absolute. . . . The old systems of meaning—the Newtonian solid geometry locating things at appropriate distances or the theoretic order of Alberti's perspective, which foreshortened— are suspect. Novelist, painter, and scientist have given up foreshortening. Plot itself was a mode of foreshortening. To accept the accidental or casual is to recognize the irrationality of the obvious, to dispense with the need for a logic accounting for everything by cause and effect, action and reaction.[11]

Sypher's examples, in the case of fiction, come largely from the *chosistes*. But his discussion applies remarkably to American writers of new fiction, many of whom share next to nothing with the French writers, except a denial of depth. There is no clearer break than this between modernist (and late Victorian) fiction and new fiction—the implicit intention to let the surface be the meaning, let the possibility of a symbolistic level of reference be consistently undercut, let the data be the system, let there be nothing between the lines, as Barthelme puts it, but white space.

6. *New fiction permits itself a degree of latitude from the illusionist tradition greater than in any body of fiction since the beginning of the novel.* Classic fiction, of course, varies in the degree of its fidelity to an illusionist aesthetic, from the dull fidelity of Zola to the involutions and indirections of dozens of others whom we might place at some kind of polar extreme. It is difficult to imagine, however, that any classic work of fiction ever represents the wish that the reader apprehend it mainly as a self-referential literary construct, or mainly allegory, or mainly myth, or mainly private vision. Always, in figures so various as Scott or James, Mme. de Lafayette or Tolstoy, we are compelled to say, in Trollope's phrase, yes, that is "the way we live now" or to say, yes, that is the way it must have been, at Bath or Lyme, Waterloo or Leningrad; that is the way it must have looked and sounded, what people must have said and thought. It is hard to see how fiction, in its classic formulations, could escape this common mimetic center without ceasing to be prose fiction and becoming something else.

Irving Howe, some years ago in an essay titled "Mass Society and Post-Modern Fiction," took note of the comparative lack of interest in social fact, in class, in institutions and manners that characterized the fiction that seemed most compelling at that time, the fiction of Salinger, Wright Morris, Herbert Gold, and Saul Bellow. Howe at that time could not have foreseen a disengagement from the mimetic impulse more thorough by far than what was occurring at that time, a progressive lack of interest not only in institutions but in the very "solidity of specification" that the novel seems to need to survive. It is partly the result of the revival of interest in pre-novelistic forms, the fabulistic, proto-realistic works that echo through much of new fiction, allowing a kind of power to grow out of the invention itself rather than depending upon the solidity with which the figures of the fiction are placed. For whatever reason, it is possible to read for many pages of Cortázar, Landolfi, and Borges, Barth, Barthelme, and Coover, with a constant delight in the craft displayed, with a constant sense of recognition, a feeling that the fiction is, in some oddly tangential way, powerfully pertinent to one's inner life, yet never once saying, yes, that is the way things look and feel, that is the way time passes, that is the way people really speak, that is the way we live now.

7. *New fiction, finally, in common with only a few scattered instances before it, seeks to represent, explicitly or implicitly, the act of writing as an act of play.* In the novels of Fielding or Jane Austen or Dickens or Thackeray, the compositional act is made to seem at once pleasurable and difficult, an act of play and an act of heavy moral responsibility. There is not much doubt, I think, that the play is subordinate to the hard work, that the energies of invention, the joys of making, are always less significant than the difficult work of making a big book into an intelligible aesthetic object, along with a heavy responsibility to the author's audience and to literature as an institution. Had the novel been invented by a Cavalier poet of the seventeenth century, perhaps, or had the example of Petronius or Rabelais really served as the cornerstone of the great tradition, the novel might have escaped its heavy burden of seriousness, both moral and vocational, and, having been conceived as a thing made with self-justifying invention and a large measure of fun, it might have been unnecessary for Flaubert to have worked so hard, to have told us he worked so hard, to have flayed the bourgeoisie so relentlessly, to have felt Emma Bovary's poison in his own vitals, to have sweat over every word.

New fiction, on the other hand, elevates play to the very center of the complex of apparent motives that animate the work. Barth, in any given work, is doing many things: working very hard, thinking, shaping, hoping, giving up and starting over, planning, expecting, learning, imitating, trying not to imitate. It does not surprise me, how could it surprise anyone, to hear, through some dubious grapevine, that Barth is not writing, that he is in despair, having written himself out. Still, can there be any doubt that writing fiction is very centrally, for Barth, an act of play? One can differ with the particulars of Robert Scholes's *The Fabulators*; but I would not choose to differ with its donnée. New fiction can be differentiated from old on the basis of its fabulation, its willingness to allow the compositional act a self-conscious prominence and to invest that act with love, a sense of game, invention for its own sake, joy.

Notes

1. "What Was New About the 'New Species of Writing'?" *Studies in the Novel,* II (Summer, 1970), 118.

2. *The Popular Novel in England, 1770–1800* (Lincoln, Nebraska, 1961), p. 5.

3. *Counterstatement* (Los Altos, Calif., 1953), p. 124.

4. The best source for this kind of experimentation is Eugene Wildman's anthology, *Experiments in Prose* (Chicago, 1969).

5. See, for example, the section entitled "Antagonism" in Renato Poggioli's *The Theory of the Avant-Garde* (New York, 1971), pp. 30–40.

6. "Notes on a New Sensibility," *Partisan Review*, XXXVI (1969), 460–477.
7. In *Writers and Issues*, ed. Theodore Solotaroff (New York, 1969), pp. 260–275.
8. *Against Interpretation and Other Essays* (New York, 1969), p. 298.
9. *Theory of Literature* (New York, 1956), pp. 235–236.
10. "Afterword" to *The Adventures of Roderick Random*, Signet Edition (New York, 1964), pp. 478, 471.
11. *Literature and Technology: The Alien Vision* (New York, 1968), p. 240 and the entire section titled "The Agnosticism of Craft."

The Myth of the Postmodern Breakthrough

GERALD GRAFF

The postmodern tendency in literature and literary criticism has been characterized as a "breakthrough," a significant reversal of the dominant literary and sociocultural directions of the last two centuries. Literary critics such as Leslie Fiedler, Susan Sontag, George Steiner, Richard Poirier, and Ihab Hassan have written about this reversal, differing in their assessments of its implications but generally agreeing in their descriptions of what is taking place. What is taking place, these critics suggest, is the death of our traditional Western concept of art and literature, a concept which defined "high culture" as our most valuable repository of moral and spiritual wisdom. George Steiner draws attention to the disturbing implications of the fact that, in the Nazi regime, dedication to the highest "humanistic" interests was compatible with the acceptance of systematic murder.[1] Sontag and Fiedler suggest that the entire artistic tradition of the West has been exposed as a kind of hyperrational imperialism akin to the aggression and lust for conquest of bourgeois capitalism. Not only have the older social, moral, and epistemological claims for art seemingly been discredited, but art has come to be seen as a form of complicity, another manifestation of the lies and hypocrisy through which the ruling class has maintained its power.

But concurrent with this loss of confidence in the older claims of the moral and interpretive authority of art is the advent of a new sensibility, bringing a fresh definition of the role of art and culture. This new sensibility manifests itself in a variety of ways: in the refusal to take art "seriously" in the old sense; in the use of art itself as a vehicle for exploding its traditional pretensions and for showing the vulnerability and tenuousness of art and language; in the rejection of the dominant academic tradition of analytic, interpretive criticism, which by reducing art to abstractions tends to neutralize or domesticate its potentially liberating energies; in a less soberly rationalistic mode of consciousness, one that is more congenial to myth, tribal ritual, and visionary experience, grounded in a "protean," fluid, and undifferentiated concept of the self as opposed to the repressed Western ego.

Excerpted from *Literature Against Itself: Literary Ideas in Modern Society* (Chicago and London: University of Chicago Press, 1979): 31–34, 52–62, 242–245. 1979 by The University of Chicago. Reprinted by permission of the publisher.

I want here to raise some critical questions about the postmodern breakthrough in the arts and about the larger implications claimed for it in culture and society. I want in particular to challenge the standard description of postmodernism as an overturning of romantic and modernist traditions. To characterize postmodernism as a "breakthrough"—a cant term of our day—is to place a greater distance between current writers and their predecessors than is, I think, justified. There are distinctions to be drawn, of course, and both here and in the final chapter of this book I shall try to draw them. But this chapter argues that postmodernism should be seen not as a break with romantic and modernist assumptions but rather as a logical culmination of the premises of these earlier movements, premises not always clearly defined in discussions of these issues. In the next chapter I question the utopian social claims of the postmodernist sensibility by questioning the parallelism they assume between social and esthetic revolution.

In its literary sense, postmodernism may be defined as the movement within contemporary literature and criticism that calls into question the traditional claims of literature and art to truth and human value. As Richard Poirier has observed, "contemporary literature has come to register the dissolution of the ideas often evoked to justify its existence: the cultural, moral, psychological premises that for many people still define the essence of literature as a humanistic enterprise. Literature is now in the process of telling us how little it means."[2] This is an apt description of the contemporary mood, but what it neglects to mention is that literature has been in the process of telling us how little it means for a long time, as far back as the beginnings of romanticism.

It is clear why we are tempted to feel that the contemporary popularity of anti-art and artistic self-parody represents a sharp break with the modernist past. It does not seem so long ago that writers like Rilke, Valéry, Joyce, Yeats, and others sought a kind of salvation through art. For Rilke, as earlier for Shelley and other romantics, poetry was "a mouth which else Nature would lack," the great agency for the restitution of values in an inherently valueless world. Romantic and modernist writing expressed a faith in the constitutive power of the imagination, a confidence in the ability of literature to impose order, value, and meaning on the chaos and fragmentation of industrial society. This faith seemed to have lapsed after World War II. Literature increasingly adopted an ironic view of its traditional pretensions to truth, high seriousness, and the profundity of "meaning." Furthermore, literature of the postwar period has seemed to have a different relation to criticism than that of the classic modernists. Eliot, Faulkner, Joyce, and their imitators sometimes seemed to be deliberately providing occasions for the complex critical explications of the New Critics. In contrast, much of the literature of the last several decades has been marked by the desire to remain invulnerable to critical analysis.

In an essay that asks the question, "What Was Modernism?" Harry

Levin identifies the "ultimate quality" pervading the work of the moderns as "its uncompromising intellectuality."[3] The conventions of postmodern art systematically invert this modernist intellectuality by parodying its respect for truth and significance. In Donald Barthelme's anti-novel, *Snow White*, a questionnaire poses for the reader such mock questions as, "9. Has the work, for you, a metaphysical dimension? Yes ( ) No ( ) 10. What is it (twenty-five words or less)?"[4] Alain Robbe-Grillet produces and campaigns for a type of fiction in which "obviousness, transparency preclude the existence of *higher worlds*, of any transcendence."[5] Susan Sontag denounces the interpretation of works of art on the grounds that "to interpret is to impoverish, to deplete the world—in order to set up a shadow world of 'meanings.' "[6] Leslie Fiedler, writing on modern poetry, characterizes one of its chief tendencies as a "flight from the platitude of meaning."[7] As Jacob Brackman describes this attitude in *The Put-On*, "we are supposed to have learned by now that one does not ask what art means."[8] And, as Brackman shows, this deliberate avoidance of interpretability has moved from the arts into styles of personal behavior. It appears that the term "meaning" itself, as applied not only to art but to more general experience, has joined "truth" and "reality" in the class of words which can no longer be written unless apologized for by inverted commas.

Thus it is tempting to agree with Leslie Fiedler's conclusion that "the Culture Religion of Modernism" is now dead.[9] The most advanced art and criticism of the last twenty years seem to have abandoned the modernist respect for artistic meaning. The religion of art has been "demythologized." A number of considerations, however, render this statement of the case misleading. Examined more closely, both the modernist faith in literary meanings and the postmodern repudiation of these meanings prove to be highly ambivalent attitudes, much closer to one another than may at first appear. The equation of modernism with "uncompromising intellectuality" overlooks how much of this intellectuality devoted itself to calling its own authority into question. . . .

FROM MODERN TO POSTMODERN

If postmodern literature extends rather than overturns the premises of romanticism and modernism, we should expect this relation to be visible not only in the themes of literature but in its forms. Consider as an example the following passage from Barthelme's *Snow White*:

> "Try to be a man about whom nothing is known," our father said, when we were young. Our father said several other interesting things, but we have forgotten what they were. . . . Our father was a man about whom nothing was known. Nothing is known about him still. He gave us the recipes. He

was not very interesting. A tree is more interesting. A suitcase is more interesting. A canned good is more interesting.[10]

Barthelme here parodies Henry James's advice to the aspiring fiction writer: "Try to be one of the people on whom nothing is lost."[11] Barthelme inverts the assumptions about character, psychology, and the authority of the artist upon which James, the father of the modernist "recipe" for the novel, had depended. In postmodern fiction, character, like external reality, is something "about which nothing is known," lacking in plausible motive or discoverable depth. Whereas James had stressed the importance of artistic selection, defining the chief obligation of the novelist as the obligation to be "interesting," Barthelme operates by a law of equivalence according to which nothing is intrinsically more interesting than anything else.[12] Such a law destroys the determinacy of artistic selection and elevates canned goods to equal status with human moral choice as artistic subject matter. In place of Jamesian dedication to the craft of fiction, Barthelme adopts an irreverent stance toward his work, conceding the arbitrary and artificial nature of his creation. Retracting any Jamesian claim to deal seriously with the world, Barthelme's work offers—for wholly different reasons—the sort of confession of the merely "make-believe" status of fiction to which James objected in Thackeray and Trollope. The novel's inability to transcend the solipsism of subjectivity and language becomes the novel's chief subject and the principle of its form.

It would seem that the Jamesian esthetic could not be stood on its head more completely. But only a surface consideration of the comparison can be content to leave it at that. James himself, in both his fiction and his criticism, contributed to the skepticism which Barthelme turns against him. T.S. Eliot wrote that Paul Valéry was "much too sceptical to believe even in art."[13] The remark applies, in greater or lesser degree, to all the great modernist worshippers at the shrine of high art, not excluding James. Consider James's view of the infinite elusiveness of experience, which is "never limited, and . . . never complete,"[14] an elusiveness he dramatized in the interminable ambiguities of his later fiction. James combined an intense dedication to unraveling the secrets of motive and action with an acutely developed sense of the ultimate impossibility of such an enterprise.

Conflicting with James's insistence on the importance of artistic selection and shaping is the curiously subjectivistic justification James came to accord to this process. He frequently asserts, in his later reflections, that the orderings of the artist cannot derive from or be determined by the raw material of life itself. As he observes in *The American Scene*:

> To be at all critically, or as we have been fond of calling it, analytically minded . . . is to be subject to the superstition that objects and places, coherently grouped, disposed for human use and addressed to it, must have a sense of their own, a mystic meaning proper to themselves to give out: to give

out, that is, to the participant at once so interested and so detached as to be moved to a report of the matter. That perverse person is obliged to take it for a working theory that the essence of almost any settled aspect of anything may be extracted by the chemistry of criticism, and may give us its right name, its formula, for convenient use. From the moment the critic finds himself sighing, to save trouble in a difficult case, that the cluster of appearances can *have* no sense, from that moment he begins, and quite consciously, to go to pieces; it being the prime business and the high honour of the painter of life always to *make* a sense—and to make it most in proportion as the immediate aspects are loose or confused.[15]

James seems to be saying there are no objective determinants guiding the act of "making a sense" of experience. The "mystic meaning" of events is not in the events themselves, or controlled by them, but in the observer. James perceives that in these circumstances there is danger that the observer may "go to pieces" unless he is adequate to the artist's task of fabricating his own sense. But though James assigns "high honour" to the fabricator and shame to the person who surrenders to confusion, one might question his valuations. Could one not say that the artist who saves himself by inventing fictions of order he knows to be arbitrary is engaging in a deception of which the confused observer is innocent? Is it less honorable to "go to pieces" in honest confusion than to create forms of coherence whose truth is admitted to be mythical? James rests his claims of honor for the artistic process on the damaging admission that artistic order is not grounded on anything outside itself.

Perceiving that the modernist's seriousness rests on admittedly arbitrary foundations, the postmodern writer treats this seriousness as an object of parody. Whereas modernists turned to art, defined as the imposition of human order upon inhuman chaos—as an antidote for what Eliot called the "immense panorama of futility and anarchy which is contemporary history"—postmodernists conclude that, under such conceptions of art and history, art provides no more consolation than any other discredited cultural institution. Postmodernism signifies that the nightmare of history, as modernist esthetic and philosophical traditions have defined history, has overtaken modernism itself.[16] If history lacks value, pattern, and rationally intelligible meaning, then no exertions of the shaping, ordering imagination can be anything but a refuge from truth. Alienation from significant external reality, from *all* reality, becomes an inescapable condition.

THE TWO POSTMODERNISMS

In carrying the logic of modernism to its extreme limits, postmodern literature poses in an especially acute fashion the critical problem raised by all experimental art: does this art represent a criticism of the distorted aspects of modern life or a mere addition to it? Georg Lukács has argued persuasively that the successful presentation of distortion as such presupposes the existence of an undistorted norm. "Literature," he writes, "must have a concept of the normal if it is to 'place' distortion correctly, that is to say, to see it *as* distortion."[17] If life were really a solipsistic madness, we should have no means of knowing this fact or representing it. But once the concept of the normal is rejected as a vestige of an outmoded metaphysics or patronized as a myth, the concepts of "distortion" and "madness" lose their meanings. This observation provides a basis for some necessary distinctions between tendencies in postmodern writing.

In Jorge Luis Borges's stories, for example, techniques of reflexiveness and self-parody suggest a universe in which human consciousness is incapable of transcending its own mythologies. This condition of imprisonment, however, though seen from the "inside," is presented from a tragic or tragicomic point of view that forces us to see it *as* a problem. The stories generate a pathos at the absence of a transcendent order of meanings. As Borges's narrator in "The Library of Babel" declares, "Let heaven exist, though my place be in hell. Let me be outraged and annihilated, but for one instant, in one being, let Your enormous Library be justified."[18] The library contains all possible books and all possible interpretations of experience but none which can claim authority over the others; therefore, it cannot be "justified." Nevertheless, Borges affirms the indispensable nature of justification. As in such earlier writers as Kafka and Céline, the memory of a significant external reality that would justify human experience persists in the writer's consciousness and serves as his measure of the distorted, indeterminate world he depicts. Borges's kind of postmodern writing, even in presenting solipsistic distortion as the only possible perspective, nevertheless presents this distortion *as* distortion—that is, it implicitly affirms a concept of the normal, if only as a concept which has been tragically lost. The comic force of characters like "Funes the Memorious" and of solipsistic worlds such as those of "Tlön, Uqbar, Orbis Tertius" lies in the crucial fact that Borges, for all his imaginative sympathy, is *not* Funes, is not an inhabitant of Tlön, and is thus able to view the unreality of their worlds as a predicament. His work retains a link with traditional classical humanism by virtue of its sense of the pathos of this humanism's demise. The critical power of absence remains intact, giving Borges a perspective for judging the unreality of the present. His work affirms the sense of reality in a negative way by dramatizing its absence as a deprivation.

Whatever tendency toward subjectivism these Borges works may contain is further counteracted by their ability to suggest the historical and social causes of this loss of objective reality. Borges invites us to see the solipsistic plight of his characters as a consequence of the relativistic thrust of modern philosophy and modern politics. If reality has yielded to the myth-

making of Tlön, as he suggests it has, "the truth is that it longed to yield."
The mythologies of "dialectical materialism, anti-Semitism, Nazism" were
sufficient "to entrance the minds of men."[19] The loss of reality is made
intelligible to the reader as an aspect of a social and historical evolution. At
its best, the contemporary wave of self-reflexive fiction is not quite so totally
self-reflexive as it is taken to be, since its very reflexivity implies a "realistic"
comment on the historical crisis which brought it about. Where such a
comment is made, the conventions of anti-realism subserve a higher realism.
Often, however, this fiction fails to make its reflexivity intelligible as a
consequence of any recognizable cause. Estrangement from reality and meaning becomes detached from the consciousness of its causes—as in the more
tediously claustrophobic and mannered experiments of Barthelme and the
later Barth.[20] Even in these works, however, the loss of reality and meaning
is seen as a distortion of the human condition.

Far different is the attitude expressed in the more celebratory forms of
postmodernism. Here there is scarcely any memory of an objective order of
values in the past and no regret over its disappearance in the present. Concepts
like "significant external reality" and "the human condition" figure only as
symbols of the arbitrary authority and predetermination of a repressive past,
and their disappearance is viewed as liberation. Dissolution of ego boundaries,
seen in tragic postmodern works like *Invitation to a Beheading* as a terrifying
disintegration of identity, is viewed as a bracing form of consciousness-
expansion and a prelude to growth. Both art and the world, according to
Susan Sontag, simply *are*. "Both need no justification; nor could they possibly
have any."[21] The obsessive quest for justification which characterizes Borges's
protagonists is thus regarded, if it is noticed at all, as a mere survival of
outmoded thinking.

It is symptomatic of the critical climate that Borges has been widely
read as a celebrant of apocalyptic unreality. Borges's current celebrity is
predicated to a large degree on a view that sees him as a pure fabulator
revelling in the happy indistinguishability of truth and fiction. Richard
Poirier, for example, urges us in reading Borges to get rid of "irrelevant
distinctions between art and life, fiction and reality."[22] But if distinctions
between fiction and reality were really irrelevant, Borges's work would be
pointless.

But then, in a world which simply *is*, pointlessness is truth. There is
no ground for posing the question of justification as a question. We can no
longer even speak of "alienation" or "loss" of perspective, for there never was
anything to be alienated from, never any normative perspective to be lost.
The realistic perspective that gives shape and point to works of tragicomic
postmodernism, permitting them to present distortion *as* distortion, gives
way to a celebration of *energy*—the vitalism of a world that cannot be
understood or controlled. We find this celebration of energy in the poetry of
the Beats, the "Projective" poets, and other poetic continuators of the nativist

line of Whitman, Williams, and Pound, in the short-lived vogue of the
Living Theater, happenings, and pop art, and in a variety of artistic and
musical experiments with randomness and dissonance. It is also an aspect of
the writing of Mailer, Burroughs, and Pynchon, where despite the suggestion
of a critical or satiric point of view, the style expresses a facile excitement
with the dynamisms of technological process.[23] Richard Poirier states the
rationale for this worship of energy, making energy and literature synony-
mous: "Writing is a form of energy not accountable to the orderings anyone
makes of it and specifically not accountable to the liberal humanitarian values
most readers want to find there."[24] Literature, in short, is closer to a physical
force than to an understanding or "criticism of life," both of which are
tame and bourgeois. This celebration of energy frequently seems to hover
somewhere between revolutionary politics and sophisticated acquiescence to
the agreeably meaningless surfaces of mass culture.

The acquiescence seems to have the upper hand over the politics in the
esthetics of John Cage. Susan Sontag says that "Cage proposes for our experience a world in which it's never preferable to do other than we are doing or
be elsewhere than we are. 'It is only irritating,' he says, 'to think one would
like to be somewhere else. Here we are now.' "* Cage, she writes, "envisages
a totally democratic world of the spirit, a world of 'natural activity' in which
'it is understood that everything is clean: there is no dirt.' . . . Cage proposes
the perennial possibility of errorless behavior, if only we will allow it to be
so. 'Error is a fiction, has no reality in fact.' "[25] Elsewhere Cage puts it this
way: "We are intimate in advance with whatever will happen."[26] Both
nostalgia and hope are impossible because history has disappeared, replaced
by an immanent present which is always, at every changing moment, the
best of possible worlds. We are "intimate" with this present, not because it
has any meaning or potential direction, but precisely because it is so pointless
that to *expect* any meaning or direction would be out of the question. If one
feels estrangement in contemplating this pointless world, it is because one
has not yet abandoned the anthropocentric expectations that are the real
source of our problem.

Alienation is thus "overcome" by the strategy of redescribing it as
the normal state of affairs and then enjoying its gratifications. Political
intransigence, from this point of view, is but a symptom of inadequate
adjustment—the inability to get beyond old-fashioned alienation and im-
merse oneself in the unitary stream of things. Calvin Tomkins, admiring
Robert Rauschenberg for his "cheerful and nearly total acceptance" of the

---

* Sontag, *Styles of Radical Will* (New York: Delta Books, 1969), 94. Sontag seems recently to have
recanted these enthusiasms. In *On Photography*, she attacks photography because of its tendency "to rule
out a historical understanding of reality" (New York: Farrar, Straus and Giroux, 1977, 33). In her earlier
work, Sontag tended to see things like "historical understanding of reality" as poor substitutes for
immediate experience.

materials of urban life, quotes the artist as follows: "I really feel sorry for people who think things like soap dishes or mirrors or Coke bottles are ugly, because they're surrounded by things like that all day long, and it must make them miserable."[27] What is interesting in Rauschenberg's statement is the way it endows urban commercial ugliness with the permanence and unchangeability of nature—one might as soon do something about it as do something about rain or wind. Whatever one may think about the urban anti-culture, the thing is *real* and is not going to go away because a few intellectuals happen not to like it, so therefore one had better learn to love it. One does not try to change the world but rather alters one's perspective (or "consciousness") so as to *see* the world in a new way.

THE NORMALIZATION OF ALIENATION

The assumption that alienation is the normal and unalterable condition of human beings has gained strength from structuralist theories of language described in my introduction: since meaning arises wholly from the play of differences within artificial sign systems, it follows that meanings are arbitrary and that everything we say in language is a fiction. Sometimes this assertion that everything is a fiction immunizes itself from criticism by claiming *itself* to be no more than a fiction. Thus Sontag tells us that "one can't object" to Roland Barthes's exposition of structuralist ideas "simply because its leading concepts are intellectual myths or fictions."[28] Robert Scholes summarizes this poststructuralist outlook as follows:

> Once we knew that fiction was about life and criticism was about fiction— and everything was simple. Now we know that fiction is about other fiction, is criticism in fact, or metafiction. And we know that criticism is about the impossibility of anything being about life, really, or even about fiction, or, finally, about anything. Criticism has taken the very idea of "aboutness" away from us. It has taught us that language is tautological, if it is not nonsense, and to the extent that it is about anything it is about itself. Mathematics is about mathematics, poetry is about poetry and criticism is about the impossibility of its own existence.[29]

The doctrine is particularly widespread in discussions of recent fiction. Raymond Federman, a theorist of "surfiction," informs us that the authentic fiction writers of our day "believe that reality as such does not exist, or rather exists only in its fictionalized version."[30] As William Gass puts it, "the novelist, if he is any good, will keep us kindly imprisoned in his language— there is literally nothing beyond."[31]

No doubt structuralism, properly understood, is only a method of analysis and need not carry the dismal ontological conclusions which such critics have derived from it. But one of its exponents, Perry Meisel, after reassuring us that "structuralism is a method, not a program or an ideology," goes on to say that "structuralism realizes that alienation is the timeless and normative condition of humanity rather than its special modern affliction."[32] For, according to Meisel, "semiotics is in a position to claim that no phenomenon has any ontological status outside its place in the particular information system(s) from which it draws its meaning(s)." From the proposition, unexceptionable in itself, that no signifier can mean anything apart from the code or sign system which gives it significance, one infers the conclusion that no signifier can *refer* to a nonlinguistic reality—that, as Meisel puts it, "all language is finally groundless." There is, then, no such thing as a "real" object outside language, no "nature" or "real life" outside the literary text, no real text behind the critical interpretation, and no real persons or institutions behind the multiplicity of messages human beings produce. Everything is swallowed up in an infinite regress of textuality.

Meisel does not hesitate to draw the social moral of all this: "the only assumption possible in a post-Watergate era," he writes, is "that the artifice is the only reality available."[33] Since artifice is the only reality, the old-fashioned distinctions between "intrinsic" and "extrinsic," literature and life, are abolished. Literature and life are thus reconciled, but only by the strategy of enclosing "life" itself in an autonomous process of textuality which cannot refer beyond its structuring activity. The gulf imposed by romantic esthetics between literary and practical discourse is closed, not by ascribing objective truth to literature, but by withdrawing it from all discourse. Fact and value are reconciled by converting fact along with value into fiction. These reconciliations are dictated not only by philosophical and linguistic theory but by "the post-Watergate era." One wonders whether the moral of the Watergate episode might not actually be that some degree of penetration of artifice, some detection of the hidden facts *is* after all possible. But structuralist skepticism does not wait to be questioned on such points. Its method of demythologizing thinking ends up teaching that no escape from myth-making is possible.[34]

The position of structuralism and poststructuralism, however, on the postmodern spectrum of attitudes is equivocal. On the one hand there is Derrida's influential invocation of "the joyful Nietzschean affirmation of the play of the world and the innocence of becoming, the affirmation of a world of signs which has no truth, no origin, no nostalgic guilt, and is proffered for active interpretation."[35] On the other hand, there is the insistence on the *risk* involved in the enterprise of doing without a truth and an origin as anchoring points outside the infinite play of linguistic differences. As Derrida puts it, "*this affirmation then determines the non-center otherwise than as a loss of the center*. And it plays the game without security."[36] As he does often, Derrida here seems to be echoing Nietzsche, who stated that "the genuine philosopher . . . risks *himself* constantly. He plays the dangerous game."[37] However, neither the joy nor the risk invoked by this view seems fully convincing. The joy of affirmation is a diluted joy, since it comes about as a consequence of the absence of any reality or meaning in life to which effort might be directed. And the element of risk in the "dangerous game" becomes minimal when (a) relativistic philosophy has eroded the concept of error, and (b) the culture of pluralism and publicity has endowed deviation and eccentricity with "charisma."

The postmodern temper has carried the skepticism and antirealism of modern literary culture to an extreme beyond which it would be difficult to go. Though it looks back mockingly on the modernist tradition and professes to have got beyond it, postmodern literature remains tied to that tradition and unable to break with it. The very concepts through which modernism is demystified derive from modernism itself. The loss of significant external reality, its displacement by myth-making, the domestication and normalization of alienation—these conditions constitute a common point of departure for the writing of our period. Though for some of this writing they remain conditions to be somehow resisted, a great deal of it finds them an occasion for acquiescence and even celebration. Unable to imagine an alternative to a world that has for so long seemed unreal, we have begun to resign ourselves to this kind of world and to learn how to redescribe this resignation as a form of heroism. And for some observers, to whom I turn in the next chapter, this loss of a reality principle is not a loss at all but a condition of political revolution.

Notes

1. George Steiner, *Language and Silence: Essays on Language, Literature, and the Inhuman* (New York: Atheneum, 1967), 162.
2. Richard Poirier, *The Performing Self: Compositions and Decompositions in the Languages of Contemporary Life* (New York: Oxford University Press, 1971), xii.
3. Harry Levin, "What Was Modernism?" *Refractions: Essays in Comparative Literature* (New York: Oxford University Press, 1966), 292.
4. Donald Barthelme, *Snow White* (New York: Bantam Books, 1968), 82.
5. Alain Robbe-Grillet, *For a New Novel: Essays on Fiction*, trans. R. Howard (New York: Grove Press, 1965), 87. Unless indicated, italics in quotations are not added.
6. Susan Sontag, *Against Interpretation* (New York: Delta Books, 1967), 7.
7. Leslie Fiedler, *Waiting for the End* (New York: Stein and Day, 1964), 227.
8. Jacob Brackman, *The Put-On: Modern Fooling and Modern Mistrust* (Chicago: Regnery, 1971), 68.
9. Fiedler, *Cross the Border—Close the Gap* (New York: Stein and Day, 1972), 64.
10. Barthelme, *Snow White*, 18–19.
11. Henry James, "The Art of Fiction," in *Criticism: The Foundation of Modern Literary Judgment*, revised edition, ed. Schorer et al. (New York: Harcourt Brace and World, 1958), 49.
12. Ibid., 47.

13. Eliot, "From Poe to Valéry," *To Criticize the Critic* (New York: Farrar, Straus and Giroux, 1965), 39.

14. James, "The Art of Fiction," in Schorer, *Criticism: the Foundation of Modern Literary Judgment*, 48.

15. James, *The American Scene* (Bloomington: Indiana University Press, 1968), 273.

16. Eliot, " 'Ulysses,' Order, and Myth," in *Selected Prose*, ed. Frank Kermode (New York: Harcourt Brace Jovanovich, 1975), 177.

17. Georg Lukács, *The Meaning of Contemporary Realism*, trans. J. and N. Mander (London: Merlin Press, 1963), 33.

18. Jorge Luis Borges, *Labyrinths: Selected Stories and Other Writings*, trans. J. Irby (New York: New Directions, 1964), 57.

19. Ibid., 17.

20. See above, 220–21.

21. Sontag, *Against Interpretation*, 27.

22. Poirier, *The Performing Self*, 40.

23. On Mailer, see above, 216–20.

24. Poirier, *The Performing Self*, 40.

25. Ibid., 93.

26. John Cage, "Diary: How to Improve the World (You Will Only Make Matters Worse) Continued," *TriQuarterly*, 18 (Spring 1970), 101.

27. Calvin Tomkins, *The Bride and the Bachelors: Five Masters of the Avant-Garde* (New York: Viking, 1965), 194.

28. Sontag, Introduction to Roland Barthes, *Writing Degree Zero* (New York: Hill and Wang, 1953), xx.

29. Robert Scholes, "The Fictional Criticism of the Future," *Tri-Quarterly*, 34 (Fall 1975), 233. Scholes's last sentence echoes a remark of T.S. Eliot's: "The poet makes poetry, the metaphysician makes metaphysics, the bee makes honey, the spider secretes a filament; you can hardly say that any of these agents believes: he merely does" ("Shakespeare and the Stoicism of Seneca," *Selected Essays* [New York: Harcourt Brace and World, 1960], 118).

30. Raymond Federman, ed. *Surfiction: Fiction Now and Tomorrow* (Chicago: Swallow Press, 1975), 7.

31. William Gass, *Fiction and the Figures of Life*, 8.

32. Perry Meisel, "Everything You Always Wanted to Know About Structuralism but Were Afraid to Ask," *National Village Voice* (September 30, 1976), 43–45.

33. Ibid.

34. Jonathan Culler argues in this vein against the *Tel Quel* critics in *Structuralist Poetics: Structuralism, Linguistics, and the Study of Literature* (Ithaca: Cornell University Press, 1975), 247–50.

35. Derrida, "Structure, Sign, and Play in the Discourse of the Human Sciences," quoted and translated by Jonathan Culler, *Structuralist Poetics*, 247. I have used Culler's translation of this passage, which is more accurate than the standard English translation by Macksey and Donato in *The Structuralist Controversy: The Languages of Criticism and the Sciences of Man*, ed. Richard Macksey and Eugenio Donato (Baltimore: Johns Hopkins University Press, 1972), 264.

36. Derrida, "Structure, Sign, and Play," in Macksey and Donato, *The Structuralist Controversy*, 264.

37. Nietzsche, as quoted by Gayatri C. Spivak, Translator's Preface to Derrida, *Of Grammatology* (Baltimore: Johns Hopkins University Press, 1976), xxx.

POSTFACE 1982:
Toward a Concept of Postmodernism

IHAB HASSAN

The strains of silence to which I attend in this work, from Sade to Beckett, convey complexities of language, culture, and consciousness as these contest themselves and one another. Such eerie music may yield an experience, an intuition, of postmodernism but no concept or definition of it. Perhaps I can move, in this Postface, toward such a concept by putting forth certain queries. I begin with the most obvious: can we really perceive a phenomenon, in Western societies generally and in their literatures particularly, that needs to be distinguished from modernism, needs to be named? If so, will the provisional rubric "postmodernism" serve? Can we then—or even should we at this time—construct of this phenomenon some probative scheme, both chronological and typological, that may account for its various trends and counter-trends, its artistic, epistemic, and social character? And how would this phenomenon—let us call it postmodernism—relate itself to such earlier modes of change as turn-of-the-century avant-gardes or the high modernism of the twenties? Finally, what difficulties would inhere in any such act of definition, such a tentative heuristic scheme?

I am not certain that I can wholly satisfy my own questions, though I can assay some answers that may help to focus the larger problem. History, I take it, moves in measures both continuous and discontinuous. Thus the prevalence of postmodernism today, if indeed it prevails, does not suggest that ideas or institutions of the past cease to shape the present. Rather, traditions develop, and even types suffer a seachange. Certainly, the powerful cultural assumptions generated by, say, Darwin, Marx, Baudelaire, Nietzsche, Cézanne, Debussy, Freud, and Einstein still pervade the Western mind. Certainly those assumptions have been reconceived, not once but many times—else history would repeat itself, forever same. In this perspective, postmodernism may appear as a significant revision, if not an original *épistémè*, of twentieth-century Western societies.

Some names, piled here pell-mell, may serve to adumbrate postmodernism, or at least suggest its range of assumptions: Jacques Derrida, Jean-

Reprinted with permission from *The Dismemberment of Orpheus: Toward a Postmodern Literature*, 2nd ed. (Madison: University of Wisconsin Press, 1982): 259–71.

François Lyotard (philosophy), Michel Foucault, Hayden White (history), Jacques Lacan, Gilles Deleuze, R. D. Laing, Norman O. Brown (psychoanalysis), Herbert Marcuse, Jean Baudrillard, Jürgen Habermas (political philosophy), Thomas Kuhn, Paul Feyerabend (philosophy of science), Roland Barthes, Julia Kristeva, Wolfgang Iser, the "Yale Critics" (literary theory), Merce Cunningham, Alwin Nikolais, Meredith Monk (dance), John Cage, Karlheinz Stockhausen, Pierre Boulez (music), Robert Rauschenberg, Jean Tinguely, Joseph Beuys (art), Robert Venturi, Charles Jencks, Brent Bolin (architecture), and various authors from Samuel Beckett, Eugène Ionesco, Jorge Luis Borges, Max Bense, and Vladimir Nabokov to Harold Pinter, B. S. Johnson, Rayner Heppenstall, Christine Brooke-Rose, Helmut Heissenbüttel, Jürgen Becker, Peter Handke, Thomas Bernhardt, Ernst Jandl, Gabriel García Márquez, Julio Cortázar, Alain Robbe-Grillet, Michel Butor, Maurice Roche, Philippe Sollers, and, in America, John Barth, William Burroughs, Thomas Pynchon, Donald Barthelme, Walter Abish, John Ashbery, David Antin, Sam Shepard, and Robert Wilson. Indubitably, these names are far too heterogenous to form a movement, paradigm, or school. Still, they may evoke a number of related cultural tendencies, a constellation of values, a repertoire of procedures and attitudes. These we call postmodernism.

Whence this term? Its origin remains uncertain, though we know that Federico de Onís used the word *postmodernismo* in his *Antología de la poesía española e hispanoamericana* (1882–1932), published in Madrid in 1934; and Dudley Fitts picked it up again in his *Anthology of Contemporary Latin-American Poetry* of 1942.[1] Both meant thus to indicate a minor reaction to modernism already latent within it, reverting to the early twentieth century. The term also appeared in Arnold Toynbee's *A Study of History* as early as D. C. Somervell's first-volume abridgement in 1947. For Toynbee, Post-Modernism designated a new historical cycle in Western civilization, starting around 1875, which we now scarcely begin to discern. Somewhat later, during the fifties, Charles Olson often spoke of postmodernism with more sweep than lapidary definition.

But prophets and poets enjoy an ample sense of time, which few literary scholars seem to afford. In 1959 and 1960, Irving Howe and Harry Levin wrote of postmodernism rather disconsolately as a falling off from the great modernist movement.[2] It remained for Leslie Fiedler and myself, among others, to employ the term during the sixties with premature approbation, and even with a touch of bravado.[3] Fiedler had it in mind to challenge the elitism of the high modernist tradition in the name of popular culture. I wanted to explore that impulse of self-unmaking which is part of the literary tradition of silence. Pop and silence, or mass culture and deconstruction, or Superman and Godot—or as I shall later argue, immanence and indeterminacy—may all be aspects of the postmodern universe. But all this must wait upon more patient analysis, longer history.

Yet the history of literary terms serves only to confirm the irrational genius of language. We come closer to the question of postmodernism itself by acknowledging the psychopolitics, if not the psychopathology, of academic life. Let us admit it: there is a will to power in nomenclature, as well as in people or texts. A new term opens for its proponents a space in language. A critical concept of system is a "poor" poem of the intellectual imagination. The battle of the books is also an ontic battle against death. That may be why Max Planck believed that one never manages to convince one's opponents—not even in theoretical physics!—one simply tries to out-live them. William James described the process in less morbid terms: novel-ties are first repudiated as nonsense, then declared obvious, then appropriated by former adversaries as their own discoveries.

I do not mean to take my stand with the postmoderns against the (ancient) moderns. In an age of frantic intellectual fashions, values can be too recklessly voided, and tomorrow can quickly preempt today or yesteryear. Nor is it merely a matter of fashions; for the sense of supervention may express some cultural urgency that partakes less of hope than fear. This much we recall: Lionel Trilling entitled one of his most thoughtful works *Beyond Culture* (1965); Kenneth Boulding argued that "postcivilization" is an essen-tial part of *The Meaning of the 20th Century* (1964); and George Steiner could have subtitled his essay, *In Bluebeard's Castle* (1971), "Notes Toward the Definition of Postculture." Before them, Roderick Seidenberg published his *Post-Historic Man* exactly in mid-century; and most recently, I have myself speculated, in *The Right Promethean Fire* (1980), about the advent of a posthu-manist era. As Daniel Bell put it: "It used to be that the great literary modifier was the word *beyond*. . . . But we seem to have exhausted the beyond, and today the sociological modifier is *post*. . . ."[4]

My point here is double: in the question of postmodernism, there is a will and counter-will to intellectual power, an imperial desire of the mind, but this will and desire are themselves caught in a historical moment of supervention, if not exactly of obsolescence. The reception or denial of postmodernism thus remains contingent on the psychopolitics of academic life—including the various dispositions of people and power in our universi-ties, of critical factions and personal frictions, of boundaries that arbitrarily include or exclude—no less than on the imperatives of the culture at large. This much, reflexivity seems to demand from us at the start.

But reflection demands also that we address a number of conceptual problems that both conceal and constitute postmodernism itself. I shall try to isolate ten of these, commencing with the simpler, moving toward the more intractable.

1. The word postmodernism sounds not only awkward, uncouth; it evokes what it wishes to surpass or suppress, modernism itself. The term thus contains its enemy within, as the terms romanticism and classicism, baroque and rococo, do not. Moreover, it denotes temporal linearity and

connotes belatedness, even decadence, to which no postmodernist would admit. But what better name have we to give this curious age? The Atomic, or Space, or Television, Age? These technological tags lack theoretical definition. Or shall we call it the Age of Indetermanence (indeterminacy + immanence) as I have half-antically proposed?[5] Or better still, shall we simply live and let others live to call us what they may?

2. Like other categorical terms—say poststructuralism, or modernism, or romanticism for that matter—postmodernism suffers from a certain *semantic* instability: that is, no clear consensus about its meaning exists among scholars. The general difficulty is compounded in this case by two factors: (a) the relative youth, indeed brash adolescence, of the term postmodernism, and (b) its semantic kinship to more current term, themselves equally unstable. Thus some critics mean by postmodernism what others call avant-gardism or even neo-avant-gardism, while still others would call the same phenomenon simply modernism. This can make for inspired debates.[6]

3. A related difficulty concerns the *historical* instability of many literary concepts, their openness to change. Who, in this epoch of fierce misprisions, would dare to claim that romanticism is apprehended by Coleridge, Pater, Lovejoy, Abrams, Peckham, and Bloom in quite the same way? There is already some evidence that postmodernism, and modernism even more, are beginning to slip and slide in time, threatening to make any diacritical distinction between them desperate.[7] But perhaps the phenomenon, akin to Hubble's "red shift" in astronomy, may someday serve to measure the historical velocity of literary concepts.

4. Modernism and postmodernism are not separated by an Iron Curtain or Chinese Wall; for history is a palimpsest, and culture is permeable to time past, time present, and time future. We are all, I suspect, a little Victorian, Modern, and Postmodern, at once. And an author may, in his or her own life time, easily write both a modernist and postmodernist work. (Contrast Joyce's *Portrait of the Artist as a Young Man* with his *Finnegans Wake*.) More generally, on a certain level of narrative abstraction, modernism itself may be rightly assimilated to romanticism, romanticism related to the enlightenment, the latter to the renaissance, and so back, if not to the Olduvai Gorge, then certainly to ancient Greece.

5. This means that a "period," as I have already intimated, must be perceived in terms *both* of continuity *and* discontinuity, the two perspectives being complementary and partial. The Apollonian view, rangy and abstract, discerns only historical conjunctions; the Dionysian feeling, sensuous though nearly purblind, touches only the disjunctive moment. Thus postmodernism, by invoking two divinities at once, engages a double view. Sameness and difference, unity and rupture, filiation and revolt, all must be honored if we are to attend to history, apprehend (perceive, understand) change both as a spatial, mental structure and as a temporal, physical process, both as pattern and unique event.

6. Thus a "period" is generally not a period at all; it is rather both a diachronic and synchronic construct. Postmodernism, again like modernism or romanticism, is no exception; it requires *both* historical *and* theoretical definition. We would not seriously claim an inaugural "date" for it as Virginia Woolf pertly did for modernism, which she said began "in or about December, 1910"—though we may sometimes woefully imagine that postmodernism began "in or about September, 1939." Thus we continually discover "antecedents" of postmodernism—in Sterne, Sade, Blake, Lautréamont, Rimbaud, Jarry, Tzara, Hoffmannsthal, Gertrude Stein, the later Joyce, the later Pound, Duchamp, Artaud, Roussel, Bataille, Broch, Queneau, and Kafka. What this really indicates is that we have created in our mind a model of postmodernism, a particular typology of culture and imagination, and have proceeded to "rediscover" the affinities of various authors and different moments with that model. We have, that is, reinvented our ancestors—and always shall. Consequently, "older" authors can be postmodern—Kafka, Beckett, Borges, Nabokov, Gombrowicz—while "younger" authors need not be so—Styron, Updike, Capote, Irving, Doctorow, Gardner.

7. As we have seen, any definition of postmodernism calls upon a fourfold vision of complementarities, embracing continuity and discontinuity, diachrony and synchrony. But a definition of the concept also requires a dialectical vision; for defining traits are often antithetical, and to ignore this tendency of historical reality is to lapse into single vision and Newton's sleep. Defining traits are dialectical and also plural; to elect a single trait as an absolute criterion of postmodern grace is to make of all other writers preterites.[8] Thus we can not simply rest—as I have sometimes done—on the assumption that postmodernism is anti-formal, anarchic, or decreative; for though it is indeed all these, and despite its fanatic will to unmaking, it also contains the need to discover a "unitary sensibility" (Sontag), to "cross the border and close the gap" (Fiedler), and to attain, as I have suggested, an immanence of discourse, an expanded noetic intervention, a "neo-gnostic im-mediacy of mind."[9]

8. All this leads to the prior problem of periodization itself, which is also that of literary history conceived as a particular apprehension of change. Indeed, the concept of postmodernism implies some theory of innovation, renovation, novation, or simply change. But which one? Heraclitean? Viconian? Darwinian? Marxist? Freudian? Kuhnian? Derridean? Eclectic?[10] Or is a "theory of change" itself an oxymoron best suited to ideologues intolerant of the ambiguities of time? Should postmodernism, then, be left—at least for the moment—unconceptualized, a kind of literary-historical "difference" or "trace"?[11]

9. Postmodernism can expand into a still larger problem: is it only an artistic tendency or also a social phenomenon, perhaps even a mutation in Western humanism? If so, how are the various aspects of this phenomenon—psychological, philosophical, economic, political—joined or disjoined? In

short, can we understand postmodernism in literature without some attempt to perceive the lineaments of a postmodern society, a Toynbeean postmodernity, or future Foucauldian *épistémè*, of which the literary tendency I have been discussing is but a single, elitist strain?[12]

10. Finally, though not least vexing, is postmodernism an honorific term, used insidiously to valorize writers, however disparate, whom we otherwise esteem, to hail trends, however discordant, which we somehow approve? Or is it, on the contrary, a term of opprobrium and objurgation? In short, is postmodernism a descriptive as well as evaluative or normative category of literary thought? Or does it belong, as Charles Altieri notes, to that category of "essentially contested concepts" in philosophy which never wholly exhaust their constitutive confusions?[13]

No doubt, other conceptual problems lurk in the matter of postmodernism. Such problems, however, can not finally inhibit the intellectual imagination, the desire to apprehend our historical presence in noetic constructs that reveal our being to ourselves. I move, therefore, to propose a provisional scheme that the literature of silence, from Sade to Beckett, seems to envisage, and do so by distinguishing, tentatively, between three modes of artistic change in the last hundred years. I call these avant-garde, modern, and postmodern, though I realize that all three have conspired together to create that "tradition of the new" which, since Baudelaire, brought "into being an art whose history regardless of the credos of its practitioners, has consisted of leaps from vanguard to vanguard, and political mass movements whose aim has been the total renovation not only of social institutions but of man himself."[14]

By avant-garde, I mean those movements that agitated the earlier part of our century, including 'Pataphysics, Cubism, Futurism, Dadaism, Surrealism, Suprematism, Constructivism, Merzism, de Stijl—some of which I have already discussed in this work. Anarchic, these assaulted the bourgeoisie with their art, their manifestoes, their antics. But their activism could also turn inward, becoming suicidal—as happened later to some postmodernists like Rudolf Schwartzkogler. Once full of brio and bravura, these movements have all but vanished now, leaving only their story, at once fugacious and exemplary. Modernism, however, proved more stable, aloof, hieratic, like the French Symbolism from which it derived; even its experiments now seem olympian. Enacted by such "individual talents" as Valéry, Proust, and Gide, the early Joyce, Yeats, and Lawrence, Rilke, Mann, and Musil, the early Pound, Eliot, and Faulkner, it commanded high authority, leading Delmore Schwartz to chant in *Shenandoah*: "Let us consider where the great men are / Who will obsess the child when he can read. . . ." But if much of modernism appears hieratic, hypotactical, and formalist, postmodernism strikes us by contrast as playful, paratactical, and deconstructionist. In this, it recalls the irreverent spirit of the avant-garde, and so carries sometimes the label of neo-avant-garde. Yet postmodernism remains "cooler," in McLuhan's sense, than older vanguards—cooler, less cliquish, and far less aversive to the pop, electronic society of which it is a part, and so hospitable to kitsch.

Can we distinguish postmodernism further? Perhaps certain schematic differences from modernism will provide a start:

Modernism	Postmodernism
Romanticism/Symbolism	'Pataphysics/Dadaism
Form (conjunctive, closed)	Antiform (disjunctive, open)
Purpose	Play
Design	Chance
Hierarchy	Anarchy
Mastery/Logos	Exhaustion/Silence
Art Object/Finished Work	Process/Performance/Happening
Distance	Participation
Creation/Totalization	Decreation/Deconstruction
Synthesis	Antithesis
Presence	Absence
Centering	Dispersal
Genre/Boundary	Text/Intertext
Semantics	Rhetoric
Paradigm	Syntagm
Hypotaxis	Parataxis
Metaphor	Metonymy
Selection	Combination
Root/Depth	Rhizome/Surface
Interpretation/Reading	Against Interpretation/Misreading
Signified	Signifier
Lisible (Readerly)	*Scriptible* (Writerly)
Narrative/*Grande Histoire*	Anti-narrative/*Petite Histoire*
Master Code	Idiolect
Symptom	Desire
Type	Mutant
Genital/Phallic	Polymorphous/Androgynous
Paranoia	Schizophrenia
Origin/Cause	Difference-Differance/Trace
God the Father	The Holy Ghost
Metaphysics	Irony
Determinacy	Indeterminacy
Transcendence	Immanence

The preceding table draws on ideas in many fields—rhetoric, linguistics, literary theory, philosophy, anthropology, psychoanalysis, political science, even theology—and draws on many authors—European and American—aligned with diverse movements, groups, and views. Yet the dichotomies this table represents remain insecure, equivocal. For differences shift, defer, even collapse; concepts in any one vertical column are not all equivalent; and inversions and exceptions, in both modernism and postmodernism, abound. Still, I would submit that rubrics in the right column point to the postmodern tendency, the tendency of indetermanence, and so may bring us closer to its historical and theoretical definition.

The time has come, however, to explain a little that neologism: "indetermanence." I have used that term to designate two central, constitutive tendencies in postmodernism: one of indeterminacy, the other of immanence. The two tendencies are not dialectical; for they are not exactly antithetical; nor do they lead to a synthesis. Each contains its own contradictions, and alludes to elements of the other. Their interplay suggests the action of an ambilectic, pervading postmodernism. Since I have discussed this topic at some length elsewhere, I can advert to it here briefly.[15]

By indeterminacy, or better still, *indeterminacies*, I mean a complex referent which these diverse concepts help to delineate: ambiguity, discontinuity, heterodoxy, pluralism, randomness, revolt, perversion, deformation. The latter alone subsumes a dozen current terms of unmaking: decreation, disintegration, deconstruction, decenterment, displacement, difference, discontinuity, disjunction, disappearance, decomposition, de-definition, demystification, detotalization, delegitimation—let alone more technical terms referring to the rhetoric of irony, rupture, silence. Through all these signs moves a vast will to unmaking, affecting the body politic, the body cognitive, the erotic body, the individual psyche—the entire realm of discourse in the West. In literature alone, our ideas of author, audience, reading, writing, book, genre, critical theory, and of literature itself, have all suddenly become questionable. And in criticism? Roland Barthes speaks of literature as "loss," "perversion," "dissolution"; Wolfgang Iser formulates a theory of reading based on textual "blanks"; Paul de Man conceives rhetoric—that is, literature—as a force that "radically suspends logic and opens up vertiginous possibilities of referential aberration"; and Geoffrey Hartman affirms that "contemporary criticism aims at the hermeneutics of indeterminacy."[16]

Such uncertain diffractions make for vast dispersals. Thus I call the second major tendency of postmodernism *immanences*, a term that I employ without religious echo to designate the capacity of mind to generalize itself in symbols, intervene more and more into nature, act upon itself through its own abstractions and so become, increasingly, im-mediately, its own environment. This noetic tendency may be evoked further by such sundry concepts as diffusion, dissemination, pulsion, interplay, communication, interdependence, which all derive from the emergence of human beings as language animals, *homo pictor* or *homo significans*, gnostic creatures constituting themselves, and determinedly their universe, by symbols of their own making. Is ". . . this not the sign that the whole of this configuration is about to topple, and that man is in the process of perishing as the being of language continues to shine ever brighter upon our horizon?" Foucault famously asks.[17] Meanwhile, the public world dissolves as fact and fiction blend, history becomes derealized by media into a happening, science takes its own models as the only accessible reality, cybernetics confronts us with the enigma of artificial intelligence, and technologies project our perceptions to the edge of the receding universe or into the ghostly interstices of matter.[18] Everywhere—even deep in Lacan's "lettered unconscious," more dense than a black hole in space—everywhere we encounter that immanence called Language, with all its literary ambiguities, epistemic conundrums, and political distractions.[19]

No doubt, these tendencies may seem less rife in England, say, than in America or France where the term postmodernism, reversing the recent direction of poststructuralist flow, has now come into use.[20] But the fact in most developed societies remains: as an artistic, philosophical, and social phenomenon, postmodernism veers toward open, playful, optative, provisional (open in time as well as in structure or space), disjunctive, or indeterminate forms, a discourse of ironies and fragments, a "white ideology" of absences and fractures, a desire of diffractions, an invocation of complex, articulate silences. Postmodernism veers towards all these yet implies a different, if not antithetical, movement toward pervasive procedures, ubiquitous interactions, immanent codes, media, languages. Thus our earth seems caught in the process of planetization, transhumanization, even as it breaks up into sects, tribes, factions of every kind. Thus, too, terrorism and totalitarianism, schism and ecumenism, summon one another, and authorities decreate themselves even as societies search for new grounds of authority. One may well wonder: is some decisive historical mutation—involving art and science, high and low culture, the male and female principles, parts and wholes, involving the One and the Many as pre-Socratics used to say—active in our midst? Or does the dismemberment of Orpheus prove no more than the mind's need to make but one more construction of life's mutabilities and human mortality?

And what construction lies beyond, behind, within, that construction?

Notes

1. For the best history of the term "postmodernism," see Michael Köhler, " 'Postmodernismus': Ein begriffsgeschichtlicher Überblick," *Amerikastudien*, vol. 22, no. 1 (1977). That same issue contains other excellent discussions and bibliographies on the term; see particularly

Gerhard Hoffmann, Alfred Hornung, and Rüdiger Kunow, " 'Modern,' 'Postmodern,' and 'Contemporary' as Criteria for the Analysis of 20th Century Literature."

2. Irving Howe, "Mass Society and Postmodern Fiction," *Partisan Review*, vol. 26, no. 3 (Summer 1959), reprinted in his *Decline of the New* (New York: Harcourt, Brace, 1970), pp. 190–207; and Harry Levin, "What Was Modernism?", *Massachusetts Review*, vol. 1, no. 4 (August 1960), reprinted in *Refractions* (New York: Oxford University Press, 1966), pp. 271–295.

3. Leslie Fiedler, "The New Mutants," *Partisan Review*, vol. 32, no. 4 (Fall 1965), reprinted in his *Collected Essays*, vol. 2 (New York: Stein and Day, 1971), pp. 379–400; and Ihab Hassan, "Frontiers of Criticism: Metaphors of Silence," *Virginia Quarterly*, vol. 46, no. 1 (Winter 1970). In earlier essays, I had also used the term "anti-literature" and "the literature of silence" in a proximate sense; see, for instance, Ihab Hassan, "The Literature of Silence," *Encounter*, vol. 28, no. 1 (January 1967).

4. Daniel Bell, *The Coming of Post-Industrial Society* (New York: Basic Books, 1973), p. 53.

5. See "Culture, Indeterminacy, and Immanence: Margins of the (Postmodern) Age," *Humanities in Society*, vol. 1, no. 1 (Winter 1978), reprinted in *The Right Promethean Fire: Imagination, Science, and Cultural Change* (Urbana: University of Illinois Press, 1980), chapter 3.

6. Matei Calinescu, for instance, tends to assimilate "postmodern" to "neo-avant-garde" and sometimes to "avant-garde," in *Faces of Modernity: Avant-Garde, Decadence, Kitsch* (Bloomington: Indiana University Press, 1977), though later he discriminates between these terms thoughtfully, in "Avant-Garde, Neo-Avant-Garde, and Postmodernism," in *Perspectives on the Avant-Garde*, eds. Rudolf Kuenzli and Stephen Foster (Iowa City: University of Iowa Press, forthcoming). Miklos Szabolcsi would identify "modern" with "avant-garde" and call "postmodern" the "neo-avant-garde," in "Avant-Garde, Neo-Avant-Garde, Modernism: Questions and Suggestions," *New Literary History*, vol. 3, no. 1 (Autumn 1971); while Paul de Man would call "modern" the innovative element, the perpetual "moment of crisis" in the literature of every period, in "Literary History and Literary Modernity," in *Blindness and Insight* (New York: Oxford University Press, 1971), chapter 8; in a similar vein, William V. Spanos employs the term "postmodernism" to indicate "not fundamentally a chronological event, but rather a permanent mode of human understanding," in "De-Struction and the Question of Postmodern Literature: Towards a Definition," *Par Rapport*, vol. 2, no. 2 (Summer 1979), p. 107. And even John Barth, as inward as any writer with postmodernism, now argues that postmodernism is a synthesis yet to come, and what we had assumed to be postmodernism all along was only late modernism, in "The Literature of Replenishment: Postmodernist Fiction," *Atlantic Monthly* 245, no. 1 (January 1980).

7. In my own earlier and later essays on the subject I can discern such a slight shift. See "POSTmodernISM: A Paracritical Bibliography," *New Literary History*, vol. 3, no. 1 (Autumn 1971), reprinted in my *Paracriticisms: Seven Speculations of the Times* (Urbana: University of Illinois Press, 1975), chapter 2; "Joyce, Beckett, and the Postmodern Imagination," *TriQuarterly* 34 (Fall 1975), and "Culture, Indeterminacy, and Immanence."

8. Though some critics have argued that postmodernism is primarily "temporal" and others that it is mainly "spatial," it is the particular relation between these single categories that postmodernism probably reveals itself. See the two seemingly contradictory views of William V. Spanos, "The Detective at the Boundary," in *Existentialism* 2, ed. William V. Spanos (New York: Thomas Y. Crowell, 1976), pp. 163–189; and Jürgen Peper, "Postmodernismus: Unitary Sensibility," *Amerikastudien*, vol. 22, no. 1 (1977).

9. Susan Sontag, "One Culture and the New Sensibility," in *Against Interpretation* (New York: Farrar, Straus, and Giroux, 1967), pp. 293–304; Leslie Fiedler, "Cross the Border—Close the Gap," in *Collected Essays*, vol. 2 (New York: Stein and Day, 1971), pp. 461–485; and Ihab Hassan, "The New Gnosticism," *Paracriticisms*, chapter 6.

10. For some views of this, see Ihab Hassan and Sally Hassan, eds., *Innovational Renovation: Recent Trends and Reconceptions in Western Culture* (Madison: University of Wisconsin Press, forthcoming).

11. At stake here is the idea of literary periodicity, challenged by current French thought. For other views of literary and historical change, including "hierarchic organization" of time, see Leonard Meyer, *Music, the Arts, and Ideas* (Chicago: University of Chicago Press, 1967), pp. 93, 102; Calinescu, *Faces of Modernity*, pp. 147ff; Ralph Cohen, "Innovation and Variation: Literary Change and Georgic Poetry," in Ralph Cohen and Murray Krieger, *Literature and History* (Los Angeles: University of California Press, 1974); and my *Paracriticisms*, chapter 7. A harder question is one Geoffrey Hartman asks: "With so much historical knowledge, how can we avoid historicism, or the staging of history as a drama in which epiphanic raptures are replaced by epistemic ruptures. . . ?" Or, again, how can we "formulate a theory of reading that would be historical rather than historicist"? *Saving the Text: Literature/ Derrida/Philosophy* (Baltimore: Johns Hopkins University Press, 1981), p. xx.

12. Writers as different as Marshall McLuhan and Leslie Fiedler have explored the media and pop aspects of postmodernism for two decades, though their efforts are now out of fashion in some critical circles. The difference between postmodernism, as a contemporary artistic tendency, and postmodernity, as a cultural phenomenon, perhaps even an era of history, is discussed by Richard E. Palmer in "Postmodernity and Hermeneutics," *Boundary* 2, vol. 5, no. 2 (Winter 1977).

13. Charles Altieri, "Postmodernism: A Question of Definition," *Par Rapport*, vol. 2, no. 2 (Summer 1979), p. 90. This leads Altieri to conclude: "The best one can do who believes himself post-modern . . . is to articulate spaces of mind in which the confusions can not paralyze because one enjoys the energies and glimpses of our condition which they produce," p. 99.

14. Harold Rosenberg, *The Tradition of the New* (New York: Grove Press, 1961), p. 9.

15. See note 5. Also, my "Innovation/Renovation: Toward a Cultural Theory of Change," *Innovation/Renovation*, chapter 1.

16. See, for instance, Roland Barthes and Maurice Nadeau, *Sur la littérature* (Paris: Presses Universitaires de Grenoble, 1980), pp. 7, 16, 19f., 41; Wolfgang Iser, *The Act of Reading* (Baltimore: Johns Hopkins University Press, 1978), *passim*; Paul de Man, *Allegories of Reading* (New Haven: Yale University Press, 1979), p. 10; and Geoffrey H. Hartman, *Criticism in the Wilderness* (New Haven: Yale University Press, 1980), p. 41.

17. Michael Foucault, *The Order of Things* (New York: Pantheon Books, 1970), p. 386.

18. "Just as Pascal sought to throw dice with God . . . so do the decision theorists, and the new intellectual technology, seek their own *tableau entier*—the compass of rationality itself," Daniel Bell remarks in "Technology, Nature, and Society," in *Technology and the Frontiers of Knowledge* (Garden City: Doubleday and Co., 1975), p. 53. See also the more acute analysis of "l'informatique" by Jean-François Lyotard, *La Condition postmoderne* (Paris: Editions de Minuit, 1979), *passim*.

19. This tendency also makes for the abstract, conceptual, and irrealist character of so much postmodern art. See Suzi Gablik, *Progress in Art* (New York: Rizzoli, 1977), whose argument was prefigured by Ortega y Gasset, *The Dehumanization of Art* (Princeton: Princeton University Press, 1968). Note also that Ortega presaged the gnostic or noetic tendency to which I refer here in 1925: "Man humanizes the world, injects it, impregnates it with his own ideal substance and is finally entitled to imagine that one day or another, in the far depths of time, this terrible outer world will become so saturated with man that our descendants will be able to travel through it as today we mentally travel through our own inmost selves—he finally imagines that the world, without ceasing to be like the world, will one day be changed into something like a materialized soul, and, as in Shakespeare's *Tempest*, the winds will blow at the bidding of Ariel, the spirit of ideas," p. 184.

20. Though postmodernism and poststructuralism can not be identified, they clearly reveal many affinities. Thus in the course of one brief essay, Julia Kristeva comments on both immanence and indeterminacy in terms of her own: "postmodernism is that literature which writes itself with the more or less conscious intention of expanding the signifiable, and thus human, realm"; and again: "At this degree of singularity, we are faced with idiolects, proliferating uncontrollably. . . ." Julia Kristeva, "Postmodernism?" in *Romanticism, Modernism, Postmodernism*, ed. Harry R. Garvin (Lewisburg, Pa.: Bucknell University Press, 1980), pp. 137, 141.

The Problem of the Postmodern

C. Barry Chabot

During the past fifteen years we have increasingly heard and read about something variously termed *fabulism* (Scholes), *metafiction* (McCaffery), *surfiction* (Federman) and, with growing unanimity, *postmodernism*.[1] The former terms were typically developed in efforts to account for apparent changes of direction and emphasis within recent fiction. *Postmodernism*, on the other hand, is a broader term and has been pressed into service to describe developments throughout the arts; it is even said that we live in a postmodern society. Any number of people obviously believe that a cultural rupture of some moment has occurred, and that its mark is discernible across the range of our cultural activities. There seems to be little agreement, however, about the precise nature and timing of the supposed break, and even less about how we can most adequately characterize its effects upon our cultural products.

I remain doubtful that a rupture of such magnitude has occurred and want here to register a minority report. Our lack of an adequate and widely accepted understanding of literary modernism makes many arguments for the postmodern initially plausible, but much of what has been termed postmodern derives quite directly from the work of earlier writers. In order to demonstrate the hesitancies, confusions, and contradictions within and between various characterizations of the postmodern, I want to investigate the work of several representative critics. For the sake of focus, I shall concentrate initially upon characterizations of our recent novel; if my conclusions are valid, they should apply as well to comparable accounts of our recent poetry and drama.

I

When Ihab Hassan writes in *Paracriticisms* that the "change in Modernism may be called Postmodernism," he emphasizes the continuity between these literary movements.[2] He locates the origins of the latter in 1938, with the publication of Sartre's *La Nausée* and Beckett's *Murphy*, but he is not primarily

Reprinted with permission from *New Literary History* 20 (Autumn 1988): 1–20.

attempting to define the sensibilities of entire eras. "Modernism," he writes, "does not suddenly cease so that Postmodernism may begin: they now *coexist*" (47). Modernism and Postmodernism for Hassan thus provide competing visions of the contemporary predicament, and it is as likely that a particular work will be informed by the one as by the other. Hassan does not completely neglect the temporal dimension implied by the terms themselves. He understands both as responses to the character of life and thought in the twentieth century. If individuals earlier in the century had reason to be apprehensive about the possibilities then available for perpetuating viable forms of life, there has subsequently been even more reason for disquiet. Modernism and Postmodernism, respectively, represent the literary equivalents of such pervasive concerns. "Postmodernism," writes Hassan, "may be a response, direct or oblique, to the Unimaginable which Modernism glimpsed only in its most prophetic moments" (53). Such sentences award the primacy of vision to postmodernism, but its perceptiveness is largely the product of its times, which have made the awful possibilities we face only too clear.

Hassan defines neither modernism nor postmodernism. Instead, he offers a catalogue of characteristic modernist concerns—urbanism, technologism, dehumanization, primitivism, eroticism, antinomianism, and experimentalism; he then glosses each, providing instances of the forms it takes within postmodernism. In regard to primitivism, for instance, Hassan writes that its modernist forms represented a use of ritual and myth to structure contemporary experience, whereas its postmodernist forms move away "from the mythic, toward the existential," initially in the work of the Beats and later "the post-existential ethos, psychedelics (Leary), the Dionysian ego (Brown), Pranksters (Kesey), madness (Laing), animism and magic (Castaneda)" (56). As his examples and parenthetical references make clear, for Hassan postmodernism is not exclusively a literary phenomenon; rather, it represents a broad cultural response to pressing contemporary issues, and is as likely to emerge within social practices as within artistic products.

Despite the potential importance of the postmodernist program, and despite his own desire to stay in sympathy with whatever is most current, Hassan's assessment of postmodernism is finally ambiguous. He concedes that modernists frequently resorted to questionable means in shoring up such artistic authority as they could muster, citing Hemingway's code as an example, but observes that postmodernism "has tended toward artistic Anarchy in deeper complicity with things falling apart—or has tended toward Pop" (59). The choice between authoritarianism and anarchy seems a devil's choice, and it is not altogether clear, to Hassan at least, that the latter is unmistakably the course of wisdom. Finally, however, Hassan's reservations about a postmodern aesthetic go much deeper. It releases new imaginative energies, but Hassan worries that we might now have entered a time when no art "can help to engender the motives we must now acquire; or if we can long continue to value an art that fails us" (59). I am not sure how to take this reservation: Does it imply that our needs are too pressing for us to fiddle with art, or that our art already fails to provide us with the necessary direction? In the end, Hassan suggests that postmodernism is in danger of being overwhelmed by the very cultural crisis that originally called it into existence.

Jerome Klinkowitz accepts Hassan's designation of postmodernism, and thus needs another term to designate work manifesting what he takes to be an independent and more recent impulse. He offers several—*Post-Contemporary, disruptivist, SuperFiction* and most recently, *self-apparent*—but there are reasons to assimilate Klinkowitz's efforts within the broader attempt to define post-modernism.[3] Klinkowitz has assumed the role of apologist for a relatively small group of recent fiction writers; he is, accordingly, eager to differentiate their particular virtues from those of other writers. Among readers of contemporary fiction, Klinkowitz is almost alone in believing that his writers form an identifiable school distinct from postmodernism. Hassan, for instance, cites several writers Klinkowitz would term disruptivists when developing his own understanding of postmodernism. I shall return to this question later, and shall assume for the present that, despite his intentions, Klinkowitz is struggling to define a version of postmodernism.

Klinkowitz locates the emergence of disruptivist fiction "with the publishing season of 1967–68, when for the first time in a long time a clear trend in literary history became evident" (ix). Disruptivist fiction is particularly adamant about the need to abandon the mimetic aspirations of the traditional novel. "If the world is absurd," writes Klinkowitz, "if what passes for reality is distressingly unreal, why spend time representing it" (32). Such statements suggest that the disruptivists believe the world is not now worth representing, whereas others suggest that representation is not possible and has always been a misplaced aspiration. Whatever the rationale, on Klinkowitz's account disruptivists are concerned with "not just the reporting of the world, but [with] the imaginative transformation of it" (32). The transformative power of the imagination enters this fiction in two ways. First, at the thematic level, it figures in the plot, as in Vonnegut's use of time travel in *Slaughterhouse-Five*. More importantly, however, it appears in the self-reflexiveness of its characters (who frequently know that they are fictive constructs) and narrators (who frequently comment on the difficulties they are having in constructing the piece at hand). Such narrative shifts frustrate whatever tendencies readers might have to suspend disbelief and take the work at hand as a representation of some common world; in the same way, they perform the instructive function of demonstrating the ways and means by which readers too make their worlds.

Hassan's postmodern always hovers on the edge of despair and enervation, but Klinkowitz's disruptivist fiction is almost programmatically playful and energetic. "The writers we're discussing are out to create a good time," writes Klinkowitz in the prologue to *The Life of Fiction* (4). These qualities are not ancillary to disruptivist fiction, and their absence is sufficient reason to read writers out of the disruptivist camp. Thus Klinkowitz terms Barth and Pynchon "regressive parodists," and apparently believes that the former's influential essay, "The Literature of Exhaustion," has retarded appreciation of the disruptivists (ix). Barth's self-reflexive characters typically feel caught in and by their self-consciousness. It is a condition they would escape, whereas in disruptivist fiction it is perceived precisely as the condition of imaginative freedom. Exuberance is also what obviously differentiates disruptivist fiction from the French New Novel. In each of his books Klinkowitz approvingly quotes Barthelme's observation that the French New Novel " 'seems leaden, selfconscious in the wrong way. Painfully slow-paced, with no leaps of the imagination, concentrating on the minutiae of consciousness, these novels scrupulously, in deadly earnest, parse out what can safely be said' " (174). Barthelme's description of the New Novel seems a catalogue of characteristics that disruptivist fiction on Klinkowitz's account is at pains to avoid.[4]

Hassan's postmodernism and Klinkowitz's disruptivist fiction are similar in the emphasis each places on the transformative potential of the imagination. This similarity might account for Hassan's running together of writers from Beckett to Sukenick into a pervasive postmodernism; Klinkowitz, on the other hand, believes that "to the newer fictionists, Beckett is as traditional as Joyce" (*LF* 2), and accordingly would differentiate sharply among modern, postmodern, and disruptivist fiction. Hassan locates postmodernism within a general sense of cultural crisis and potential calamity; although he has written a cultural history, *The American 1960s*, Klinkowitz concentrates on the writers in question and rarely alludes to larger cultural issues. This difference in the ways they situate their work might account for a corresponding difference in tone: Hassan is prophetic, edgy, uncertain that the imagination will prove equal to the tasks at hand; Klinkowitz can be as bouncy as the authors he values, and since he sets the imagination no particular problems to solve, he need not doubt its adequacy.

Alan Wilde also finds an affirmation at the core of what he terms postmodernism, but its character is far less exuberant and has quite different sources. *Horizons of Assent: Modernism, Postmodernism, and the Ironic Imagination* is a closely reasoned study of the shift in the novel during this century from modernism, through what Wilde terms "late modernism," to postmodernism. Wilde pays particular attention to the characteristic uses and meanings of irony; he argues that these shift as the century progresses, and that each of his three phases corresponds to a characteristic form of irony.

For Wilde modernism is characterized by what he terms disjunctive or absolute irony, "the conception of equal and opposed possibilities held in a state of total poise, or, more briefly still, the shape of an indestructible, unresolvable paradox."[5] Wilde distinguishes absolute irony from an earlier and more pervasive form, which he terms "mediate irony." It "imagines a world lapsed from a recoverable . . . norm" (9) and has as its goal the recovery of that earlier wholeness. The modern ironist, by way of contrast, confronts a world apparently in such fundamental disarray that no recovery of previous states seems possible. The modern ironist nonetheless attempts to impose a shape or order, and for his efforts achieves "not resolution but closure—an aesthetic closure that substitutes for the notion of paradise regained an image . . . of a paradise fashioned by man himself" (10). Since the order achieved by the modern writer is exclusively aesthetic, he ends at a remove from the world he would make cohere. With no course of action clearly preferable to any other, the modern ironist is finally inactive as well as detached, unable to commit himself to the world without thereby destroying the order he has struggled to create.

Wilde illustrates his definition of the modernist program primarily through references to the novels of E. M. Forster and Virginia Woolf. In the work of other, generally younger writers, especially those who come to attention during the thirties, he sees a subtle shift indicative of what he terms the "late modern" sensibility. His chief examples of the late modern are Christopher Isherwood and Ivy Compton-Burnett. These writers are typically less concerned with depth than with surfaces; as a result, the relations between language and the world are thought to be less problematic than among the modernists, and appearances are again held to be valuable in understanding people and events. The obvious pleasure that Isherwood and his narrators take in some aspects of their worlds not only contrasts with the discomfort typical of the modernists, it also implies that they have partially overcome the detachment characteristic of the latter.

In their participation in their worlds, the late modernists anticipate what Wilde terms postmodernism. Although he terms Woolf's *Between the Acts* "still the most impressive of *postmodern* novels," Wilde argues that postmodernism "is essentially an American affair" (48,12).[6] On Wilde's account, postmodernists typically deploy what he terms "suspensive irony." It involves the perception of "experience as random and contingent . . . rather than—the modernist view—simply fragmented" (27). Nonetheless, postmodernism does not press for or impose order, even one limited to the aesthetic realm; instead, the contingent world is simply accepted. Modernist paradox thereby gives way "to quandary, to a low-keyed engagement with a world of perplexities and uncertainties, in which one can hope, at best, to achieve what Forster calls 'the smaller pleasures of life' and Stanley Elkin, its 'small satisfactions' " (10).

Wilde isolates two strands within postmodernism. The first consists roughly of Klinkowitz's disruptivists, especially Ronald Sukenick and Raymond Federman, but Wilde attends less to their statements of intention than the effects of their practice. On Wilde's reading, Sukenick and Federman, for all their overt hostility to modernism, end by unintentionally reproducing, in an attenuated form, many modernist dilemmas: "they are," he writes, "modernism's lineal descendents (or perhaps its illegitimate sons), patricides manqués" (144). Wilde's other strand of postmodernism employs "generative irony: the attempt, inspired by the negotiations of self and world, to create, tentatively and provisionally, anironic enclaves of value in the face of—but not in place of—a meaningless universe" (148). The world envisioned in these works is even more contingent than that found in modernist fiction, but its narrators and characters accede to that condition, recognizing that it cannot be redressed. Instead, they recognize that their worlds contain pleasures as well as pains, and therefore choose not to distance themselves, in the manner of their predecessors, from the phenomenal world. Elkin's *The Living End*, Apple's "The Oranging of America" and "Disneyad," and several of Barthelme's later stories serve as Wilde's primary examples of this postmodernism. It embodies "a vision that lacks the heroism of the modernist enterprise but that, for a later and more disillusioned age, recovers its humanity" (165).

Wilde's characterization of postmodernism does not, like those by Hassan and Klinkowitz, place a premium upon the imagination. For Hassan, the postmodern imagination must redeem a world on the brink of calamity, and its prospects for success are at best problematic; for Klinkowitz, the world similarly requires redemption, but he apparently has no doubt that the postmodern imagination is equal to the task. On Wilde's account, postmodern writers find the world fully as contingent, but he finds in them a willingness to endure the random and a capacity to identify sources of gratification within it. Both Klinkowitz and Wilde believe that an affirmative moment defines postmodern fiction, but they identify its sources differently. For Klinkowitz, what is affirmed is finally the supposedly transformative power of the imagination; for Wilde, on the other hand, it is the phenomenal world itself, which, amidst its various turnings, upon occasion throws up gratifying possibilities.

II

The efforts by Hassan, Klinkowitz, and Wilde to define postmodernism are representative of many others, and display many of the same strengths and weaknesses. They bring contemporary writers to our attention, provide insights into their particular ambitions, and begin to place them within the strands of literary and cultural history. Each defines postmodernism, however, in ways that are not only distinct but in the end mutually exclusive. Wilde's late modern, for instance, is not the same as Hassan's postmodern, even though both are located in the thirties; and Hassan links the fiction of Beckett and Sukenick, whereas Klinkowitz sees the latter as being in rebellion against the former. The primary difficulties in the way of the very concept of postmodernism, in other words, involve its definition and inclusiveness.

As the term suggests, postmodernism is invariably defined vis-à-vis modernism—postmodernism is what comes after and in opposition to modernism. But there is little agreement about the nature of modernism, many characterizations of it enjoying some degree of currency within the profession. In Wilde's account, for instance, modernism is equivalent to the use of a particular form of irony, what he terms absolute irony. I have no quarrel with his readings of Forster and Woolf, but I find it difficult to extend the term so defined to cover the work of other writers typically termed modernists, such as Fitzgerald and Hemingway, or Stevens and Hart Crane. One wonders, in other words, if Wilde's postmoderns would seem equally distinct from modernism if they were read within the context of earlier American instead of British writers. Perhaps the differences that Wilde finds derive as much from differences between the national literary traditions, differences obscured by his framework, as from any supposed change in the literary sensibility that has occurred over time. Although I frequently find Wilde's readings of individual works compelling, such doubts leave me with questions about the history he constructs from them.

Unlike Wilde, Klinkowitz does not venture detailed accounts of the succession of literary sensibilities during the century. His conception of disruptivist or self-apparent fiction is the most narrow of the three surveyed. It identifies writers of a particular school, but then claims that it represents an entire generation of writers come of age during 1967–1968. In *Literary Disruptions* he writes of a "generational gap" between Barth and Barthelme, which "has obstructed the critical understanding of new fiction" (175). When he reduces the relations between disruptivist and other fiction to the terms of generational conflict, Klinkowitz introduces several difficulties. One of his disruptivists, Kurt Vonnegut, is in fact eight years older than John Barth, and his first novel was published in 1952, four years before Barth's *The Floating Opera*; Klinkowitz is thus in the anomalous position of having a rebellious son who in fact arrives on the scene earlier than the figurative father. Such local anomalies, however, are the least of Klinkowitz's conceptual difficulties. I want to discuss three that particularly disable his argument.

First, Klinkowitz is concerned largely with younger or at least recently arrived writers who clearly feel a need to make a space for themselves on the literary scene. They do so in part by issuing manifestos and granting interviews in which they attempt to differentiate their own efforts from those of earlier and already established writers. As an apologist for these writers, Klinkowitz takes them at their word, rarely questioning either announced goals, the measure of their success in meeting them, or their statements concerning the position of their own work in regard to that of other writers. A curiously naive species of literary history is the result, especially when one considers that Klinkowitz writes at the same time that Harold Bloom and others have been demonstrating how complicated the relations among writers can be. Klinkowitz's literary sons (and they are all sons) overcome their literary fathers with little difficulty, and the latter never survive to disfigure the former's efforts. We now know to be suspicious of such characterizations of literary succession, where literary influence is conceived purely as a negative affair and breaks between literary generations appear absolute.

Second, Klinkowitz, like the writers he admires, is so intent upon celebrating this generation that he fails to recognize the ways in which it simply continues or modifies the literary heritage. Wilde, for instance, observes that "the Surfictionists recall ('in attenuated form') nothing so much as the aesthetic manifestos of the early decades of the century" (144). When Sukenick and Federman engage in polemics against the novel as currently practiced and invent neologisms to identify themselves, they continue the tradition and rhetoric of Pound, Breton, and other poets earlier in the century. Indeed, one way of understanding these writers involves recognizing the extent to which they have adapted to the writing of fiction many of the practices common to poets during the teens and twenties. Fitzgerald, Hemingway, and Faulkner did not issue manifestos, nor did they devote much energy to berating other novelists to their own advantage. Poets of that time, especially those who self-consciously considered themselves part of the avant-garde, did engage in such activities, and the Surfictionists seemingly follow their example, simply adapting it to the conditions of another time and genre. This adaptation is particularly clear in the case of Sukenick, who wrote a dissertation and first book on the poetics of Wallace Stevens. In his own subsequent fiction Sukenick adapts Stevens's poetics to the condition of the contemporary novel, but large portions of the poet's work survive the adaptation virtually unaltered. Klinkowitz simply passes over such borrowings, either because he does not notice them, because they weaken his case, or because he believes the transportation of poetic doctrines and practices to fiction in itself constitutes a significant innovation. Whatever the reason, the neglect of such continuities with writers earlier in the century casts doubt upon Klinkowitz's account of the disruptivists.

Although Wilde does not use the language of generations and is characteristically more cautious in suggesting the kinds of departures that constitute postmodernism, his own account of the phenomenon encounters similar problems. Stanley Elkin is one of Wilde's exemplary postmoderns. Elkin wrote a dissertation on Faulkner and has said in an interview that Saul Bellow is probably the writer who has influenced him most strongly. "To the extent that I imitate anyone," he continued, "I think I may—in dialogue—imitate Saul Bellow."[7] Few people, including Bellow himself, would consider Bellow a postmodern writer, and Faulkner is certainly one of the foremost American modernists. Like Faulkner and Bellow, Elkin writes an extremely rhetorical prose. Although each possesses a distinctive voice and puts it to distinctive ends (consider, for instance, the differences between Faulkner's Flem Snopes and Elkin's Ben Flesh in *The Franchiser*), it seems excessive to posit an additional difference between them of the kind usually associated with the transition between modern and postmodern.

Modernism, in its usual usage, is a fairly capacious term, one covering a range of literary practices. A final difficulty in the way Klinkowitz and others typically propose definitions of the postmodern involves their violation of modernism in this larger sense. *Modernism* is not a term equivalent to *Imagist, Futurism, Surrealism, Vorticism*, and the like, which refer to specific literary schools or movements; instead, it is the term invoked to suggest what such particular and divergent programs have in common. It is a *period* concept; and its use involves the claim that in the end, and whatever their obvious differences, the individual energies of the time possess enough family resemblances that it makes sense to refer to them collectively. Modernism refers to whatever Ezra Pound and Wallace Stevens, Ernest Hemingway and William Faulkner, to name only American writers whose credentials as modernists seem beyond question, have in common. By its very nature, then, *modernism* is a second-order concept.

Since modernism is a period concept, one encompassing many divergent specific movements, it is likely to be surpassed or replaced only by a concept of the same kind and with comparable reach. The emergence of surrealism, for instance, did not represent the overcoming of modernism so much as the emergence of another dimension within it. When we consider the various claims being made for the emergence of what is being called "postmodernism," we must ask whether the tendencies in question resemble in kind surrealism or modernism. Klinkowitz, as we have seen, believes that the disruptivists form an identifiable "school" (x); we have also seen that they are unmistakably indebted to modernist poets for their means of self-promotion and their aesthetic. There are thus reasons to believe that these writers represent, like the surrealists, a late development within modernism rather than its replacement. The rhetoric used in clearing themselves a place, of course, makes larger claims; but I understand the rhetorical intensity as itself in part a legacy from modernism, and in part as deriving from the felt urgency, at this late date, of claiming some necessarily marginal territory as its own.

Unlike Klinkowitz, Hassan recognizes that modernism is a period concept. He acknowledges the diversity of literary modernism when he catalogues its various schools and movements. His lists, however, fall short of providing definitions for either modernism or its supposed successor, because he does not indicate what the items on either list have in common, or what differentiates them from other contemporary cultural phenomena. He provides something of an anatomy without a conception of the whole the various organs and limbs finally compose. His attention is on the immediate future, or better on the question of whether we shall have one, and does not pause over what might be considered academic questions.

The situation in regard to Wilde's characterization of recent literary history and the emergence of the postmodern is somewhat more complicated. Wilde defines modernism narrowly, as the consequences that follow from the use of what he terms absolute irony. The emergence more recently of what Wilde terms suspensive or generative irony provides the grounds for claiming that it constitutes a new or postmodern sensibility. The narrow conception of modernism, in other words, is what lends credence to the claims for postmodernism; but, as mentioned earlier, I doubt the adequacy of Wilde's characterizations of modernism. My doubts take two forms. First, I doubt that it is possible to say that the entire range of modern novelists employ absolute irony. It seems that Wilde has mistaken a form of modernism for modernism itself, much as if he had identified it with, say, Pound's Imagism. Second, even if Wilde could make a reasonable case for the pervasiveness of absolute irony in this body of fiction, I do not believe he would thereby be identifying its most distinctive feature. I do not believe, in other words, that one can define modernism formally, despite its own obvious formal intensities; as a period concept, modernism must be approached more broadly and its distinctive features sought in the relationships it establishes with both the literary tradition and the immediate cultural context.

Horizons of Assent is in most respects the best book now available on our recent fiction, and Wilde's failure to develop a satisfactory account of postmodernism is therefore especially instructive. By its nature the postmodern is conceived in contrast to the modern—the era, sensibility, or set of literary strategies it would supplant. The initial plausibility of Wilde's description of postmodernism turns out to depend upon his prior conception of modernism. When that conception is found wanting, the claims for an emergent postmodernism are simultaneously thrown into doubt. In the absence of an adequate and widely accepted conception of modernism, we shall probably continue to be presented with claims in behalf of an emergent postmodern; but at least for the near term I doubt that upon inspection any will prove any more substantial than those already proposed by Hassan, Klinkowitz, and Wilde.[8]

III

In a series of recent essays, Fredric Jameson has been developing his own conception of postmodernism. It is explicitly a period concept, and thus does not fall prey to the difficulties enumerated above. Jameson believes that postmodernism has become the cultural dominant for the entire social order;

accordingly, its force is to be found as much in the economy, the cinema, philosophy, and architecture as in literature itself. Indeed, Jameson says that his own formulation of postmodernism initially took shape in response to the continuing debates concerning the nature of contemporary architecture.[9] Since Jameson's use of the term is so distinctive among literary critics, it will be instructive to see if it proves more adequate to its appointed task.

At crucial points in these essays, after lengthy discussions of various cultural manifestations of what he terms postmodernism, Jameson alludes to its characteristic economic forms. His conception of economic postmodernism clearly derives from Ernest Mandel's *Late Capitalism*. Mandel argues that Western capitalism has evolved through three distinct stages: market capitalism, monopoly capitalism, and, since the 1940s, what Jameson calls multinational capitalism. This latest form simultaneously clarifies the logic of capitalism and, to an unprecedented degree, expands its reach, drawing the entire globe within its ambit. In his contribution to *The 60s, Without Apology*, Jameson suggests that the upheavals of that period parallel the culminating moments of the transition from monopoly to multinational capitalism, a shift that was largely completed by the early seventies. The postmodern, or so Jameson argues, is the culture appropriate to this last phase of capitalism, just as realism and modernism, respectively, had been appropriate to its earlier forms (PC 78).

Jameson enumerates a number of constitutive features of this postmodern culture—among them, "a new depthlessness," "a consequent weakening of historicity," "a whole new type of emotional ground tone" (PC 58), and the dissolution of the individual subject—but a new sense of space seems to hold a privileged position. The preoccupation of modernism with "the elegiac mysteries of *durée* and of memory" (PC 64) has been replaced within the postmodern by a comparably intense concern with spatial questions. This apparent shift makes Jameson's interest in contemporary architecture especially relevant. He analyzes John Portman's postmodern Bonaventura Hotel in Los Angeles, and suggests that the building aspires less to be a part of its environment than to be "a total space, a complete world, a kind of miniature city" (PC 81), capable of replacing the city itself. Its interior is a stage for continual movement via escalators and exposed elevators; but what most distinguishes the building is the way it deprives patrons of spatial coordinates, so that they are often unable to relocate shops on its balconies. Jameson believes that the confusion felt by the visitor to the Bonaventura Hotel is the architectural equivalent of a more fundamental confusion felt by inhabitants of the postmodern era: namely, our inability "to map the great global multinational and decentred communicational network in which we find ourselves caught as individual subjects" (PC 84). Postmodern architecture, in other words, reproduces the experiential conditions of multinational capitalism.

In a review of two recent novels, Don DeLillo's *The Names* and Sol

Yurick's *Richard A.*, Jameson illustrates how this difficulty manifests itself within fiction. The latter is a version of the common conspiracy novel (the postmodern, says Jameson, effects a new relation with the forms of popular culture [PC 54–55]); it uses the image of the telephone system to suggest the ways in which people's lives have become interconnected. That image represents Yurick's attempt to conceptualize or map the locations of his characters within a world as disorienting as Portman's hotel. DeLillo's narrator is an American abroad, an employee of a risk insurance firm, who is increasingly unable to assess the risks in an increasingly dangerous world. He picks up pieces of information, fragments of puzzling knowledge, but cannot make them cohere into anything resembling a map of his surroundings. Each of these novels, according to Jameson, struggles with the special spatial dilemma of contemporary life: "That dilemma can be schematically described as the increasing incompatibility—or incommensurability—between individual experience, existential experience, as we go on looking for it in our individual biological bodies, and structural meaning, which can now ultimately derive only from the world system of multinational capitalism" (R 116). The solutions found in these works differ markedly: Yurick constructs an image that evokes the interconnections that cannot be directly experienced, whereas DeLillo renders the experience of living amidst fragments that, however suggestive of some larger order, resist our effort to piece them together.

Jameson's account of the postmodern is immensely suggestive. He seems to be a person unable to forget or ignore anything; his work, accordingly, invariably contains striking analogies and connections among the most disparate phenomena. I have only sketched a portion of his argument, but it should be clear that his conception of the postmodern differs strikingly from those discussed earlier. In particular, Jameson's postmodern is systematically a period concept, one that reaches not only across various movements and genres, but as well across the various arts and other social institutions in the contemporary world. Its very reach, however, produces an order of difficulties distinct from those discussed in regard to Hassan, Klinkowitz, and Wilde.

As we have seen, Jameson coordinates an apparent preoccupation with space with the establishment of a genuinely multinational economic system. He recognizes, of course, that the economic system became increasingly international throughout the earlier period of monopoly capitalism, as previously isolated cultures were penetrated and opened as markets. Jameson believes, however, that the effects upon local cultures of these earlier penetrations were comparably benign and that they are now being dramatically transformed as the logic of multinational capitalism takes hold on a global scale. I am not in a position to judge the adequacy of such sweeping claims; I do question, however, some of the cultural consequences Jameson would derive from them. In particular, I question his claim that contemporary arts are uniquely concerned with locating the individual within some "postmodern hyperspace" (PC 83). Jameson himself makes substantial use of Kevin Lynch's *The Image of the City*, which argues, according to Jameson, that the "alienated city is above all a space in which people are unable to map (in their minds) either their own positions or the urban totality in which they find themselves" (PC 89). Such cities and the confusions to which they give rise predate postmodernism, but Jameson nowhere differentiates specifically postmodern forms. Similarly, since at least the early years of this century Western culture has been exploring the implications of an increasingly interconnected world; such explorations have taken various forms, such as the use of artistic resources drawn from other cultures, and the depiction of travel through distant and disorienting lands. The culminating achievement of Jameson's most recent book, *The Political Unconscious*, is his reading of Conrad's *Lord Jim*, one of many exemplary works concerned with such issues.[10] Neither experiences of spatial dislocation nor the existence of a multinational world, in other words, are unique to the last decade. The manifestations of both might have changed and become more pronounced, but Jameson would then have to demonstrate how differences in intensity have become differences in kind, such that one can speak of a distinctly postmodern disorientation. I suspect that Jameson's reliance upon Mandel's economic stages compels him to make claims for corresponding cultural transformations that he had not as yet adequately supported.

As we have seen, architecture holds a special place within Jameson's conception of postmodern culture. It is not only the art primarily concerned with the spaces we inhabit, but the recent debates within architecture have also informed Jameson's own formulations in important ways. Within architecture, the claims for postmodernism have developed in an especially clear way, and Jameson has largely appropriated these claims for more sweeping purposes. I believe that the reason postmodernism has emerged with special clarity within architecture has to do largely with the remarkable agreement within that field about the nature of modernism, the aesthetic it would replace. Architectural modernism consists largely of the so-called International Style. The increasingly strident reaction against the main tenets of this style is carried out in the name of postmodernism. The comparative uniformity of architectural modernism lends credibility to the claims of its new rivals that they constitute a genuinely postmodern alternative.

The situation within architecture, in other words, is quite different from that within the other arts, particularly literature. Literary modernism, as we have seen, has been characterized by a great diversity of separate movements and styles. It possesses nothing comparable to the Seagram Building. Since many different and competing aesthetic programs collectively constitute literary modernism, the claims of any particular program to supersede literary modernism per se must be scrutinized with some care; upon inspection, as we have seen, such programs are likely to represent new alternatives within modernism, not alternatives to it. The claims for the emergence of a genuine architectural postmodernism, on the other hand, possess a greater initial credibility due to the more monolithic quality of its predecessor.

Different cultural spheres, then, seemingly require different conceptualizations in terms of periods. By way of explanation, it might be said that different spheres evolve at different paces, depending upon a welter of factors, including both internal dynamics and their locations within the culture as a whole. In the case at hand, however, it is probably more to the point that the parallel between literary and architectural modernism was never more than an analogy. That is, roughly contemporary movements within architecture and literature were both termed modernism, but their contemporaneity and designations were all that they had in common. The mere fact that both have been termed modernism has clearly tempted many to claim more substantial similarities between them, or to see both as manifestations of an overarching cultural shift; but such findings have invariably been metaphoric or analogic: architectural and literary modernism have about as much in common as any two contemporaries named John Smith.

Jameson, in brief, errs in attempting to apply the debate within contemporary architectural circles to contemporary culture generally. What might be true of one art need not be true of others. In particular, a genuine postmodern alternative might be emerging within architecture; but we have less reason to believe that a corresponding phenomenon is occurring within literature, due to the different nature of what is called literary modernism. A rhetoric of postmodernism might be common to both fields, but in the latter it is misplaced, at most a sign of impatience. Since Jameson is attempting to develop a period concept that encompasses all of social life, he presumes that changes occur across a broad front and thus discounts the conditions specific to discrete cultural spheres. As a Marxist, Jameson knows that contending energies are likely to be operative at any particular time, and that resolutions among them achieved in one sphere need not have occurred elsewhere. Social life changes unevenly. In his work on postmodernism, however, Jameson's awareness of these facts remains theoretical; whenever he gets to actual cases, postmodernism seems to be progressing apace in every cultural sphere.

If Jameson sometimes argues that significant changes are occurring within all cultural spheres, at other times his argument for an emergent postmodern culture takes a different form: "The first point to be made about the conception of periodization in dominance, therefore, is that even if all the constitutive features of postmodernism were identical and continuous with those of an older modernism—a position I feel to be demonstrably erroneous but which only an even lengthier analysis of modernism proper could dispel—the two phenomena would still remain utterly distinct in their meaning and social function, owing to the very different positioning of postmodernism in the economic system of late capital, and beyond that, to the transformation of the very sphere of culture in contemporary society" (PC 57). Jameson here argues that the conditions under which cultural production and reception take place have so changed that culture itself has been thoroughly transformed. I in fact agree with this assessment, but would not go on to say that we therefore now have a postmodern literary culture. American literary modernism was crucially shaped by its relations with the whole of contemporary social life; but it is best *defined* by the set of strategies it developed in response, and thus by the relations it established with the contemporary social order. Consistency would seem to demand that a proper literary postmodernism be defined in the same manner; that is, not alone by the social conditions in which it reaches us, but as well by the strategies it deploys for existing within those conditions.

Jameson is currently embarked upon an anatomy of contemporary culture; literary matters obviously figure in this undertaking, but only in a subsidiary manner. The entire undertaking is prone to the kind of error we have already seen in regard to his generalization of architectural debates. It is instructive to compare the difficulties encountered by Jameson in developing a conception of postmodernism with those encountered by Klinkowitz and Wilde. The latter, as we saw, generated initially plausible definitions of the postmodern by countering it with an impoverished sense of modernism. In particular, they failed to acknowledge that modernism is a second-order, period concept, and thus proposed definitions of postmodernism that could as well or better be conceived as developments within modernism itself. Jameson, on the other hand, knows that modernism is a period concept. His generalization of the situation within architecture, however, provides him with a fairly monolithic modernism against which he can conceive a postmodern alternative. Architectural modernism, in brief, serves the same function in Jameson's formulations that absolute irony serves in Wilde's. Since he conceives postmodernism as a period concept, Jameson then wants to locate parallel developments in other cultural spheres. In the process, however, he typically minimizes crucial differences among the spheres, thereby creating the erroneous appearance of a culture undergoing change in a fairly uniform manner. Jameson knows that cultural change is an uneven affair, but the ambition to describe an entire cultural transformation apparently leads him to pay more attention to claims for cultural change, and then to lend his voice to them, than the available evidence seems to warrant.

IV

Our survey of difficulties encountered in proposing definitions of some emergent postmodernism leads to several proposals. First, before we can speak meaningfully of the postmodern we require an adequate conception of modernism. That conception, at least in regard to literary modernism, must guard against mistaking one of its constitutive movements (Surrealism, for example) for modernism itself; it must, that is, be a period concept, able to clarify what its different and competing movements have in common. That definition, too, should be specific to literature. The existence of something termed modernism in other cultural realms does not mean that these various artistic modernisms have much in common. Different cultural realms have different histories, needs, and opportunities; and these differences combine to assure that "modernism" will mean different things in each. Finally, we should profit from the example of Wilde and at least initially confine our investigations of literary modernism to individual national traditions. Otherwise we too are likely to mistake differences between national literatures for developments within literature itself. Different national literatures differ in the same ways that literature differs from architecture; since at any given time a national literature represents a specific disposition of cultural forces, each reacts uniquely to any attempt to introduce new and necessarily competing aesthetic programs. The distinctive colorations achieved by literary modernism within the British and American traditions are largely due to the native traditions, with their existing relations among competing interests.[11] It seems only prudent, therefore, that we attend to the configuration achieved by literary modernism within single national literatures before venturing more expansive characterizations of it. This research strategy was recently pursued successfully by June Howard, whose *Form and Function in American Literary Naturalism* conceives the work of Jack London and others as responses to the particular disposition of social and literary forces in the United States at the turn of the century.[12] I am suggesting, in short, that we pursue a comparable program in regard to American literary modernism, for until we have an adequate conception of literary modernism, all claims for anything called postmodernism, like those addressed here, are likely to be premature.

It might be argued that these difficulties in establishing the canon and shape of a nascent postmodernism are only to be expected. The argument might invoke the authority of Thomas Kuhn, and claim that such critics are attempting to describe a shift between prevailing paradigms, and that such confusions are characteristic of transitional periods, times that lack the securities provided by stable intellectual coordinates. The tools of the old order are not appropriate to the new, assuring that those who use them will fail; the intellectual tools of the new order, on the other hand, are either unfamiliar or not yet to hand, with the result that their use is uncertain. Such arguments beg the question. They assume that we are in fact witnessing the emergence of some genuinely postmodern culture, whereas I want to question that assumption. It seems to me at least equally plausible that what some are calling postmodernism is actually a late development or mutation within modernism itself. I have presented several arguments in support of my contention: (1) that no satisfactory and widely accepted account of postmodernism now exists; (2) that much of what is called postmodern in fact derives directly from modernism; and (3) that most arguments for its existence achieve their initial plausibility largely through impoverished characterizations of modernism, especially characterizations that neglect its nature as a second-order concept.

I suspect that the term's currency has more to do with impatience than with actual conceptual shifts. Modernism has been with us for the better part of the century. Its own restless search for innovation in part informs efforts to move beyond it. Some contemporary writers want to claim for their own efforts as radical a departure from now established strategies as that achieved earlier in the century. All honor seems to belong to the founders, and these writers want to avoid thinking of themselves as like Kuhn's normal scientists, working out the residual problems left them by the true innovators. Comparable motives inspire their academic apologists. In the end, as Frank Kermode has shown, there is considerable satisfaction in believing that one inhabits a cusp between eras, not the least of which is the belief that one is replicating the heroic phase of modernism.[13] We might sympathize with such desires, but it seems to me that we should receive announcements of the postmodern's arrival as skeptically as we do commercials for other new products in the marketplace.

Whatever the merits of my arguments, the term "postmodern" has entered our lexicon and will doubtless continue to be used. Too many factors conspire to keep it in circulation, not least of which is inertia, the tendency for anything once set in motion to continue on its way. At the moment, however, the term is an empty marker. It holds a place in our language for a concept that might one day prove necessary; in the meantime, it is the recipient of the ambitions and apprehensions that our prospects for the future evoke.

Notes

1. See Robert Scholes, *Fabulation and Metafiction* (Urbana, Ill., 1979); Larry McCaffery, *The Metafictional Muse: The Work of Robert Coover, Donald Barthelme, and William Gass* (Pittsburgh, 1982); and Raymond Federman, "Surfiction—Four Propositions in Form of an Introduction," in *Surfiction: Fiction Now and Tomorrow*, ed. Raymond Federman (Chicago, 1975), pp. 5–15.

2. Ihab Hassan, *Paracriticisms: Seven Speculations of the Times* (Urbana, Ill., 1975), p. 43; hereafter cited in text.

3. The first two terms appear in Jerome Klinkowitz, *Literary Disruptions: The Making of a Post-Contemporary American Fiction* (Urbana, Ill., 1975), the third in his *The Life of Fiction* (Urbana, Ill., 1977), and the last in his *The Self-Apparent Word: Fiction as Language / Language as Fiction* (Carbondale, Ill., 1984). Unless otherwise indicated, all quotations are from *Literary Disruptions*.

4. See Donald Barthelme, "After Joyce," *Location*, 1 (1964), 13–16.

5. Alan Wilde, *Horizons of Assent: Modernism, Postmodernism, and the Ironic Imagination* (1981; rpt. Philadelphia, 1987), p. 21; hereafter cited in text.

6. This claim obviously puts Wilde's conception of postmodernism at odds with Hassan's and in line with Klinkowitz's and Rother's. See also James Rother, "Parafiction: The Adjacent Universe of Barth, Barthelme, Pynchon, and Nabokov," *boundary 2*, 5, (1976), 21–43.

7. Stanley Elkin, "An Interview with Stanley Elkin," conducted by Scott Sanders, *Contemporary Literature*, 16 (1975), 140.

8. The tendency to reduce modernism to some caricature of itself in order to get a definition of postmodernism off the ground is especially strong when critics define both terms simply against each other and in isolation from the implicit series of period concepts; see, e.g., David Lodge, *The Modes of Modern Writing: Metaphor, Metonymy, and the Typology of Modern Literature* (Ithaca, 1977).

9. Fredric Jameson, "Postmodernism, or The Cultural Logic of Late Capitalism," *New Left Review*, 146 (1984), 53–92, hereafter cited in text as PC; "Periodizing the 60s," in *The 60s Without Apology*, ed. Sohnya Sayres et al. (Minneapolis, 1984), pp. 178–209, hereafter cited as P; Review of *The Names*, by Don DeLillo, and *Richard A.*, by Sol Yurick, *The Minnesota Review*, ns 22 (1984), 116–22, hereafter cited in text as R; "The Politics of Theory: Ideological Positions in the Postmodernism Debate," *New German Critique*, 33 (1984), 53–65; and "Wallace Stevens," *New Orleans Review*, 11 (1984), 10–19.

10. Fredric Jameson, *The Political Unconscious: Narrative as a Socially Symbolic Act* (Ithaca, 1981), pp. 206–80.

11. See the opening sentences of Jeffrey Herf, *Reactionary Modernism: Technology, Culture, and Politics in Weimar and the Third Reich* (New York, 1984): "There is no such thing as modernity in general. There are only national societies, each of which becomes modern in its own fashion." Herf studies a phenomenon much wider than literary, architectural, or any other specific cultural modernism, but his research strategy resembles my proposals.

12. June Howard, *Form and Function in American Literary Naturalism* (Chapel Hill, N.C., 1985).

13. Frank Kermode, *The Sense of an Ending: Studies in the Theory of Fiction* (New York, 1967).

GENRE

Yuppie Postmodernism

David Kaufmann

Keep reminding yourself that the commentary on reality . . . calls for a method completely different from that required for a text. In the one case theology is the basic science, in the other philology.

—Walter Benjamin

The recent past always presents itself as if destroyed by catastrophes.

—T. W. Adorno

Downward mobility has virtually no ritual face . . . there is no equivalent to Horatio Alger stories for the downwardly mobile.

—Katherine S. Newman

What are we to make of the '80s? If, as Habermas has argued, we assume that a crisis only deserves the name if it is experienced as such, how do we account for the commercial success of crisis narratives during the longest period of sustained economic growth in the history of the United States?[1] If things were really going so well for the upper classes during the Reagan years, how can we understand the taste among those classes for stories of anomie, weightlessness and apocalypse? In this essay, I will investigate one aspect of this problem by looking closely at the convergence of two important but often overlooked cultural phenomena of the last decade: the coming to consciousness of a new character type, the Yuppie, and the unprecedented expansion of trade paperback fiction. I shall maintain that one of the most salient features of this literature has been its use of *parataxis*, a disjunctive style marked by its avoidance of grammatical subordination. For the sake of my argument, I will take Raymond Carver as a synechdoche for a wide range of predominantly white, frequently male, and consistently paratactic authors. It will be my contention that this style and this fiction enact a thorough-going naturalization of modernist aestheticism and, along with the creation of the ideal type of the Yuppie, mark the literary expression of a larger, critical socio-historical realignment.

Reprinted with permission from *Arizona Quarterly* 47 (Summer 1991): 93–116. Copyright © 1991 by Arizona Board of Regents.

I.

According to a rather lengthy spread in *Newsweek*, 1984 was the year of the Yuppie.[2] It produced the first Yuppie ads, the first Yuppie products and the first Yuppie presidential candidate. The driven professionals whom *Newsweek* featured in its report were remarkable for their youth, their apparent sophistication and their commitment to the pursuit and ostentatious display of wealth. It is important to remember, though, that *Newsweek* did not invent Yuppies, nor did it discover them. The magazine's canonization of this new class within the New Class signals instead the acknowledgment and dissemination of a new ideal type.

It cannot be a coincidence that the Year of the Yuppie dovetailed neatly with America's emergence from the recession of 1982–83. As the *Newsweek* article pointed out, these young professionals were trying to buck the tide. At a time when the median income for families in the 25-to-34 age bracket was declining, Yuppies were beating out other members of their age cohort by taking home 23% of the nation's net income.[3] And what they took home, they spent. If Yuppies seemed at the time to embody the glamour of wealth in the age of a newly triumphant Reaganomics, they also marked a reaction to what seemed like the renewed threat of downward mobility. As Katherine S. Newman has noted in *Falling from Grace*, a study of the experience of defeated economic expectation, the median income of Americans declined 14% between 1972 and 1982. In the last four years of that period, 56% of the population had incomes that fell behind inflation.[4] Depending on the parameters one uses, at least ⅕, and perhaps ⅓, of all Americans have fallen from the economic and social positions they held in 1973.[5]

These figures point to a crux in Newman's argument: blue collar workers are not the only ones who suffered in the last fifteen years. In 1985 alone, 600,000 middle management jobs evaporated as a result of corporate mergers.[6] But even in the face of widespread *déclassement*, "the culture of meritocracy," that is, the dominant ideological presuppositions that bind together the managerial classes, seems unable to lay the moral burden of unemployment on larger structural changes or business trends. Rather, the tendency is to blame the unemployed individual. Newman's book describes a fascinating blindness among members of the managerial elite: the cognitive dissonance that widespread unemployment causes could easily call into question the workings of the corporate system. Instead, the *victims* of that system's cyclical squeezes get blamed. The unemployed manager becomes a cognitive threat whose predicament is personalized and thus denied. In the face of that threat, the Yuppie and the cult of the tangible markers of success flourished. The system, it seemed, could work very well indeed; hence the scores of the visibly elect who teemed around Wall St. In the face of ideological dislocation, the new type of the Yuppie became a tentative solution to the larger cultural problem of how to come to terms with the specter of economic and/or status decline.

Nineteen-eighty-four was also the year of *Bright Lights, Big City*, the first Yuppie bestseller. In September, Gary Fisketjon, a young editor at Vintage Books, launched a new line of trade paperbacks devoted to contemporary fiction and called, somewhat paradoxically, Vintage Contemporaries. It is worth noting that the trade paperback field, once hailed as the low-price savior for an inflated hardcover industry, was not doing well in early 1984.[7] In January, John Dessauer argued in *Publisher's Weekly* that book executives had made a grave error in previous years: they had mistaken pricing for marketing. As lower cover prices would never generate sufficient sales, publishers would have to pay attention to the intricacies of marketing.[8] Seven months after this manifesto, Fisketjon inaugurated his series, and in both interviews and press releases he stressed the importance of marketing.[9] But where Dessauer had touted advertising and direct sales, Fisketjon talked about only one thing: cover design.

Fisketjon's marketing plan was remarkably uncomplicated. All the titles in the fledgling series were going to share the same package: they would all have the same trim size, design, and typography. Their cover art would be similar. They were meant to be instantly recognizable as part of a line whose avowed aim was to present "the Best of a New Generation." Their high visibility now seems like an attempt to overcome one of the peculiarities of the business, the virtual lack of trademark identification in trade publishing.[10] Of course, there had been trademark identification in mass-market publishing for years. It is worth noting that an earlier experiment with uniform formats failed precisely because Fisketjon did not honor the distinction between trade and mass-market publishing. He had originally tried to market Don DeLillo as a mass-market author: he released a series of DeLillo's books in a lurid, mass-market format. As he told an interviewer, the problem with packaging books as trash—and the word is Fisketjon's—is that people who buy books that look like trash want books that read like trash.[11] Apparently, people judge books by their cover. The hierarchical division between mass market and trade, between "serious" and "trash" guides, if not determines, the customer's expectations and choices: the attempt to blur these distinctions with DeLillo led to commercial failure. So Fisketjon tried again. This time, though, he repackaged DeLillo in a uniform *trade* edition and was remarkably successful. Ironically, Fisketjon's fiasco brought him his greatest glory. It taught him how to import a mass-market technique into a more upscale market, how to peddle fiction whose definition in the marketplace depended on its distance from "trash."

The cover price of the first Vintage Contemporaries also helped define both the series and its audience. At $5.95 a pop, the books cost almost three dollars more per unit than mass-market paperbacks in the same year.[12]

Possession of these books constituted an announcement of affluence. They were not—as their price and larger trim size advertised—what Fisketjon called "trash," were not mass-market. This was quality stuff; this was *literature*. In fact, the uniform packaging of the series played on the hunch that these books constituted a major literary event, that they formed a canon in the making.[13]

The Vintage Contemporary line was, in short, the Mustang of the publishing world. Sleek, aimed at a specific upscale audience, it gained its popularity from its apparent exclusiveness, from the prestige it called on and seemed to embody. In fact, one could go farther, and claim that Vintage Contemporaries helped extend the hegemonic reach of this new ideal type beyond the confines of the urban and the professional.

Of course, all my claims would be hyperbolic speculation if *Bright Lights, Big City*, the only original in the initial list of seven books, had not succeeded so spectacularly. In a field where a book is doing well if it sells more than 7500 copies, McInerney's novel—whose first printing consisted of 15,000 units—sold more than 300,000 copies in the two years after it was published. While it is clear that McInerney's popularity boosted the rest of the series, we must remember that Fisketjon had insured such a reflex action when he insisted on the uniform design. He made doubly sure of it by his remarkably canny use of blurbs—those little puffs from the press or other authors that punctuate the back covers and flaps of books. The original Vintage Contemporary line included Thomas McGuane's *The Bushwhacked Piano* and Raymond Carver's *Cathedral*. Accordingly, McGuane and Carver— who had been McInerney's teacher at Syracuse—provided blurbs for *Bright Lights, Big City*. Another blurb likened MacInerney to McGuane. The nexus of endorsements underscored the aura of uniformity and excellence the series cultivated: it also provided a system of internal reference. If you liked McInerney, you should read Carver: if you liked McGuane, then you'd love *Bright Lights, Big City*. You could enter the series at any point and be directed to other titles that would provide similar satisfactions.

Let us stress, however, that the Vintage series could not be a series in the strictest sense: these are not Harlequins or Nancy Drews. If the editors had submitted to this temptation and tried to create a uniform series, their product would have turned into category fiction—the very genres of pure entertainment against which "literature" defines itself. By the same token, there had to be some consistency between books in order not to frustrate the reader's expectations. Certain similarities of style and content had to be maintained as the list grew. In short, for the series to be successful, it had to satisfy opposite demands. It had to be diverse enough to count as literature and similar enough to ensure continued product loyalty. During his tenure at Vintage, Fisketjon was able to do all this with great success, and other publishing houses—Scribner's, Penguin, Bantam, and Harper & Row, to name a few—launched their own series of contemporary trade paperback fiction along similar lines. In the end, and despite Dessauer's depressing prognostications, trade paperback fiction was one of the most unlikely success stories of the decade.[14]

I would like to suggest that the most important similarity that bound the original Vintage list—or bound together the writers affiliated by their blurbs—was not one of content, but rather one of style. Carver and McInerney share a commitment to a resolute parataxis. Fisketjon hardly invented or commissioned paratactic writing: all he did was capitalize on paratactic works that already existed and market them to a willing audience. Of course, we cannot reduce the glut of trade paperback fiction to the syntactic peculiarities of a few writers. But if we follow the bouncing blurbs, we can begin to understand the success of *this* particular brand of fiction at *this* time. Carver bears a triple burden in the story I am reconstructing here. He was McInerney's teacher, the cornerstone of Fisketjon's editorial plans when he first came to Random House, and a critically respected writer. For the sake of argument, then, we will look closely at *his* work before expanding our purview. But first we will have to analyze why parataxis should have been so compelling.

II.

We can begin to chart the import of Carver's short sentences and refusal to subordinate by looking to the start of his early story, "Fat":

> I am sitting over coffee and cigarettes at my friend Rita's and I am telling her about *it*.
> Here is what I tell her.
> It is late of a slow Wednesday when Herb seats the fat man at my station.
> This fat man is the fattest person I have ever seen, though he is neat-appearing and well-dressed enough. But it is the fingers I remember best.[15]

Apart from a temporal marker and a brief qualification about the man's appearance, this prose is disjunctive, a quality that is underscored by its one-sentence paragraphs. The narrator is a waitress and we are meant to assume that the paratactic structure of her sentences simulates working-class speech. This laconism also reveals, as the story goes on, that the *it* which the narrator wants to recount is not anything she can articulate or conceptualize: she can only narrate *around* it. In fact, the story she tells is disturbingly inconsequential. It turns on the somewhat grotesque good manners of an obese diner who cannot help but eat and the fantasy of weight and power he calls up in an all-too-thin and emotionally victimized waitress.[16]

Rita does not understand that elusive *it*:
"That's a funny story," Rita says, but I can see she doesn't know what to make of *it*.
I feel depressed. But I won't go into *it* with her . . .
She sits there waiting, her dainty fingers pulling her hair.
Waiting for what? I'd like to know.
It is August.
My life is going to change. I feel *it*.[17]

The narration has fallen apart into a series of apparently empty impersonal pronouns with no stable antecedent. The sentences get shorter and the distance between them gets broader: how does one move from flat declaration about the month to the conviction that life is going to change? What is Rita waiting for? For the punchline of the story, for the conceptualization which will render that "it" intelligible. The punchline does not come, of course; just a series of what appear to be non-sequiturs and a statement of faith based on an inarticulate emotion.

What are we to make of this story? At best, "Fat" is a tale in which hallucinations of power either obscure or misunderstand the objects that elicit them. The narrator cannot admit that she yearns for power, cannot understand her fascination with the fat man: "I know now I was after something. But I don't know what."[18] This quest without a definable object thus marks a warning against trying to provide too much context to that *it*. It might well be that the point of the tale rests on such incomprehensibility. The paratactic sentence structure is not a stylistic quirk but is rather integral to the construction of the story: the inability to subordinate, to organize material in anything other than chronological order, gets folded back into a larger inability to conceptualize and articulate. The crisis that the everyday grotesqueness of the fat man precipitates remains as enigmatic as it is inexpressible.

This conjunction of incomprehension and inexpressibility—which manifests itself in empty epiphanies brought on by an oddness in the everyday—runs through Carver's work. More often than not, however, these moments of crypto-illumination turn not on empowerment or dreams of positive change. Frequently they center on divorce, death, disappointment, and poverty, as in "Gazebo":

Then I go, "Holly, these things, we'll look back on them too. We'll go 'Remember the motel with the crud on the pool?' I go, you see what I'm saying Holly?
But Holly just sits there on the bed with her glass.
I can see she doesn't know.
I go over to the window . . . I stay there. I pray for a sign from Holly.
I pray for Holly to show me.
"Duane" Holly goes.
In this too, she was right."[19]

Again, the laconism of the sentences and their arrangement in single-sentence paragraphs isolate actions and perceptions, recast them as irreducible and pathos-ridden data whose pathos depends on the sheer vulnerability they expose. Duane is waiting for a sign, for an epiphany. What he gets is a moment in which the impoverishment to which they have fallen becomes brutally clear, a moment in which hope and direction have been so diminished that the narrator's name is in fact the only true thing that Holly can say.

If Carver's use of parataxis is a stylistic correlative of a thematics of incomprehensibility and loss, it is also shown to be a defense against that loss. Hence the beginning of "Why Don't You Dance?":

> In the kitchen, he poured himself another drink and looked at the bedroom suite in his yard . . . things looked much the way they had in the bedroom— nightstand and reading lamp on his side of the bed, nightstand and a reading lamp on her side.
> His side, her side.
> He considered this as he sipped the whiskey.[20]

At no point in this story does the narrator have the man acknowledge, nor does the narrator explain, the absence of the woman who only exists in the passage as a possessive pronoun. "Why Don't You Dance?" represents and enacts an elaborate ritual of denial and mute revenge in which the man sells off the offending bedroom furniture—a fetish of his former relationship— to a young couple who are aware of his pain but do not understand it. In this case, parataxis can be seen as the stylistic equivalent of the defense Freud calls "isolation," the process which allows "the insertion of a hiatus into the temporal sequence of thoughts or acts"[21] and deprives potentially threatening material of its affect.[22] In short: parataxis serves as both the register on the level of style of trauma and an attempt to metabolize it at the same time. In the world of Carver's characters, parataxis serves as the defense against an everyday world which has devolved into an enigma or has been deformed by the reaction to shock.

There is a strong family relation between Carver's blue-collar protagonists and figures in works by other writers such as Bobbie Ann Mason.[23] It would be tempting to write off the incomprehension of their characters in the face of a world grown alien as an element of residual class bias on the part of the readers who have made these writers successful, if not on the part of these writers themselves.[24] But incomprehension and denial are not limited to the working classes who people contemporary trade fiction. The unnamed, well-educated narrator of *Bright Lights, Big City* begins his novel with a sweeping disavowal: "You are not the type of guy who would be at a place like this at this time of the morning."[25] Several pages later he expands on this negative self-definition: "Your presence here is only a matter of conducting an experiment in limits, reminding yourself of what you aren't."[26] If he is not a downtown hedonist, just what *is* he? The narrator maintains that he dreams of a sober domesticity and indicates that his ex-wife is the cause of his downward spiral into coke addiction and sheer randomness. He seems to want to claim that she made him do it. But this regressive passivity has deeper roots. As it happens, his wife's desertion is not the primary trauma. She is nothing more than a stand-in for the real love of his life, his mother, whose death he so strongly represses that he does not realize that his most recent self-destructive binge neatly coincides with the anniversary of her passing.[27] As with Carver, McInerney's use of the present tense and his wittily disjunctive prose are meant to signal both a hidden trauma and the means by which that trauma is overcome. Like Brett Easton Ellis's *Less Than Zero*, McInerney's novel is structured—rather schematically, it must be admitted—around the terrors and denials attendant on individuation.

The foregrounding of shock and denial and the remarkable prevalence of paratactic constructions serve as distinguishing features of a number of highly successful young writers of this decade. The arguments I have made in this essay could be extended to the work of Ellis, Susan Minot, David Leavitt, and Tama Janowitz, to name just a few. We can begin to account for the popularity of this fiction by noting that the thematics and stylistics outlined above serve a strongly ideological function. The cool surfaces of contemporary paratactic prose—a coolness that is taken to a terrifying extreme in the work of Frederick Barthelme—mark a deliberate denial of sentimentality and affect. Parataxis makes it more difficult to map cause and effect in anything other than a chronological relation; it separates will from action and desire from will. It magnifies the importance of the interpretation which it does not, or cannot, provide. It renders enigmatic the world it appears to describe—this fiction is, after all, low mimetic. It can serve to obscure, if not destroy, a story's pathos, thus encouraging the readers to view the sorrows of others as an aesthetic or as an epistemological problem. Furthermore, the disjunctive humor and the fascination with the grotesque which mark this prose are not only the ciphers of suffering, they are ways of denying pain. The anaesthetization which this fiction describes and enacts acts to legitimize self-interest by making the situations of others either funny, horrifying, or incomprehensible.

At the same time, this fiction solicits the opposite response. It invites the reader to indulge in an identification which allows him or her a thrill of resentment. We have all been victimized just like the "hero." *Bright Lights, Big City* invites such a foreshortened projection by making the book about the person it addresses, about the "you" who is *both* the reader and the narrator.[28] The fiction discussed here thus presents its readers with a double pitfall that its ambiguous position in the literary marketplace seems to determine. It invites its audience to underidentify or overidentify, to treat it with the disinterestedness accorded to "literature" or with the blatant sensationalism that marks mass-market "trash." In either case, the suffering, the shock, which constitute the subject both in and of these texts get mishandled and misplaced.

But such a reduction of what has become a sizeable body of work to mere ideological obfuscation is dangerous, in that it can all-too-easily collapse into a victimization theory which lends a supernatural efficacy to the merely existent. While it is important to see how denial, distance, and self-indulgence are the markers of Yuppie culture, it is equally important to remember that these fictions are demonstrably *about* suffering and shock. So, while we should ask what ideological consolations these works provide, we might also want to ask why it is that readers who identify so defensively with a socially dominant class position would want to read about alcoholic, blue-collar divorcees, or the unemployed. Alternatively, why would they want to trace the odd brutalities of upper middle-class life in the works of a McInerney or a Leavitt?

There is a strong temptation to truncate the discussion here and reduce the fiction under discussion to a reflection of contemporary life, to claim that paratactic fiction reveals immediately some truth about the current dispensation. But that would be, in the terms of the Benjamin quotation that figures above this essay, to mistake philology for theology, text for the world. Far better, then, to reconstruct the philological background to this parataxis before seeking a mediation back to the realm that produces both Yuppies and the fictions marketed at them.

It is a commonplace that Carver's style seems to draw on Hemingway's example, an opinion repeated by Carver's most famous student, Jay McInerney.[29] Such a genealogy makes Carver the latest example of a rugged realism. But this superficial affiliation cannot account for the odd grotesques in Carver's fictions nor for the humor of his stylistic disjunctions. It is in fact more worthwhile to compare Carver with the most influential author of short fiction from the '60s—Donald Barthelme. I will argue that the disjunctions of trade paperback fiction are best read as a naturalization of the fiercely anti-mimetic work of writers like Barthelme.

Barthelme's early work eschews the conventions of low and high mimetic fiction. Here is the beginning of "The Indian Uprising" which was first published in book form in 1968:

We defended the city as best we could. The arrows of the Comanches came in clouds. The war clubs of the Comanches clattered on the soft, yellow pavements. There were earthworks along the Boulevard Mark Clark and the hedges had been laced with sparkling wire. People were trying to understand. I spoke to Sylvia. "Do you think this is the good life?" The table held apples, books, long-playing records. She looked up. "No."[30]

The unnamed city, with its yellow pavements (are these streets paved with gold?) is fabular and its referents are confusing. The story juxtaposes

two apparently heterogeneous literary codes—the Western and the tale of
domestic manners—in such a way as to liberate them both from the tram-
mels of referentiality and verisimilitude. The extreme parataxis of this
game frustrates the search for extra-literary meaning, a goal of unknowing
that Barthelme thematizes when he writes, "People were trying to understand."

If this prose is not an index of the world, then it cannot help but turn
back on itself, in a mode of formalism or aestheticism. It marks an attempt
to play with the very stuff of literature, with language and convention.
Barthelme was of course hardly the only writer of his generation to exploit
the purely literary aspects of his art: Barth, Hawkes, Sukenick, Coover, and
Abish are just a few of the others who have mined this vein. Barthelme is
particularly interesting for our purposes in that his work is insistently fragmented (see, for instance, "Eugenie Grandet"), paratactic, and resolutely
uncomfortable with politics. In "The Rise of Capitalism" (collected in 1972),
Barthelme plays clichés of the critique of capitalism ("A hierarchy of function-
aries interposes itself between the people and the leadership"[31]) against the
clichés of bourgeois domesticity ("Friends for dinner! The crudités are prepared, green and fresh. . . . The good paper napkins are laid out . . ."[32]).
Sentimentality—in this case, an overemphasis on the details of everyday
life—is juxtaposed with the frozen figures of social scientific language. The
two combine in the following personification: "Capitalism arose and took off
its pajamas. Another day, another dollar."[33] The wickedly surreal irony here
stems, of course, from the odd literalization of the cliché "the rise of capitalism" as if capitalism marked not a relation but a thing. If capitalism creates
a bourgeois sentimentality of the quotidian, it also produces a sentimentalism
of critique: each is guilty, it would seem, of reifying language. Each claims
that its clichés are in fact referential. Barthelme's aesthetic anarchism, then,
is based on the defamiliarization techniques which we recognize not only
from the Russian Formalists but also from the works of early Modernism. In
Barthelme's practice, the crossing of literary codes is not meant to reveal the
world, but to promote the autonomy of literature on the one hand, and to
reanimate dead language on the other.

If this all-too-cursory description of Barthelme's work though the
early '70s is accurate, then we can historicize this work in the terms
Peter Bürger sets out in his *Theory of the Avantgarde*. For Bürger, the
development of aestheticism in late nineteenth century Europe allowed
the latent possibilities of art to become fully open to cognition. The
growth of an autonomous sphere for the aesthetic opened the door to the
full conceptualization of art and therefore to its sublation by the avantgarde.
The avantgarde used techniques of shock in order to radicalize the defamiliarization which they took as the very idea of the artwork and to make it a
category of general validity.[34] In short, the avantgarde sought through the

use of enigma to induce the audience to break down the boundaries that separated art from life. Using liberal doses of shock therapy, the Dadaists and Surrealists hoped to return art's expressive utopianism to the impoverished realm of the everyday.

The limits of Bürger's relevance for our discussion should be as obvious as they are instructive. Although Barthelme owes a great debt to surrealist fabulation, he does not seem to want us to change our lives. According to Bürger, the shock techniques of the avantgarde were meant—in their utopian formulation—to tear through aesthetic immanence and destroy the borders that separate art and life. But Barthelme, whose work was shocking enough to be considered avantgarde even into the '80s, seems to want to secure these borders, not to tear them down.[35]

If Bürger's book is a strong reflection on the period in which it was written—it was first published in Germany in 1974—we can explain its inability to account for Barthelme by claiming it is also a strong discussion of the dilemma of *European* art. But Bürger is just not accurate about America, where aestheticism did not really take in the late nineteenth century. In fact, one of the burdens of American avantgardes since the death of the WPA has been to liberate art as far as possible from its dependence on other spheres of activity.[36] The relative triumph of Abstract Expressionism after the War marks the first general victory for autonomous art in the States. Serge Guilbaut's provocative but ultimately muddled account of this victory suffers from its narrow focus and generally unmediated account of the reception of this art. Nevertheless, he is most likely accurate in his intuition that the development of the Cold War made autonomous art acceptable to the art audience, museums, and the general public.[37] The liberty of the artist testified to the liberty of the society he lived in. There are numerous articulations of this idea. One could appeal to Schlesinger's famous defense of alienation in a free society in *The Vital Center*, but it might be just as informative to quote Meyer Schapiro, whose Marxist roots are impeccable and who should be therefore somewhat more ambivalent about preaching a full-blown aestheticism. Nevertheless, here he is in 1950:

> Artists today who would welcome the chance to paint works of broad human content for a larger audience . . . find no sustained opportunities for such an art; they have no alternative but to cultivate in their art *the only or surest realms of freedom—the interior world of their fancies, sensations and feelings, and the medium itself.*[38]

Freedom has come to rest in a psychological hermeticism or formalism: it has turned inward towards art itself. In the free world, free art is either a sign of or a refuge from the liberties that America could stand for.

The notion that the aesthetic could be both a realm of autonomy and authenticity (both are implied in Schapiro's description) was hardly limited to the visual arts: it was apparent in the conceptualizations of bebop and cool jazz as well as in literature. Richard and Carol Ohmann have written convincingly about the reception of *Catcher in the Rye* and the way critics both acknowledged and contained the novel's subversive content.[39] One could go a step further and say that a certain, sanitized subversion was expected from the novel, that the novel *as a form* could be taken as a position of resistance against what Holden would call the "phoniness" of the suburban and corporate worlds. Such a polemical aestheticism underwrote both the position of the tweedy academic defenders of art like Trilling, and the more outlandish, because hairier, exponents of expressive individualism like the Beats. According to one historian of the period, both sides shared an antipathy towards suburbia and conformity, and a faith in "the importance of dissent, the need for independent thinking, the value of personal resistance."[40] Such a stance undergirds Richard Yates' *Revolutionary Road*, a bitter and now remarkably dated book from 1961. In it, a suburban couple dreams of breaking out from the strifling conformity of commuter life into an existence of aesthetic expressiveness. Of course, as a mad and therefore truly authentic character predicts, they fail. Yates' novel is low mimetic and in no way bodies forth the dissonant autonomy or the rigorous introspection imagined by a Schapiro or an Adorno. In fact its thematization of an ideology of aestheticism cannot, or will not, actually allow that ideology to determine the structure of the book. A thorough-going aestheticism had to wait for Barthelme, Barth and company, who of course undermined the notion of authenticity on which the ideology was based. This aestheticism had to wait for that fiction which critics from the late '50s until the mid-'80s have called postmodern.

If I am accurate in my sense that avantgardist and formalist works provide the background for the odd defamiliarizations of contemporary trade paperback fiction, that fiction turns out to be exactly what Dwight Macdonald called "midcult": it is characterized by the apparent domestication of the avantgarde for middlebrow consumption. Such a view, however, misses the important innovation in this work. The shock—the enigmatic refusal of easy conceptualization—that featured as an important structural aspect of American autonomous art is no longer seen as a way of dividing art from life. Rather, shock and enigma are seen as being flatly mimetic of contemporary experience. It is of course a commonplace in discussions of postmodernity to argue that what differentiates this period is, in fact, the aestheticization of life. Thus, my description can be taken as an extension of the work of commentators like Jameson, Baudrillard, and Debord. But there is a difference here that is paramount. In the work of Carver, McInerney, Ellis, and Mason, life is not only remade in the image of rock videos, but is seen to be as incomprehensible as "high" art. Shock is no longer reserved for art: it constitutes the experience of the quotidian.

III.

How can we conceptualize what is troped as beyond conceptualization; how can we explain this migration of shock from the aesthetic to everyday experience? To put it another way: how is it that Yuppie culture will want simultaneously to disseminate and deny the trauma these tales describe? Is it merely bad faith on their readers' parts, an ideological rationalization for a post-political self-indulgence?[41]

To account for this remarkable preponderance of crisis narratives let us look at one of Habermas's more recent metanarratives of this crisis, a lecture entitled "The Crisis of the Welfare State and the Exhaustion of Utopian Energies." Habermas here analyzes the condition he calls "die neue Unübersichtlichkeit," which is translated as "the new obscurity" but might better, although more clumsily, be called "the new unsurvey-ability." According to Habermas, the welfare state compromise marked an attempt to realize in society the aspirations of nineteenth-century emancipatory movements: its utopian seed lay in the dream of liberating the worker from the heteronomy of wage labor.[42] Underlying the welfare state, then, is the desire to live in a world in which work is afforded dignity, in which the worker can live in spontaneous freedom and benefit from social justice; a world in which capitalism is humanized by democracy.[43] In short, the welfare state was guided by the twin beacons of post-Enlightenment utopian thought, by an autonomy and a solidarity based on labor.

This conception of the welfare state and the utopian energies that guided it date in America (though not without recurrent struggle) from the 1930s and in Germany from the 1940s. The consensus began to suffer in the late '60s. Habermas locates two reasons for this crisis. First of all, while the welfare state was designed to protect and legitimize capitalism, it was not supposed to interfere with the mechanisms of investment: it is therefore vulnerable to the pressures of a world economy and unable to play a substantial role in the domestic one. The state, given a mandate it cannot fulfill, is blamed for failures of a capitalism it cannot quite protect. What is more, bureaucratic protection against risk tends to undermine the very autonomy it is supposed to protect by colonizing aspects of the everyday, such as schools, family, and daycare.[44]

The withdrawal of support for the welfare state that results from the bureaucratization of the everyday and the swings and dips of capitalism is aided by a revision of the utopian horizons—the dreams of future fulfillment and collective orientation—that guided that state. As Claus Offe has argued, in an age marked by the growth of service labor and deskilling, work no longer serves as the key category for sociological self-definition and therefore for solidarity: religion and region are as important for the expression of needs as class and calling.[45] The ideal of autonomous labor—of labor itself—can no longer serve as a utopian orientation for the state.[46]

Though Habermas's lecture is remarkably free of the social-scientific language that usually marks his prose, the main characters of his story—"system" (the economic and state institutions of material reproduction) and "lifeworld" (the autonomous realm of symbolic reproduction)—should be familiar to anyone who has followed his work since *Legitimation Crisis*. These categories are not without their problems and have been subjected to great scrutiny and criticism, most notably by Nancy Fraser.[47] Fraser's elegant deconstruction of Habermas's dyad reveals how ideological and how limited the opposition really is, how bound it is to prevailing modes of patriarchal oppression. Nevertheless, Fraser shows that one of the strengths of Habermas's schema is that it charts the deep interrelations and interdependencies between system and lifeworld. Hence the model is descriptively (though perhaps not normatively) useful in that it allows us to see how state management of economic crises causes crisis tendencies to appear in non-economic forms, how steering difficulties manifest themselves as deformations of everyday life. One can best describe this process in psychoanalytic terms: crises of economic reproduction are repressed, displaced, and return in odd guises. They become visible as crises of symbolic reproduction.[48] Thus we can say that the realignment of the American economy since the end of the Vietnam War—the move from economies of scale to economies of scope[49] and the erosion of American financial and productive hegemony by the globalization of the world economy—has exerted enormous pressures on the reproduction both of economic institutions and the organizations of everyday life. Most tellingly, it has deformed the structures of representation through which we depict our lives to ourselves by undermining the very institutions of solidarity through which individual and collective identities are interpellated and asserted. As the constellations on which the welfare compromise was based disintegrate, so the horizon of hope—that is, the collective and universalizable orientation toward an improved future we call utopia—has been undercut, if not destroyed. The *character* of the Yuppie has been so important for this decade because it embodies both the decade's predicament and its denial of that predicament. The Yuppie as a type manifests the fear of the defeat of the expectations on which the welfare state has rested. It also bears witness to contemporary means for metabolizing that predicament through an overwhelming, because compensatory, materialism. The fiction that has crystalized around the type of the Yuppie registers this new structure of feeling.[50] The use of parataxis in this prose signals both the loss of complexes of meaning as well as ways of dealing with that loss.

We therefore cannot blame it all on Ronald Reagan. In fact, Reagan's victory in 1980 was an effect of the decline of the utopian energies that animated the welfare state and not its cause. Ironically, the motifs of Reagan's first years—with their return to a strident anticommunism, their attempt to re-sanctify the embattled family and its "values," and their evocations of a no longer existent small-town life—marked an attempt to revive a number of the utopian underpinnings of the post-War liberal consensus. In fact, Reagan's victory in 1980 reflects an attack not on the welfare state as such, but rather on the specific configurations it took in the late '60s and early '70s—that is, in the years before the American economy seemed to cave in. As Stanley Kelley, Jr. has argued, Reagan's victories were not based on the lack of viability of New Deal issues but on lack of confidence in the Democrats' ability to work the economy.[51] Americans voted against OPEC, Jimmy Carter, and Welfare Queens, not against Social Security or Medicare. Accordingly, we can see that one of the truly brilliant aspects of Reagan's first campaign was its capacity to lend the pathos of revolution to established ideological positions. Reagan tried to reorient us toward the future by turning us toward the past.

It should not come as a surprise, then, that the '80s were years of odd and ironic nostalgia. Nostalgia marks a longing for a set of certainties—or rather pseudo-certainties—that have been lost. Irony marks the fact that they *have* been lost, that they no longer make any sense. From appropriation art to reruns of "Leave It to Beaver," baby boomers keep returning to the scene of their past, both in a mood of regression and of painful individuation. Andreas Huyssen has argued that postmodernist art is remarkable for the "search for cultural tradition and continuity, which underlies all the radical rhetoric of rupture, discontinuity, and epistemological breaks."[52] One could argue, with all the usual caveats about false immediacy, that the same is true for Yuppie culture at large: the experience of those ruptures and breaks has made ambiguous fetishes of the artifacts of the past.

This regressive and mystified fascination with the inoperative ideological products of the '50s and the '60s marks, by definition, a doomed endeavor: the dream of a return that is by now impossible. And it has been met by a counter-tendency, which is directed toward the future. Reagan's crypto-crusade against liberalism coincided with a resurgence of "anti-liberal" communitarian thought. The communitarian attack was not geared against the welfare state that Reagan both assailed and supported, but against the tradition of *classical* liberalism. Alan Ryan has made a convincing case that communitarianism is not, *per se*, inimical to liberalism, but rather tends to be anti-contractarian which is another thing entirely.[53] Nevertheless, people have found the muddled affiliation between communitarianism and the critique of liberalism quite attractive. Communitarian thought has flourished in a number of fields: one need only think of MacIntyre's *After Virtue*, Sandel's *Liberalism and the Limits of Justice*, and Bellah's *Habits of the Heart*. (The last of these was, interestingly enough, a bestseller as well.) Furthermore, the draw of the term community is strong outside the academy as well—Scott Peck's second book bears the term community proudly in its subtitle and *Tikkun* magazine was started to promote progressive Jewish *communitarian* thought. It should be obvious that the ideal of community—abstract as it may sometimes be—has a strong semantic charge. It marks a frequently progressive attempt to recover the utopian horizons that have been lost in the last twenty years.

I can summarize my argument in the following way. The depletion of the older utopian horizons and the unsurveyability of the future have led to three reactions: stunned incomprehension and shock coupled with denial; regressive fetishization of the past; and attempts to conceptualize new images of fulfillment.

If trade paperback fiction of the sort I have discussed in this essay has manifested a reaction to the structural changes of the last two decades, it should come as no surprise that it has also served up a number of ciphers of fulfillment and solidarity. At the end of Carver's "A Small, Good Thing" (from *Cathedral*) the parents of a young boy who is killed on his birthday drive down in the middle of the night to their local mall. They want to confront a baker who has been harassing them by phone because they never picked up the boy's birthday cake. The baker apologizes, feeds them, and begins to talk:

> They listened carefully. Although they were tired and in anguish, they listened to what the baker had to say. They nodded when the baker began to speak of loneliness, and of the sense of doubt and limitation that had come to him in his middle years. He told them what it was like to be childless all these years. To repeat the days with the ovens endlessly full and endlessly empty . . .
> They listened to him. They ate what they could. They swallowed the dark bread. It was like daylight under the florescent trays of light. They talked on into the early morning, the high pale cast of light in the windows, and they did not think of leaving.[54]

Even as the sentences begin to loosen up and get longer, the three people engage in what can only be called a secular communion over bread and coffee. The most remarkable thing here is the level of inter-subjective communication Carver envisions compared with the tenacious lack of communication in his earlier stories. It is also interesting to note that the baker's expressions of pain and need are answered by the couple: they move from listening to speaking. They engage in a conversation about need—in an act of solidarity—that is so compelling or so satisfying that they do not leave.

Such ciphers of utopia are not uncommon in paratactic trade paperback fiction—one thinks of the unnamed narrator of *Bright Lights, Big City* genuflecting on the pavement, eating freshly baked bread, and having the epiphany that he must change his life, or of the children at the end of Susan Minot's *Monkeys*, marching up the gangplank together after dispersing their mother's ashes.

Nevertheless, these moments are only ciphers, promissory notes for a deferred future, images whose content has yet to be inscribed. For they are either proleptic (as in McInerney's case) or mute (as in *Monkeys*), or reduced to chance moments between atomized individuals (as in "A Small, Good Thing"). To a certain extent, this gingerly attempt to figure utopia is ideological in that it supports the existent by remaining within it. These figures of solidarity arise from and are caught within the very horizons whose depletion they protest against. But, just as new social and economic configurations have created new needs, so they have only just begun to generate anticipatory intimations of new forms of solidarity and fulfillment. Trade paperback fiction, with its alienation of the everyday and its paratactic structures, is both part of the problem—it reduces suffering to entertainment—and, only tentatively, part of the solution—it articulates suffering, and creates a new (and albeit, limited) mode of publicity and circulation for the expression of needs.[55] The success of trade paperback lines, like the ambivalent and tenuous hegemony of Yuppie culture that brought them to the forefront, is itself as interesting as it is ambiguous. It bears witness to the shock of the new it can neither conceive nor deny. The suffering and the trauma which these fictions disavow and yet display apply pressure to a present they support and beyond which they aspire.[56]

Notes

1. Here is Habermas: "The crisis cannot be separated from the viewpoint of the one who is undergoing it—the patient experiences his powerlessness *vis-à-vis* the objectivity of the illness only because he is a subject condemned to passivity and temporarily deprived of the possibility of being a subject in full possession of his powers." [Jürgen Habermas, *Legitimation Crisis* (Boston: Beacon, 1975) 1.] Crisis, then, is the perception of the loss of autonomy: its resolution, according to Habermas, "effects a liberation of the subject caught up in it." I will argue in this article that in the last ten or fifteen years Americans have been caught in a crisis—viscerally experienced but indirectly articulated—of expectations: global economic shifts have resulted in the decline, not the rise, of personal wealth. This decline comes into direct conflict with the ideological faith in economic progress on which the Cold War welfare-state consensus was based.

2. "The Year of the Yuppie," 31 December 1984, 16–29.

3. "The Year of the Yuppie," 16–17, 28–29.

4. Katherine E. Newman, *Falling from Grace* (New York: Pantheon, 1989), 21.

5. Newman, 40.

6. Newman, 34.

7. It is important to discriminate between trade and mass-market paperbacks. Trade paperbacks are distributed by book wholesalers and sold in bookstores. Trades have an advantage over mass-market paperbacks—the rack-sized books distributed by magazine wholesalers and found in drugstores and airport terminals—in that fewer copies need to be sold. On average, a publisher has to sell 50,000 units of a mass-market paperback before turning a profit; a trade paperback might break even at 7500 copies. What is more, trade paperbacks have a longer shelf-life than their mass-market counterparts.

8. John Dessauer, "Trade Paperbacks: No Panacea," *Publisher's Weekly*, 225:2 1984), 39–41.

9. "Vintage Series Showcases 'Best of A New Generation,' " *Publisher's Weekly*, 226:10 (1984), 48; Joann Davis, "A Talk With Editor Gary Fisketjon," *Publisher's Weekly*, 226:8

(1984), 69; E. Graydon Carter, "Leading the Gliterary Life," *Esquire* December 1986, 161–62.

10. Leonard Shatzkin, *In Cold Type* (Boston: Houghton Mifflin, 1982), 3.

11. Carter, 165.

12. Chandler B. Grannis, "Title Output and Average Prices: 1984 Final Figures," *Publisher's Weekly* 228:8 (1985), 44.

13. The notion that one is getting in on the ground floor, that there is a kind of entrepreneurship in cultural capital is evident from the blurb on the back cover of the anthology *20 Under 30*, edited by Debra Spark and published by Scribner's in 1986: "When literary prizes are awarded in the future, many of the recipients will be authors first noticed in 20 UNDER 30." It is interesting that the copywriter here sees success in terms of prizes: the value of the book will be that others will recognize these authors later. You will be able to say you knew them when, etc.

14. Production of trade fiction increases every year. In 1987, new titles numbered 295; in 1988, they totaled 345, whereas hardcover fiction titles dropped both years. In the same period, there was a 19% decline in mass-market fiction title production. See Chandler B. Grannis, "Titles and Prices, 1988; Final Figures," *Publisher's Weekly* 240:8 (1989), 224–25.

15. Raymond Carver, *Where I'm Calling From* (New York: Vintage, 1989), 64; emphasis mine.

16. "But here's the *thing*. When he [her lover/husband] gets on me, I suddenly feel I am terrifically fat, so fat that Rudy [her lover/husband] is a tiny *thing* and hardly there at all" (69; emphasis mine).

The "thing"—the point of the story, perhaps—lies in that odd hallucination of weight and the reduction of Rudy into a meaningless thing. This fantasy reduces others to "things." In fact, one could say that the "thing," the "it" of the story, is just the "thingness," the reification of other people: it describes a zero-sum game in which the empowerment of some depends on the dehumanization of others.

17. Carver, 69; first, second and fourth emphases mine.

18. Carver, 67.

19. Carver, 146.

20. Carver, 155.

21. J. Laplanche and J. B. Pontalis, *The Language of Psychoanalysis* (New York: Norton, 1973), 232.

22. Here is Freud: ". . . the experience is not forgotten, but instead is deprived of its affect, and its associative connections are suppressed or interrupted so that it remains as though isolated and is not reproduced in the ordinary process of thought." Sigmund Freud, *Inhibitions, Symptoms, and Anxiety* (New York: Norton, 1959), 46.

23. Such uses of parataxis are hardly limited to Carver. At the end of the title story of Bobbie Ann Mason's critically and financially successful collection, *Shiloh*, Leroy and Norma Jean make an ambivalent pilgrimage to the Civil War battlefield. At the site of this Confederate defeat, Norma Jean tells her husband that she wants a divorce, although she cannot tell him why. Leroy's estrangement from his setting is total. When he tries to account for his life, he concentrates on discrete details that do not make a coherent narrative. He strings details together in an almost Biblical parataxis of genealogical succession, but unlike the Bible he leaves whole generations out. Unlike the Bible, he cannot find what Auerbach calls the "vertical connection" that binds the apparently discontinuous moments of this world to the masterplot of salvation history. He cannot construct a story that will bring the insides of history to bear on the outsides—a problem underscored by the fact that the story is narrated in the present tense, as if immediacy were a bar to comprehension. See Bobbie Ann Mason, *Shiloh and Other Stories* (London: Chatto & Windus, 1983) 15–16. For the "vertical connection," see Erich Auerbach, *Mimesis* (Princeton: Princeton University Press, 1953), 17.

24. Alternatively, one could argue, following Marcuse, that identification with these

characters marks an understanding that in the present economic dispensation the exigencies of the market affect all members of society, even the professional. See Herbert Marcuse, *Counterrevolution and Revolt* (Boston: Beacon Books, 1972), 9–16.

25. Jay McInerney, *Bright Lights, Big City* (New York: Vintage, 1984), 1.

26. McInerney, 4.

27. McInerney, 157, 161.

28. The two greatest financial successes of white trade paperback fiction, Jay McInerney and Brett Easton Ellis, provide their readers with complicated forms of identification. Perfect exemplars of an age which was supposed to say no and yet still remain hedonistic, *Bright Lights, Big City* and *Less Than Zero* actively disavow the excitements of drugs and sex they promote. Furthermore, as I have indicated above, both seem to blame the absence of parents—of authority—for the present mess their protagonists are in. This curious resentment might in fact be a mediated acknowledgment of a twin set of problems: the decline in the standard of living which faces this generation and the depletion of utopian horizons, which I will discuss later in this essay.

29. Jay McInerney, "Raymond Carver: A Still, Small Voice," *New York Times Book Review*, 6 August 1989, 24.

30. Donald Barthelme, *Sixty Stories* (New York: G. P. Putnam's Sons, 1981), 108.

31. Barthelme, 205.

32. Barthelme, 207.

33. Barthelme, 207.

34. Peter Bürger, *The Theory of the Avantgarde* (Minneapolis: University of Minnesota Press, 1985), 18.

35. One need only read the attack by Charles Newman to see that there was still a charge to his work into this decade. See *The Postmodern Aura* (Evanston: Northwestern University Press, 1985), 76–80.

36. The fate of the first generation of American aestheticists was to relocate for a greater or lesser period on more favorable turf—that is, in Europe. One thinks here of James, Whistler, and Sargent. It could be argued that a second generation of aesthetes—Eliot and Pound—also moved to Europe. For the absence of an American aestheticism and therefore an avantgarde, see Andreas Huyssen, *After The Great Divide* (Bloomington: University of Indiana Press, 1986), 167–68. One can square this interpretation with Jackson Lears's discussion of fin-de-siecle aestheticism by noting that 1) the late nineteenth-century variety was anti-progressive; 2) it was also instrumental, that is, *therapeutic* or *religious*. It is also worth noting that Lears does not mention the Armory Show. See T. J. Jackson Lears, *No Place of Grace* (New York: Pantheon, 1981), 77–78, 190–92.

37. See *How New York Stole the Idea of Modern Art* (Chicago: University of Chicago Press, 1983), 198–99. See also Paul Carter, *Another Part of the Fifties* (New York: Columbia University Press, 1983), 156–57 and T. J. Jackson Lears, "A Matter of Taste: Corporate Cultural Hegemony in a Mass-Consumption Society," *Recasting America*, ed. Lary May (Chicago: University of Chicago Press, 1989), 38–53.

38. *Modern Art* (New York: Braziller, 1979), 176.

39. "Reviewers, Critics, and *The Catcher in the Rye*," *Critical Inquiry* 3:1 (1976), 33–7.

40. Richard H. Pells, *The Liberal Mind in a Conservative Age* (New York: Harper and Row, 1985), 380.

41. See Todd Gitlin, "Postmodernism: Roots and Politics," *Dissent* (Winter 1989): 100–8, esp. 105.

42. *Die Neue Unübersichtlichkeit* (Frankfurt: Suhrkamp 1985), 147.

43. Habermas, 148.

44. Habermas, 150–52.

45. *Disorganized Capitalism* (Cambridge: MIT Press, 1985), 129–50 and Habermas, 159–60.

46. Habermas, 161.

47. See Nancy Fraser, "What's Critical About Critical Theory," *Unruly Practices* (Minneapolis: University of Minnesota Press, 1989), 113–43; for a summary of other criticism of the system-lifeworld dichotomy, see David Ingram, *Habermas and the Dialectic of Reason* (New Haven: Yale University Press, 1987), 168–71.

48. Jürgen Habermas, *The Theory of Communicative Action* (Boston: Beacon Books, 1984–87), 2 vols., vol II, 141–43, 385–89.

49. *The Condition of Postmodernity* (New York: Blackwell, 1989), 179–80.

50. For a fascinating and very different discussion of similar phenomena see Fred Pfeil, "Postmodernism as a 'Structure of Feeling,' " *Marxism and the Interpretation of Culture*, ed. Cary Nelson and Lawrence Grossberg (Urbana: University of Illinois Press, 1988), 381–404.

51. "Democracy and the New Deal Party System," *Democracy and the Welfare State*, ed. Amy Guttmann (Princeton: Princeton University Press, 1988), 191, 198–201.

52. Huyssen, 169.

53. "Communitarianism: The Good, the Bad and the Muddly," *Dissent* (Summer 1989), 350, 352–54.

54. Carver, 405.

55. Here I am drawing on Albrecht Wellmer's suggestion against Adorno, that the work of art is the medium, not the model, for utopia. Wellmer's argument seems to fulfill the pragmatic promise of Habermas's approach, but does not retain the deep pathos of Adorno's vision. If one wanted to redeem Adorno's more stringent utopianism of art, one would have to historicize the strong theory of mimesis one finds in his work and in Benjamin's. I should also note that this essay was written before the publication of Richard Wolin's "Utopia, Mimesis, and Reconciliation: A Redemptive Critique of Adorno's *Aesthetic Theory*," *Representations* 32 (Fall 1990): 33–49. See Albrecht Wellmer, "Reason, Utopia, and Enlightenment," *Habermas and Modernity*, ed. Richard J. Bernstein (Cambridge: MIT Press, 1985), 65–66 and Seyla Benhabib, *Critique, Norm, and Utopia* (New York: Columbia University Press, 1986), 329–53. See also Stephen K. White, *The Recent Work of Jürgen Habermas* (New York: Cambridge University Press, 1989), 144–54.

56. This article is dedicated to the memory of my aunt, Sandra Schoenberg Kling, a sociologist, who first introduced me to critical theory. I would like to thank Deborah Kaplan, Tom Moylan, Jonathan Freedman, and Kirsten Gruesz for their help.

Where Are the Missing Contents?
(Post)Modernism, Gender, and the Canon

Ellen G. Friedman

In the postmodern condition, Jean-François Lyotard writes about "missing contents" and the "unpresentable" in the literature of modernity.[1] What are missing and unpresentable, and what this literature expresses nostalgia for, according to Lyotard, are the master narratives that sustained Western civilization in the past and that have now been delegitimated. By calling into question the Western paternal narratives of philosophy, religion, and history, as well as the great quest and goal narratives, modernity has provoked a "crisis in narrative" resulting in a literature that can present the sense of loss but not what is lost (78–81). Fredric Jameson, in his introduction to the English translation of Lyotard's book, observes that these master narratives have not disappeared. Rather, they have gone underground, protected in the culture's unconscious, a site from which they still wield power (xii).

Indeed, the yearning for fathers, for past authority and sure knowledge that can no longer be supported, permeates male texts of modernity. A clear example of this condition is Donald Barthelme's novel *The Dead Father*. The plot follows a brother and sister's journey to bury their reluctantly dead father. The size of a Titan, this father is introduced as "[d]ead, but still with us, still with us, but dead" (3). On the way to the burial site, the daughter asks, "Tell me . . . did you ever want to paint or draw or etch?" The dead father answers, "It was not necessary . . . because I am the Father. All lines my lines. All figure and all ground mine, out of my head. All colors mine. You take my meaning" (18, 19). The narrative ends with the dead father speaking "resonantly" and "grandly" from his hole in the ground even as the bulldozers approach. Although he is buried, he is not silenced.

The missing father as irresistible presence is even more striking in Thomas Pynchon's new work, *Vineland*, since it begins as a daughter's quest for her mother. The mother, Frenesi, who was a sixties radical, abandons her infant daughter, Prarie, as well as her husband, Zoyd, the man Prarie presumes is her father. Frenesi leaves her husband and child to run away

Reprinted by permission of the Modern Language Association of America from *PMLA* 108 (March 1993): 240–52.

with Brock Vond, a powerful member of the FBI. As Prarie searches for her mother, evidence mounts that Brock is also looking for Frenesi. In fact, as Brock's presence in the narrative increases, the importance of the quest for the mother diminishes. Indeed, the final meeting between mother and daughter is anticlimactic. The narrative focus, by this time, has moved to Brock. Although he is an elusive, rarely glimpsed figure, he is also an inescapable, controlling presence, with an insidious power and a talent for locating his victims' vulnerabilities. His colleagues call him "Death from Slightly Above." For Pynchon, Brock is an avatar of the paranoic systems that drive American culture, but he is more than that. Ten pages from the end of the book, he appears to Prarie and tells her, "I'm your father. . . . Your real Dad" (375, 376).

With these words, Brock presents himself, in Lyotard's terms, as the missing contents. Hearing these words, Prarie finds her world destabilized. Zoyd, the man who claimed her as his daughter and raised her, may not be her father. As a result, her focus shifts, significantly, from a quest for her mother to a quest for her father. When the FBI suddenly relieves Brock of his funds and other resources, he loses his source of power but not the force he represents, which persists in Prarie's yearning for him. Pynchon emphasizes the nature of this father figure by replacing Zoyd—a local joke who argues the state into supporting him by an annual leap through a plate glass window—with the imperious and relentless Brock. Thus *Vineland* follows Lyotard's paradigm of modernity, in which master narratives are yearned for but cannot be raised. As soon as Brock tells Prarie that he is her father, a statement that may or may not be true, he disappears from her life, leaving her at the end of the novel—as the texts of modernity are left— in a condition of loss. In this state, she focuses on her past, frozen in the oedipal backward glance. As Pynchon turns away from the quest for the mother, he suggests that the longing for the lost father is inevitable, because the father's order is the only one that Pynchon can imagine.

The emphatic reign of Oedipus in current explanatory cultural narratives is honored even in philosophical works that propose alternatives. In *Anti-Oedipus: Capitalism and Schizophrenia*, a work provocatively resisting oedipal determinism, Gilles Deleuze and Félix Guattari sum up a position taken by cultural and orthodox psychoanalysts: "They all agree that, in our patriarchal and capitalist society at least, Oedipus is a sure thing. . . . They all agree that our society is the stronghold of Oedipus. . . ." Moreover, as Deleuze and Guattari concede, Oedipus is not an invention of these analysts; rather, he "is demanded, and demanded again and again . . ." (174–75). The oedipal preoccupation with fathers—missing, lost, or otherwise inaccessible—is a compulsive theme in male modernism. It is the great theme of William Faulkner's *Absalom, Absalom!* and *Light in August*. The missing father is the link to the past that, for the protagonists, determines identity. That sons are refused their fathers renders these narratives tragedies.

A variation on the search for the father is the profoundly nostalgic conviction that the past has explanatory or redemptive powers. This belief is expressed as the futile desire to stop time or to understand, recoup, or re-create the past, summoning it into the present. Such a desire, of course, informs Gatsby's obsession with Daisy and illuminates the narrative voice in T. S. Eliot's *Four Quartets*. The object of the longing in the poem's final lines is clear: "And the end of all our exploring / Will be to arrive where we started and know the place for the first time" (208). This futile desire underlies Ernest Hemingway's portrait of Jake's impotence in *The Sun Also Rises*. For Jake, who has lost the tie between past and present in the conflagration of the war, meaning evaporates or degenerates into the sentimentalism of Cohn or the ersatz religions of bullfighting and fishing. In the rituals that mark these sports, Jake attempts to locate meaning, but the inadequacy of such attempts to replace the missing contents is emphatically represented in Jake's impotence. He never acquires the father's power; he remains forever the yearning son. Similarly, the center of Ezra Pound's directive to "make it new" is *it*, signifying past texts, past ideologies, the determining word of the father that controls all narratives. James Joyce's final work is about the "wake" of Finnegan—the mythic, protean father who never stays quite dead but reasserts himself repeatedly in multitudinous reincarnations.

Women's works of modernity, however, show little nostalgia for the old paternal order, little regret for the no longer presentable. The master narratives are not buried in the unconscious of these texts, nor do they create a vacuum that longs to be filled. Although all the texts of modernity express a yearning for the unpresentable, female texts often evoke this unpresentable as the not yet presented. As Lillian Robinson wisely observes, patriarchal myths and traditions are "essentially external to any central female project" (29). Thus the lack of nostalgia for them in women's narratives seems natural. In fact, reading the texts of modernity through the lens of gender reveals how gender inflects the missing contents and how this inflected unpresentable relates to the canon. This essay offers such a reading in the hope of advancing discussions of sexual difference in the modernism-postmodernism debate, a project proposed by Craig Owens (61, 77). In an essay on feminism and postmodernism, E. Ann Kaplan similarly suggests that "we must continue to articulate oppositional discourses" (43). For her, as well as for Owens, such discourse is a precondition to imagining what lies beyond opposition.[2]

Two revisions of *Don Quixote*, neither by Cervantes, highlight these issues of sexual difference and opposition. "Pierre Menard, Author of *Don Quixote*," a story by Jorge Luis Borges, relates the attempt of the early-twentieth-century writer Pierre Menard to re-create, word for word, the text of Cervantes's *Don Quixote*. Menard, the narrator reports, "did not want to compose another *Don Quixote*—which would be easy—but *the Don Quixote*." He plans to achieve this goal without forgetting European history between Cervantes's time, 1602, and his own, 1918. The problem is to re-create the exact text within a twentieth-century perspective, not to translate the text into contemporary terms: "Any insinuation that Menard dedicated his life to the writing of a contemporary *Don Quixote* is a calumny of his illustrious memory." Borges describes Menard's project in this way: "To be, in some way, Cervantes and to arrive at *Don Quixote* seemed to him less arduous—and consequently less interesting—than to continue being Pierre Menard and to arrive at *Don Quixote* through the experiences of Pierre Menard" (48, 49).

This plot is an exemplar of the missing contents Lyotard identifies in the narratives of modernity. Menard attempts to write a text, already in existence, in which the original assumptions, historical context, and quest are no longer alive. In fact, the allusion to Cervantes's *Don Quixote* constitutes a second level of missing contents, since that story centers on the pursuit of knights, armor, chivalry, and the worldview they represent—missing contents that are still presentable in Cervantes's time, at least as objects of satire and as vehicles of moral instruction. Indeed, Borges's story almost perfectly illustrates Lyotard's theories on the condition of modernity. Menard, explaining his project, remarks: "To compose *Don Quixote* at the beginning of the seventeenth century was a reasonable, necessary and perhaps inevitable undertaking; at the beginning of the twentieth century it is almost impossible. It is not in vain that three hundred years have passed. . . ." Thus, as Menard confesses, missing contents are unpresentable, and yet the longing for them informs his project. Perhaps no statement more poignantly expresses the futility of this longing than the narrator's flat description of Menard's efforts: "He dedicated his conscience and nightly studies to the repetition of a pre-existing book in a foreign tongue" (51, 54).

As it turns out, Menard does succeed in re-creating several pieces of Cervantes's text: "the ninth and thirty-eighth chapters of Part One of *Don Quixote* and a fragment of the twenty-second chapter" (48).[3] Yet he also does *not* succeed, because the two apparently identical texts differ in style, theme, textual ambiguity, and other elements determined by and within the works' separate historical contexts. For instance, when Cervantes wrote the words "truth, whose mother is history" in the seventeenth century, he was composing, according to the narrator, a "mere rhetorical eulogy of history." The same words written by Menard—who, as a contemporary of William James, defines history not as an "investigation of reality, but as its origin"—mean something else entirely. While the "text of Cervantes and that of Menard are verbally identical," the narrator comments, "the second is almost infinitely richer" (53, 52). This judgment aside, Borges's point is that although Menard has, after great effort, reproduced the letters that blacken some pages in *Don Quixote*, he cannot reproduce the text. It has passed over to the unpresentable. It has become unrecoupable missing contents. The imagination informing this story is deeply nostalgic, as is much of Borges's fiction. His stories relate quests that look backward toward some teleological sense of reality or truth, for which, in the domain of modernity, it no longer seems reasonable to search.

Like Borges, Kathy Acker centers a narrative on Cervantes's text, appropriating the title *Don Quixote*. While Acker's *Don Quixote* also concerns the unpresentable and missing contents, it does not call nostalgically to the unpresentable, does not silently invoke lost or disappeared master narratives. Although the missing contents in Acker's work are also unpresentable, they are composed of the not yet presented. Rather than look backward, her narratives look forward.

Acker's quest novels obsessively depict the search for individuality, for selfhood, in the context of the cultural construction of identity. For this search to proceed, Acker's protagonists must move beyond the border of culture to conceive of themselves as individuals, as other than complaint products of their culture.[4] This quest, like the one Borges depicts, is unreasonable; it cannot be completed, for even in Acker's delirious narratives, it is impossible to step outside culture and thus to shed the culturally constructed self.

During a moment of revelation in the abortion scene that begins Acker's *Don Quixote*, the protagonist resolves to embark on such a quest for selfhood. Dressed in green paper and positioned on the operating table with knees raised as masked medical figures prepare to invade her body, she is struck with the sudden knowledge that her identity is not her own. This understanding moves her to adopt subversive strategies to disengage from the forces that have compelled her identity: "When a doctor sticks a steel catheter into you while you're lying on your back and you do exactly what he and the nurses tell you to . . . you let go of your mind. . . ." Once she can conceive of surrendering the constructed self, she can also formulate the quest to acquire her own "name": "She needed a new life. She had to be named" (9–10).[5]

The quest for a new life and a name structures several of Acker's works. Yet unlike male quest novels, such as *The Magic Mountain* and *A Portrait of the Artist as a Young Man*, Acker's texts locate the means of acquisition outside culture, since they are unavailable in the context of patriarchy. To constitute the self differently, the quester must find an alternative site for such constitution. Acker moves her protagonists toward this site through the appropriation of male texts, a strategy she explains in the epigraph to part 2: "Being born into and part of a male world, she had no speech of her own. All she could do was read male texts which weren't hers." The male texts represent the limits of language and culture within which the female quester attempts to acquire identity. Once inside the male text, the quester, by her very posture, subverts it: "By repeating the past, I'm molding and transforming it." In the Borges story, replication is the issue. For Acker the appropriation of *Don Quixote* is a strategy of subversion. Her description of the textual appropriation used by Arabs applies to herself: "They write by cutting chunks out of all-ready written texts and in other ways defacing traditions: changing important names into silly ones, making dirty jokes out of matters that should be of the utmost importance to us . . ." (39, 48, 25).[6]

Acker's purpose in appropriating well-known texts is profoundly political. Through plagiarism, Acker proposes an alternative to the classical Marxist explanation of the sources of power. With Jean Baudrillard she believes that those who control the means of representation are more powerful than those who control the means of production. Plagiarism undermines the assumptions governing representation. Sherrie Levine, an artist who also uses appropriation, explains: "The whole art system was geared to celebrating . . . objects of male desire. Where, as a woman artist, could I situate myself? What I was doing was making this explicit: how this oedipal relationship artists have with artists of the past gets repressed; and how I, as a woman, was only allowed to represent male desire" (96–97). In plagiarizing, Acker does not deny the masterwork itself, but she does interrogate its sources in paternal authority and male desire. By placing the search for modes of representing female desire inside male texts, Acker and others clearly delineate the constraints under which this search proceeds. She also suggests that the alternative nature of, and location for, the missing contents in women's texts is in the not yet presented.[7]

Modernism and postmodernism reveal a pattern of bifurcation: two unpresentables, two sets of missing contents. As male texts look backward over their shoulders, female texts look forward, often beyond culture, beyond patriarchy, into the unknown, the outlawed. Marguerite Duras, commenting on this disengagement from master narratives, remarks, "[T]o put society into question is still to acknowledge it. . . . I mean the people who do that, who write about the refusal of society, harbor within them a kind of nostalgia. They are, I am certain, much less separated from it than I am" (qtd. in Suleiman 15). Such separation is evident not only in Duras's work but in many other female texts of modernity; in Acker's narratives, for instance, the protagonists repeatedly demonstrate the inadequacy of patriarchal culture, past or present, as the arena for identity. The liberating image common to these writers is the nomad who seeks sanctuary in the interstices of culture and replaces Oedipus as the protagonist of culture and the unconscious. Nearly all Acker's central characters are nomadic. In Marilynne Robinson's Housekeeping, the protagonist, Ruthie, feigns suicide in order to live as a drifter. It gives her license to become "strange" without having that strangeness defined and perhaps tempered and shaped by society.[8]

Before Duras, Acker, and Robinson, a generation of women innovators set the precedent for these contemporary nomads (see Friedman and Fuchs, "Contexts"). In Djuna Barnes's Nightwood, the character Robin, whose various identities are shaped by the nearest dominating presence, maintains at the core a "desperate anonymity" (168). Like strangeness and nomadism, anonymity is a strategy to elude cultural construction, a precondition for raising the not yet presented in these women's texts. Robin's husband, Felix, a man obsessed with the past, observes that Robin's "attention had . . . been taken by something not yet in history. Always she seemed to be listening to the echo of some foray in the blood that had no known setting . . ." (44). Barnes engages in a critique of the backward oedipal glance with her portrait of Felix's son, the child of a man stuck in this glance:

> [A]s time passed it became increasingly evident that this child, if born to anything, had been born to holy decay. Mentally deficient and emotionally excessive, an addict to death; at ten, barely as tall as a child of six, wearing spectacles, stumbling when he tried to run, with cold hands and anxious face, he followed his father. . . .
>
> (107)

The dual central characters in Jane Bowles's *Two Serious Ladies* also follow strange, nomadic paths (Friedman and Fuchs, "Contexts" 20–22). The non sequiturs of their conversation, their paradoxical pronouncements, the eccentric movements through time and space are motivated less by loss than by hope. Reviewers have characterized the novel as unusual, even bizarre. Edith Walton, for example, finds it pathological, noting that "[t]here is hardly a character in the book who could be called really sane," while John Ashbery remarks, "No other contemporary writer can consistently produce surprise of this quality, the surprise that is the one essential ingredient of great art" (30). Although *Two Serious Ladies* offers both plot and recurring images, its main structural materials are sentences reminiscent, though not imitative, of Gertrude Stein. These sentences often occur in discrete, monadic units, not dependably connected to what precedes or follows, and only haphazardly make sense. Yet they are resonant and nervously interesting. For instance, Miss Goering, one of the "serious ladies" of the title, muses, "Most people have a guardian angel; that's why they move slowly." In a political discussion she cautions, "Just remember . . . that a revolution won is an adult who must kill his childhood once and for all." One feels that these statements are penetrable with effort but that such penetration is not the point. A man at a party asks Miss Goering, with seeming disingenuousness, to spend the night at his house because, as he says, "We have an extra bedroom." Although he is sincere, Miss Goering speaks to what she assumes is his subtext: "[I]t is against my entire code, but then, I have never begun to use my code, although I judge everything by it" (12, 143, 19).

Readers who surrender to this vermiculate reasoning cannot reliably use it to calibrate anything else in the text. It is neither a proper window to the figure of Miss Goering nor a mechanism to untie textual knots. Bowles's husband, Paul, has revealed that Bowles named her character for the murderous Nazi Hermann Goering. Yet this information does not illuminate. In contrast to surrealism's yoking of two disparate images to yield a meaning-charged third image, Bowles's yoking of the Nazi with her character seems baldly bizarre, though not strictly meaningless. The meaning is simply not revealable in the available context. Although her images and sentences deliberately resist obvious hermeneutics, whether of surrealism or psychoanalysis, they seem to seek resolution in a logic not yet grasped. Unlike male texts, which force the condition of strangeness on the characters, Bowles's and other women's texts seek that condition, for only in the domain of anonymity, strangeness, orphanhood, nomadism, or madness does it seem appropriate to await and perhaps awaken the not yet presented, which for these authors composes the missing contents in Western culture.

In an essay on the writer's block that afflicted Bowles for decades, Millicent Dillon describes the notebooks Bowles filled with fragments of her unfinished novel, *Out in the World*. Dillon, revising the ideas advanced in her biography of Bowles, speculates that the fragments represent a "mode of expression that was attempting to manifest itself through [Bowles] but that she could not accept":

> The cast of her mind and feelings was expressing its intention in this form—through fragmentation and repetition—but she took the result to be only failure. If it is true that her work was psychically blocked, it is also true that had she been able to view this fragmentation as a valid expression of her own narrative vision, the fragmentation could have led her to further development. . . . I now see the history of her later writing as a flight from the form that she was being impelled toward by her very nature.
>
> ("Experiment" 140–41)

In fact, when her husband suggested, "Just for the first page have the character come in, see this, do that," Jane would answer, "No, that's your way, that's not my way. I've got to do it my way and my way is more difficult than yours" ("Experiment" 140). Both Jane and Paul Bowles placed themselves in the avant-garde, but Jane's way involved an element unknown to either of them: the not yet presented to which Jane could not commit herself but whose absence is strongly felt in most of her narratives, including *Two Serious Ladies*.

Although Paul Bowles sets many of his stories in an exotic Arab Moroccan culture that he paints as dangerous to certain unworthy Westerners, Western culture, nevertheless, calibrates the stories' underlying sensibility and values. In his most celebrated story, "A Distant Episode," a professor of linguistics—made arrogant by his ample Western purse, his status as an American professor in a "primitive" culture, and most of all his knowledge of the local dialects of Moghrebi—easily falls prey to a group of thugs, the Reguiba, who, with deft ironic cruelty, cut out his tongue. They turn him into a dancing clown and subsequently sell him to a wealthy client. In the process, the Professor, as he is called, loses memory, consciousness of his humanity, and language. Unable to understand what is said to him, he is transformed into a sleeping, eating, defecating, dancing machine. When, at the story's climax, he reawakens to language and thus to his situation, his recognition sends him howling with bereavement into the sunset. Like much of the literature of modernity, this narrative centers on unrecoupable loss, which Paul Bowles offers as the defining condition of modern life. He moved to Morocco to escape his culture; he clothed his narratives in strange and sinister details. But as "A Distant Episode" suggests, the missing contents in his vision—unlike his wife's vision but like the vision of other male authors of modernity—are to be found in the past, a past that is decidedly Western.

The narrative of *Two Serious Ladies* concerns oedipal missing contents, as Mrs. Copperfield, the novel's other main character, reveals when she articulates her longing to replace God the Father, who seems to have disappeared:

When people believed in God they carried Him from one place to another. They carried Him through the jungles and across the Arctic Circle. God watched over everybody, and all men were brothers. Now there is nothing to carry with you from one place to another, and as far as I'm concerned, these people might as well be kangaroos; yet somehow there must be someone here who will remind me of something . . . I must find a nest in this outlandish place.

(40; ellipsis in text)

Bowles's narrative juxtaposes two quests, Miss Goering's for sainthood and Mrs. Copperfield's for happiness, that differ in form and substance. Both characters, however, act in ways that contradict their declared objectives. Miss Goering, for instance, moves near a glue factory on Staten Island, where she engages in a number of dull, accidental liaisons. Mrs. Copperfield becomes compulsively attached to a prostitute while on vacation in Panama with her husband, whom she abandons. The characters meet twice, once at the beginning of the novel and once toward the end. Each time, the plot neither compels nor justifies their meeting. Although both questers are quirky and both share a fondness for non sequiturs, their stories have little in common, not even on the level of metaphor. When they meet again at the end of the book, their statements to each other seem just short of random. Yet the inconsistency, randomness, and contradiction contribute to the narrative's seductive and liberating strangeness. Near the end of the novel, Mrs. Copperfield declares, "I *have* gone to pieces, which is a thing I've wanted to do for years. I know I am as guilty as I can be, but I have my happiness, which I guard like a wolf, and I have authority now and a certain amount of daring . . ." (197). Mrs. Copperfield resists the nostalgic, self-declared quest to find a substitute for the missing God the Father in favor of a more fruitful route to happiness, "going to pieces." Similarly, Bowles's writing repeatedly falls to pieces, refuses to organize itself according to nostalgic scripts, and, in spite of the author herself, moves with unconscious daring toward something she cannot name. This proposing and then resisting nostalgic scripts is Bowles's signature quality, evident in the eccentric movement of her unresolved narrative logic. In the final lines of *Two Serious Ladies*, Miss Goering reflects, "Certainly I am nearer to becoming a saint . . . but is it possible that a part of me hidden from my sight is piling sin upon sin as fast as Mrs. Copperfield?" (201).

Unlike Bowles, Anaïs Nin quite consciously and stubbornly pursued the not yet presented, an endeavor that caused her great suffering since the literary circles in which she moved often dismissed her efforts as trivial and nonliterary. Nin's search was confined to the psyche, as mediated by psychoanalysis, out of which she hoped to draw the return of the repressed, her version of the not yet presented.[9] Although this repressed, by its very nature, does represent a "past" of sorts, it has never occupied the symbolic and thus does not resemble Lyotard's unpresentable, which previously provided the dominant cultural narratives. In a rhapsodic passage of her 1937 *Diary*, Nin describes her vision:

> I mastered the mechanisms of life the better to bend it to the will of the dream. I conquered details to make the dream more possible. With hammer and nails, paint, soap, money, typewriter, cookbook, douche bags. I created a dream. . . . Through the markets, the whorehouses, the abattoirs, the butcher shops, the scientific laboratories, hospitals, Montparnasse, I walk with my dream unfurled, and lose myself in my own labyrinths, and the dream unfurled carries me. . . . I am passionate and fervent only for the dream, the poem. . . . Something is happening to me of which I am not afraid; it is an expansion of my consciousness, creating in space and loneliness. It is a vision, a city suspended in the sky, a rhythm of blood. It is ecstasy. Known only to the saints and the poets. . . . I may explode one day and send fragments to the earth.
>
> (2: 152–53)

As this passage suggests, Nin uses a variety of metaphors to tease the not yet presented onto her page—metaphors from religion, psychoanalysis, poetry, politics. Her most persistent terms come from female anatomy. In fact, Sharon Spencer has called Nin's feminine writing "music of the womb." The literary men Nin knew, including Henry Miller and Edmund Wilson, saw her diary as a waste of her creative powers and energies. They used the image of the womb to argue the diary's insular inadequacy as art. Lawrence Durrell cautioned, "You must make the leap outside of the womb, destroy your connections" (qtd. in *Diary* 2: 232). He urged that she rewrite *Hamlet*, a telling recommendation for a modernist since *Hamlet* is an exemplary representation of how the future is propelled by the past, by the power of the dead father. Such a recommendation was insensitive to Nin's project, which was to excavate woman's consciousness. In a statement that anticipates the imagery with which Hélène Cixous and contemporary feminists describe feminine writing, Nin writes:

> Woman never had direct communication with God anyway, but only through man, the priest. She never created directly except through man, was never able to create as a woman. . . . Woman's creation far from being like man's must be exactly like her creation of children, that is it must come out of her own blood, englobed by her womb, nourished with her own milk.
>
> (*Diary* 2: 233)

A second prominent image for the domain out of which the not yet presented is summoned is madness. In *House of Incest*, Nin links madness to freedom: "There is a fissure in my vision and madness will always rush through. . . . Lean over me, at the bedside of my madness and let me stand without crutches" (39). Her sense of the not yet presented is consistent with the ideas put forward in *The Newly Born Woman*, by Hélène Cixous and Catherine Clément, who speak in psychoanalytic terms about the identification of women with the fissures in the social structure: "Women bizarrely embody this group of anomalies showing the cracks in an overall system" (7). Nin searches for women's expression in the imaginary zone, a repository for what culture excludes. Bordering on obsession, the not yet presented is the most compelling force in Nin's writing. As *House of Incest* draws to a close, Nin offers an image of a dancer "listening to a music we could not hear, moved by hallucinations we could not see" (71).

Nin's *Spy in the House of Love* follows the pattern of male identity-quest novels until the final passage. The protagonist, Sabina, who is dubbed "Dona Juana," seeks her identity through a series of lovers, each of whom speaks to an aspect of her but none of whom helps her to coalesce the fragments of herself into a whole. She metamorphoses into another role—mother, seductress, sister, mother earth, wife—as each lover appears to her in his role of Don Juan, Wagnerian hero, father, brother, artist, or musician. Unsuccessful in establishing her identity conventionally—that is, in relation to a man, as Virginia Woolf famously observed that women characters generally do—she is admonished, "Yours is a story of non-love . . ." (117). Yet this identity quest has a deviant ending: the protagonist does not resign herself to convention or receive punishment for her sins (as does Don Juan), nor does she come to an understanding of her task (as do Stephen Dedaelus and Hans Castorp). She remains fragmented; a state of irresolution is preferable to any of the old scripts, none of which serves her purpose. Her remedy, as the last line of the novel suggests, is to stay sick: "In homeopathy there is a remedy called pulsatile for those who weep at music" (140). Homeopathy attempts to cure patients by prescribing small doses of what made them ill. Sickness, in the context of patriarchal culture, may show the way to another kind of health.

The work of HD, as replete with allusions to Western texts and myths as are the works of Joyce, Pound, and Eliot, also refuses the poignant solace of oedipal nostalgia. Indeed, critics have associated HD's use of myths, ancient history, and hieratic symbols with the modernist (male) mainstream, but for the most part they concentrate on biography. Her prose fiction, which constitutes almost half her canon, is deeply autobiographical, as the introductions by her daughter, Perdita Schaffner, to several volumes attest. When viewed through a modernist lens, however, her narratives—despite their allusive tapestry—follow the female paradigm of missing contents. In *The Waste Land*, Eliot slices through the millennia with a sexual theme because one of his purposes, modulated by nostalgia, is to demonstrate the vulgarity of contemporary life, the superiority of high culture. For instance, the "change of Philomel, by the barbarous king / So rudely forced" is, nevertheless, transfigured: "yet there the nightingale / Filled all the desert with inviolable voice" (56). No such transfiguration, Eliot implies, results from or accompanies contemporary instances, such as the sordid "seduction" of the typist by the "the young man carbuncular" or Lil's abortion (62). Eliot measures the poverty of modern life by such losses. HD does not approach the past with reverence, as Eliot does, but views it, in Henry James's metaphor, as the carpet in which to discover a figure illuminating contemporary life. Eliot and HD share a mythic method and a sense of missing contents, but their purposes in this method, as well as their construction of these contents, differ along gender lines. Both seek revelation in summoning the past, but they deviate in their configuration of revelation. For Eliot the revelation is religious and transcendent; for HD, particularly in *Palimpsest* and *Hermione*, it is psychological and concerns earthly life. While Eliot's pilgrim—whether in *The Waste Land* or in *Four Quartets*—seeks higher ground, HD's protagonists search for a way to be in the world.

Palimpsest, HD's first published novel, proceeds in three sections, each of which depicts a woman's quest. The three protagonists (Hipparchia, Raymonde, and Helen), each a version of a single persona, are linked by similar doubts and strivings through twenty centuries, from 75 BC to 1926; the three sections also share a pattern of repeated allusions and images. HD, influenced by her tenure as a patient of Freud, uses myth and ancient history to describe the territory of the unconscious, a place for excavating the object of her protagonists' quests. Each of the three sections of *Palimpsest*, whose title describes the book's method of superimposing one narrative on another, begins with the protagonist expressing doubt, which leads to her self-abnegation; the course of self-abnegation is then refused as she moves, or is moved, toward hope for affirmation. In the process, each protagonist rejects ordinary life to pursue a goal she cannot define, a decision that makes her an outsider and renders her strange in the context of her society. Each section more clearly articulates the object of the quest, although this object is never precisely identified. Part 1, set in Rome in 75 BC, focuses on the visionary poet Hipparchia, who follows the example of her mother in renouncing the conventional female role and chooses to "cast [her] lot with cynics, not with women seated at the distaff" (3). Part 2 also centers on a woman writer, Raymonde, an American poet living in postwar London. In the third metamorphosis, the text's persona appears as Helen, a woman on an archaeological expedition to Egypt in 1925. Expanding on the thoughts of Raymonde, Helen articulates her quest: "She wanted to dive deep, deep, courageously down into some unexploited region of the consciousness, into some common deep sea of unrecorded knowledge and bring, triumphant, to the surface some treasure buried, lost, forgotten" (179). Clearly, this quest for missing contents enters new territory ("unrecorded knowledge") for its "treasure." And although what is being sought may have been "buried, lost, forgotten," it is definitively not the comforting embrace of the father but something that, despite the efforts of visionary women questers (Hipparchia and Raymonde) through the millennia, has not yet surfaced.

The narratives of Joyce Carol Oates, though variously experimental, are fairly faithful to the practice of realism in the late twentieth century. But even Oates invests her texts with a sense of the not yet presented when she offers her characters hints of an option that has yet to materialize. In her bildungsroman *Because It Is Bitter, and Because It Is My Heart*, she builds steadily to a poignant sense of missing contents as she chronicles the lives of two young people in the 1960s and 1970s, an African American man who goes to Vietnam and a white woman who gets married. Oates undermines a satisfying sense of closure in the achievement of these ordinary destinies by infusing the text with irresolution and frustrated yearning. She separates her two central characters from the rest of society and links them immutably to each other by making them coconspirators in the accidental death of a classmate, the circumstances of which they never reveal publicly. Oates also provides them with somewhat unusual longings for working-class inhabitants of a small town. Jinx, the African American youth, longs for a college basketball scholarship, and Iris secretly longs for Jinx, with whom she is in love, although she sets her course more conventionally toward college and marriage. They wage the typical battles of their class: for Jinx, against bigotry, a community hostile to success, the lure of drugs; for Iris, against violent street life, inertia, indifferent and incapable parents addicted to alcohol and gambling. But their real nemesis is nastier than these predictable barriers. Jinx has all the ingredients for success: a caring, hardworking mother, a stable family life, intelligence, talent, and ambition. Yet for Jinx to succeed, he must betray his brother or watch his brother betray him. Rather than choose, he surrenders to failure and to the prescribed role for young African American men at the time—probable death in Vietnam. Iris, who is a virtual orphan (her mother dies of a liver disease related to her alcoholism, and her gambler father abdicates his parental responsibility), marches determinedly, if halfheartedly, toward conventional success but never feels identified with it. In the last line of the novel, she asks her future mother-in-law and the dressmaker adjusting her wedding gown, "*Do* you think I'll look the part?" (405). Both characters yearn to be protagonists in the master narrative chronicling their rise to success, their achievement of self-produced identity, their arrival in the middle class. Jinx learns that this narrative does not account for the complications of his life; it is not devised for him. Iris, although she has fought to enter this narrative, finds that she cannot believe in it, so she walks perfunctorily through its chapters. The master narrative fails Jinx and Iris because it is defunct, even irrelevant, in the world of the author and the world of the narrative. The novel provides this insight and moves toward it not with nostalgia but, particularly for Iris, with a sense of intense yearning for possibilities that have not yet come into range. As an inhabitant of a realistic novel, Iris cannot embark on a nomadic quest for the not yet presented as Ruthie does in Robinson's post-modern narrative *Housekeeping*. Nevertheless, Oates has made the missing contents in Iris's world almost palpable.

Although Deleuze and Guattari target late capitalist rather than patriarchal oppression in summoning a figure to oppose Oedipus, they also put forward the nomad (among others). Michel Foucault summarizes their reasoning:

> The first task of the revolutionary . . . is to learn . . . how to shake off the Oedipal yoke and the effects of power, in order to initiate a radical politics of desire freed from all beliefs. Such a politics dissolves the mystifications of power through the kindling, on all levels, of anti-oedipal forces . . . forces that escape coding, scramble the codes, and flee in all directions: *orphans* (no daddy-mommy-me), *atheists* (no beliefs), and *nomads* (no habits, no territories).
>
> (xxi)

They consider a variety of writers who seem to have broken out of the oedipal stranglehold: "Strange Anglo-American literature: from Thomas Hardy, from D.H. Lawrence to Malcolm Lowry, from Henry Miller to Allen Ginsberg and Jack Kerouac, *men* who know how to leave, to scramble the codes. . . . They overcome a limit, they shatter a wall, the capitalist barrier" (*Anti-Oedipus* 132–33; emphasis mine). Deleuze and Guattari propose that the schizophrenic writer Antonin Artaud is one of the few who escaped the oedipal economy, but most of the nomadic writers they are able to summon do not live up to the nomadic rhetoric. These writers "fail to complete the process, they never cease failing to do so. The neurotic impasse again closes— the daddy-mommy of oedipalization, America, the return to the native land—or else the perversion of the exotic territorialities, then drugs, alcohol, or worse still, an old fascist dream" (*Anti-Oedipus* 133). Indeed, Allen Ginsberg's Whitmanesque claim to the "native land" and his Eastern "exotic territorialities"; William Burroughs's use of drugs and alcohol; Jack Kerouac's pro-McCarthyism, pro-Eisenhower conservatism, and anti-Semitism; and, of course, the beats' pervasive misogyny all suggest that the understanding shaping these writers' nomadism is different from, and ultimately less radical than, the understanding of the women writers discussed in this essay. One wonders what Deleuze and Guattari would conclude from a study of the nomadic patterns of women writers. From the vantage point of the 1990s, Kerouac's *On the Road*, in particular, seems fecklessly rebellious. In fact, the work of the beats, generally, is infused neither with nostalgia for the unpresentable nor with yearning for the not yet presented. The master narratives, strangely, seem more alive in the beats' work than they do in works of modernity. They are the contexts of the beats' rebellion. The beats, in their very opposition, legitimate master narratives and thus position themselves, in some ways, outside modernity.

From the first generation of innovative women writers, female texts generally show little allegiance to the past. Stein's texts, unlike the works of her contemporaries Pound, Eliot, and Joyce, do not engage in nostalgia for the fathers' texts and myths. Stein captures the obsessiveness of this backward look in "Patriarchal Poetry":

> Patriarchal Poetry
> Their origin and their history.
> Patriarchal Poetry their origin and their history
> their history patriarchal poetry their origin patriar-
> chal poetry their history their origin patriarchal
> poetry their history patriarchal poetry their origin
> patriarchal poetry their history their origin.
>
> (115)

With the word *their*, Stein proposes a schism between her texts and patriarchal texts. She sets hers free from tradition, free from "*their* history their origin"; her texts are formally nomadic, spinning free of nostalgic modes. They resist nostalgic resonance, resist the imposition of narrative, resist outside attempts to construct them according to familiar orders and patterns. In "Rooms" of *Tender Buttons*, she writes, "Act so that there is no use in a centre" (498; see DuPlessis). Her works, when compared with the works of male modernists, focus on the present without bearing the burden of regret for what has passed. Stein does not elaborate the present as a tragic condition of no choice or as a condition to escape; rather, it is a place of hope and sometimes joy. There is hardly a nostalgic moment in her work. In *The Mother of Us All*, Susan B. (Anthony) asserts, "We cannot retrace our steps," though, she adds with irony, "going forward may be the same as going backwards" (201). Even in the most radical expressions of rebellion and discontent, male texts of modernity are suffused with nostalgia for a past order, for older texts, for the familiar sustaining myths. This shared sense of order, these shared texts and shared myths bind male postmodernism to male modernism and male modernism to the long reach of the male Western narrative tradition. Male texts of modernity have little trouble acquiring membership in the canon. Despite the different sociological and historical positions they represent, they have similar memories, similar allegiances, the same father, and the same laws.[10]

In "Composition as Explanation," Stein writes:

> Those who are creating the modern composition authentically are naturally only of importance when they are dead because by that time the modern composition having become past is classified and the description of it is classical. That is the reason why the creator of the new composition in the arts is an outlaw until he is a classic, there is hardly a moment in between. . . .
>
> (514)

It is instructive that many male modernists and even contemporary postmodernists like Pynchon are already, in Stein's terms, "past" and thus classical or, in current terms, canonical. It is instructive, too, that few female modernists or postmodernists, including Stein herself, are "past." They—Stein, Barnes, Bowles, Nin, Acker—remain outlaws, outside the canon because there is little in the backward, oedipal glance for them. Instead, they aim their gaze unabashedly and audaciously forward.[11]

Notes

1. To simplify terminology, I follow Jardine's example and use the term *modernity* to designate the literature usually included under the rubrics "modernism" and "postmodernism," but in passages requiring a distinction, I use *modernism* or *postmodernism*, assigning these terms according to common practice.

2. For the idea of nostalgia as a strategy to resist feminism, see Doane and Hodges. In a 1983 essay, Owens proposed introducing sexual difference into the modernism-postmodern debate. By now, this introduction is well under way. See, for instance, Friedman and Fuchs, *Breaking*; Jardine; Suleiman; and Waugh. I am grateful to Charles B. Harris for directing me to these points in Owens and Kaplan.

3. In reading this manuscript, Sharon Magnarelli observed that one of the passages Menard succeeds in replicating—part of Cervantes's ninth chapter—concerns a truncated text. Cervantes's narrator is unable to conclude the adventure introduced in the previous chapter because he does not have the rest of the text, but he finds a manuscript that translates the text from the Arabic. The chapter offers a *mise en abîme*, since the Arabic translation makes the story's completion possible and at the same time involves the text and the reader in a series of backward glances. Thus, in Borges's tale, Menard reproduces a reproduction, replicating a text that is itself a replication.

4. For an interesting exploration of a view more radical than Acker's, one arguing

that women do reserve an essential, female aspect not liable to patriarchal imprinting, see Fuss.

    5. I have adapted some of the material on Acker from Friedman.

    6. Acker's use of Arabs to illustrate her point is significant since they, like women, represent an "other" of Western culture.

    7. Winnett proposes that the paradigms of female writing differ from those of male writing; her excellent discussion focuses on the problem of applying an oedipal paradigm of pleasure to women readers (see esp. 505–07).

    8. On Acker's nomads, see Dix, who uses the theoretical model provided by Deleuze and Guattari in *A Thousand Plateaus*. Robinson's *Housekeeping* can also be described as a quest for the mother. Unlike Pynchon's *Vineland*, it does not turn into a quest for the father, a figure whose absence in Robinson's narrative gets very little attention. See Ravits.

    9. Nin writes, "I took psychoanalysis and made a myth of it" (*Diary* 2: 152).

    10. Jameson makes a similar observation, though, like most other critics, he assumes that male modernism speaks for all modernism: "Not only are Picasso and Joyce no longer ugly; they now strike us, on the whole, as rather 'realistic'; and this is the result of a canonization and an academic institutionalization of the modern movement generally . . ." ("Postmodernism" 56). Lyotard observes, "The activity men reserve for themselves arbitrarily as *fact* is posited legally as the *right* to decide meaning" ("One Thing" 119).

    11. I am grateful to Marjorie Perloff and Miriam Fuchs for their thoughtful readings of this essay in draft form. A shorter version of this paper was presented at the American Literature Conference in San Diego, May 1990.

Works Cited

Acker, Kathy. *Don Quixote*. New York: Grove, 1986.

Ashbery, John. "Up from the Underground." Rev. of *The Collected Works of Jane Bowles. New York Times Book Review* 29 Jan. 1967: 5+.

Barnes, Djuna. *Nightwood*. 1937. New York: New Directions, 1961.

Barthelme, Donald. *The Dead Father*. New York: Farrar, 1975.

Baudrillard, Jean. "Simulacra and Simulations." *Selected Writings*. By Baudrillard. Ed. Mark Poster. Stanford: Stanford UP, 1988. 166–84.

Borges, Jorge Luis. "Pierre Menard, Author of *Don Quixote*." *Ficciones*. 1956. Trans. Anthony Bonner. New York: Grove, 1962. 45–55.

Bowles, Jane. *Two Serious Ladies*. 1943. *My Sister's Hand in Mine: An Expanded Edition of the Collected Works of Jane Bowles*. New York: Ecco, 1978. 1–201.

Bowles, Paul. "A Distant Episode." *Collected Stories: 1939–1976*. Santa Barbara: Black Sparrow, 1981. 39–50.

Cixous, Hélène, and Catherine Clément. *The Newly Born Woman*. Trans. Betsy Wing. Minneapolis: U of Minnesota P, 1986.

Deleuze, Gilles, and Félix Guattari. *Anti-Oedipus: Capitalism and Schizophrenia*. 1972. Trans. Robert Hurley, Mark Seem, and Helen R. Lane. New York: Viking, 1977.

———. *A Thousand Plateaus*. Trans. Brian Massumi. Minneapolis: U of Minnesota P, 1987.

Dillon, Millicent. "Jane Bowles: Experiment as Character." Friedman and Fuchs, *Breaking* 140–47.

150 ◆ ELLEN G. FRIEDMAN

———. *A Little Original Sin: The Life and Work of Jane Bowles.* New York: Holt, 1981.

Dix, Douglas Shields. "Kathy Acker's *Don Quixote*: Nomad Writing." *Review of Contemporary Fiction* 9.3 (1989): 56–62.

Doane, Janice, and Devon Hodges. *Nostalgia and Sexual Difference: The Resistance to Contemporary Feminism.* New York: Methuen, 1987.

DuPlessis, Rachel. "Woolfenstein." Friedman and Fuchs, *Breaking* 99–114.

Eliot, T.S. *Four Quartets. Collected Poems* 173–209.

———. *T.S. Eliot: Collected Poems, 1909–1962.* New York: Harcourt, 1963.

———. *The Waste Land. Collected Poems* 51–76.

Foucault, Michel. Introduction. Deleuze and Guattari, *Anti-Oedipus* xv–xxiv.

Friedman, Ellen G. " 'Now Eat Your Mind': An Introduction to the Works of Kathy Acker." *Review of Contemporary Fiction* 9.3 (1989): 37–49.

Friedman, Ellen G., and Miriam Fuchs, eds. *Breaking the Sequence: Women's Experimental Fiction.* Princeton: Princeton UP, 1989.

———. "Contexts and Continuities: An Introduction to Women's Experimental Fiction in English." Friedman and Fuchs, *Breaking* 3–51.

Fuss, Diana J. " 'Essentially Speaking': Luce Irigaray's Language of Essence." *Hypatia* 3 (1989): 62–80.

HD [Hilda Doolittle]. *Palimpsest.* 1926. Rev. ed. Carbondale: Southern Illinois UP, 1968.

Jameson, Fredric. Introduction. Lyotard, *Postmodern Condition* vii–xxii.

———. "Postmodernism; or, The Cultural Logic of Late Capitalism." *New Left Review* 146 (1984): 53–94.

Jardine, Alice A. *Gynesis: Configurations of Woman and Modernity.* Ithaca: Cornell UP, 1985.

Kaplan, E. Ann. "Feminism/Oedipus/Postmodernism: The Case of MTV." *Postmodernism and Its Discontents.* Ed. Kaplan. New York: Verso, 1988. 30–44.

Levine, Sherrie. "Art in the (Re)Making." *Art News* May 1986: 96–97.

Lyotard, Jean-François. "One Thing at Stake in Women's Struggles." *The Lyotard Reader.* Ed. Andrew Benjamin. Cambridge: Blackwell, 1989. 111–21.

———. *The Postmodern Condition: A Report on Knowledge.* 1979. Trans. Geoff Bennington and Brian Massumi. Theory and History of Literature 10. Minneapolis: U of Minnesota P, 1984.

Nin, Anaïs. *The Diary of Anaïs Nin.* Ed. Gunther Stuhlmann. 7 vols. New York: Harcourt, 1966–80.

———. *House of Incest.* 1936. Chicago: Swallow, 1958.

———. *A Spy in the House of Love.* 1954. New York: Bantam, 1968.

Oates, Joyce Carol. *Because It Is Bitter, and Because It Is My Heart.* New York: Dutton, 1990.

Owens, Craig. "The Discourse of Others: Feminists and Postmodernism." *The Anti-aesthetic: Essays on Postmodern Culture.* Ed. Hal Foster. Port Townsend: Bay, 1983. 57–77.

Pynchon, Thomas. *Vineland.* New York: Little, 1990.

Ravits, Martha. "Extending the American Range: Marilynne Robinson's *Housekeeping.*" *American Literature* 61 (1989): 644–66.

Robinson, Lillian. "Canon Fathers and Myth Universe." *New Literary History* 19 (1987): 23–35.

Robinson, Marilynne. *Housekeeping*. 1981. New York: Bantam, 1982.

Spencer, Sharon. "The Music of the Womb: Anaïs Nin's 'Feminine Writing.' " Friedman and Fuchs, *Breaking* 161–73.

Stein, Gertrude. "Composition as Explanation." *Selected Writings* 511–23.

———. *The Mother of Us All. Selected Operas and Plays of Gertrude Stein*. Ed. John Malcolm Brinnin. Pittsburgh: U of Pittsburgh P, 1970. 159–202.

———. "Patriarchal Poetry." *The Yale Gertrude Stein*. Ed. Richard Kostelanetz. New Haven: Yale UP, 1980. 106–46.

———. "Rooms." *Tender Buttons. Selected Writings* 498–509.

———. *Selected Writings of Gertrude Stein*. Ed. Carl Van Vechten. New York: Vintage-Random, 1972.

Suleiman, Susan Rubin. *Subversive Intent: Gender, Politics, and the Avant-Garde*. Cambridge: Harvard UP, 1990.

Walton, Edith. "Fantastic Duo." Rev. of *Two Serious Ladies*, by Jane Bowles. *New York Times Book Review* 9 May 1943: 14.

Waugh, Patricia. *Feminine Fictions: Revisiting the Postmodern*. New York: Routledge, 1989.

Winnett, Susan. "Coming Unstrung: Women, Men, Narrative, and Principles of Pleasure." *PMLA* 105 (1990): 505–18.

Moving with the Mainstream:
A View of Postmodern American
Science Fiction

BOB DONAHOO

"It's an experimental novel, an allegory, a lunar geography, an artful autobiography, a cryptic scientific tract, a work of science fiction."
—Don DeLillo, *Ratner's Star*

For all the recent evidence that science fiction has finally jettisoned its cult status and begun to receive serious critical consideration, it is important to acknowledge that texts on the cutting edge of that success are recognizably different from many that preceded them and from much that dominates the popular idea of what science fiction writing is. In short, science fiction's plunge into postmodernism has meant more than catching up to date with "literary" fiction; it has changed the nature of science fiction texts themselves. Most significantly, the further science fiction has plunged into postmodernism, the further it has challenged its own genre identity; it has turned its eyes from the goal of imaginative science and instead gone in quest of a soul.

This is not to say that "souls" has been missing from traditional American science fiction. Far from it. The early American science fiction stories collected and canonized in Tom Shippey's *The Oxford Book of Science Fiction Stories* make clear that authors such as Jack Williamson and John Campbell wrote about the human soul as well as extrapolated science, and that the effects of science on that soul were crucial to their imaginations.[1]

However, the soul searching in postmodern American science fiction is not the search for or pondering about the human soul common in traditional science fiction; rather it centers on the soul of American science fiction itself. The question postmodern science fiction raises—in its most postmodern, self-reflexive mode—is, "What is science fiction about?"

Signs of the centrality of this question can crop up in any bookstore, signs such as *Slam*, Lewis Shiner's 1990 hardback novel (published by Doubleday, not Ace or Tor or Spectra),[2] displayed not in the science fiction/fantasy section near the *Star Trek* novelizations, but between Sidney Sheldon and

This essay was written expressly for this volume and is published here for the first time.

Danielle Steele, not that far from collector's editions of Steinbeck! More recently, at least two other science fiction genre writers have joined Shiner on the mainstream shelves: Orson Scott Card (*Lost Boys*, 1992)[3] and David Eddings (*The Losers*, 1992).[4] And then there is the case of William Gibson and Bruce Sterling's 1991 collaboration, *The Difference Engine*.[5] Though technically still belonging to the science fiction genre, its alternate time-line plot of a Victorian England dominated by computers is a long way from what readers of Isaac Asimov, Robert Heinlein, or Ray Bradbury—much less fans of *Star Wars* and *Star Trek*—have come to expect.

Scholars and theorists have, of course, noted the change. Istavan Csicsery-Ronay, Jr., for instance, has termed the new development an "SF of implosion" in direct contrast to "the conventions of expansionist SF."[6] Bruce Sterling, in his preface to *Mirrorshades*, a defining volume of postmodern science fiction's most hyped subgenre, cyberpunk, argues that such writing is a "modern reform" of a flabby genre: "For the cyberpunks, . . . technology is visceral. It is not the bottled genie of remote Big Science boffins; it is pervasive, utterly intimate. Not outside us, but next to us. Under our skin; often, inside our minds."[7] By implication, whatever postmodern science fiction is—cyberpunk or some other label created by writers, critics, or marketing executives—it has a more internal and present focus than traditional science fiction. It is less about "them," defined as either Bug-Eyed Monsters (BEMs) or extrapolated heroes, and more about us, defined as contemporary psychological and social problems, hopes, and fears. Lewis Shiner captures the idea of the distinction succinctly: "The pulp tradition is a tradition of childish, self-centered fantasy. I think it's time to grow up."[8]

A huge part of this "growing up" has been an increased awareness of the literary world in which science fiction is produced—an awareness carefully and intelligently explored by Brian McHale's essay "POSTcyberMODERNpunkISM." McHale argues that almost since its inception science fiction has lagged behind contemporary mainstream literary movements, but the lag time has steadily decreased to the point where there now exists a "feedback loop . . . between SF and postmodernist fiction. That is, we find postmodernist texts absorbing materials from already 'postmodernized' SF, and SF texts incorporating models drawn from already 'science-fictionized' postmodernism, so that certain elements can be identified which have cycled from SF to mainstream postmodernism and back to SF again, or from mainstream fiction to SF and back to the mainstream again."[9]

The relationship McHale suggests goes a long way to explain the presence of science fiction writers on the mainstream book shelves, and it begins to suggest the face of postmodern science fiction. For in seeking to grow up, in forming part of a feedback loop with mainstream fiction, science fiction is actually altering its stance toward technology and science. The result is fiction that increasingly rejects *as its focus* an attempt to understand, attack or defend, or even purely extrapolate science and technology. Rather, postmodern science fiction seeks to use science and technology as a source for extended metaphors to explore realities of life in the postmodern world. Oddly, in doing so, it also seeks to underline its status as "genre fiction"— to create a level of self-awareness that, in the final analysis, argues for the genre's increased respect as a kind of "home world" for postmodern life.

To explain what I mean by this idea, I want to look at a number of science fiction works; however, let me make clear that this is no attempt to form a canon for postmodern American science fiction. The great number of science fiction texts constantly disgorged in both magazines and books makes any claim for having a basis to create a canon ludicrous. However, by focusing on a range of texts from authors praised by both critics and readers, a reasonable description of the directional arc of contemporary science fiction can come into view.

To see that arc, it's useful to begin with a text rarely discussed in recent years by science fiction critics: Kurt Vonnegut's first novel, *Player Piano*.[10] Published in 1952, *Player Piano* stands at the cusp of the postmodern era, though well before Jean-François Lyotard and Fredric Jameson made the term critically fashionable. Its setting is a near-future labor market in which humans of average IQ and ability have been relegated to idleness or unfulfilling work by machines of ever-increasing efficiency and ability. In its distrust of technology, it typifies New Wave science fiction (see Csicsery-Ronay, 187), but its ending offers an omen for the postmodern science fiction that would follow. Their armed revolt against a technologically dominated society having failed, the four leaders of a rebel group—Dr. Paul Proteus (the novel's protagonist), Finnerty (a disgruntled engineer), Lasher (a clergyman), and Professor von Neumann—prepare to surrender to authorities and accept certain execution. As readers, we are brought to verge of a revelation, some sense of the meaning of "it all." However, Vonnegut opts to create not a critique of technology and science but a metaphor for his understanding of the human condition. Instead of an answer, we're given a shrug, a move that argues a typically postmodern reading of the novel: it stands as an ambiguous sign, expressing and not expressing Vonnegut's extratextual pessimism. The technological extrapolation hasn't been the point, just the method. The novel isn't about science or the future; it's about one man's sense of what it was like to live and work in post–World War II America.

Famously, of course, Vonnegut would eventually work to distance himself from science fiction,[11] but that stands beside the point. What's important is that the move most postmodern science fiction writers opt to make is exactly the one Vonnegut elects in this passage: the shift in focus from imaginative extrapolation of science to creation of metaphor; the rejection of Truth in favor of truths. Identifying this authorial move and looking for it in postmodern science fiction texts brings to the surface a number of different ideas. Many of the writers, not surprisingly, echo Vonnegut's cool pessimism, but more distinctively, they display other, more specific focus shifts, often shifts that foreground contemporary issues.

Consider William Gibson's early but pivotal short story "Burning Chrome," the tale in which he began to develop his idea of the cyberspace matrix and create the background for his novel *Neuromancer*.[12] In our thinking of his work as a developing metaphor and a focus shift, the role of gender in the tale claims attention. After all, gender is the hinge to the tale's two parallel plot lines: the heist tale in which Bobby Quine ("a cowboy. . . . a cracksman, a burglar, . . rustling data and credit in the crowded matrix . . .")[13] and his trusty sidekick, Automatic Jack, enter the matrix to rob— "burn"—Chrome, "as ugly a customer as the street ever produced, but she didn't belong to the street anymore. She was one of the Boys, Chrome, a member in good standing of the local Mob subsidiary" (180). The second plot line concerns Bobby's and Automatic Jack's romantic/sexual relationship to "Rikki Wildside," a young girl whom Bobby sees as the inspiration for his caper but whom Jack recognizes as looking out for herself, hoping for a chance to become a "simstim" star. Clearly, both plots rely on male-female confrontations.

However, the male-female distinctions are also confused in both plots. Chrome is a "she," described as having "a sweet little heart-shaped face" (180)—an allusion to Thomas Pynchon's picture of women in *The Crying of Lot 49*.[14] But she's also "one of the Boys," holding a position of power traditionally associated with males. Rikki, while functioning as a traditional sex-object of pulp fiction, bears a masculine name. More pointedly, the process of "burning" Chrome is metaphorically made equivalent to rape. The burn begins with Bobby "driv[ing] the Russian program into its slot" (168), and, after having "breached the first gate" (173), Jack narrates the process with the phrase "Ride 'em, cowboy" (173). At the climactic moment, Bobby cries out, " 'Burn the bitch down. I can't hold the thing back—' " (187). The escapade ends with these lines:

We've done it.
The matrix folds itself around me like an origami trick.
And the loft smells of sweat and burning circuitry.
I thought I heard Chrome scream, a raw metal sound, but I couldn't have.

(188)

In penetrating and taking that which defines Chrome as Chrome, Bobby and Jack act out a classic form of female-bashing: the destruction of the female who has dared to cross the boundary into the male power hierarchy. Such a plot suggests that this fiction is no more grown up than science fiction that reduces all women to either castrating bitches or buxom Barbarellas.

But then the second plot kicks in. For Rikki, far from standing by her man (or men), uses the physical assets of her feminine body to raise money working as a futuristic prostitute in Chrome's House of Blue Lights. Rather than profit from Bobby's "big score" (190), she buys her own ZIESS IKON eyes and a ticket to Hollywood, abandoning Bobby and Jack without regrets or good-byes. In short, she acts out the role of the independent woman. In both plots, Gibson makes no authorial comment on the action. Rikki and Chrome are allowed simply to vanish from his texts into the texts of their own lives. By Gibson's refusal to privilege either of these plots, readers can't be sure which gender pattern—burn the bitch or independent woman—is "correct" in his future. We can only be certain that both exist there and that judgment on either is withheld.

Recognizing this aspect of the tale underscores that Gibson, like Vonnegut, is dealing with an issue, not of technology or life in the future, but of life in his present (the 1980s), when the narrowing or at least altering gender gap created a great deal of uncertainty about what—if any—were the proper "male" and "female" roles in society. He has both shifted attention from the future technology in the tale to the issue of gender roles and created a metaphor for 1980s gender confusion. In short, Bruce Sterling would seem to describe this fiction accurately when he claims that the tales in *Burning Chrome* "paint an instantly recognizable portrait of the modern predicament."[15]

This shift from technological extrapolation to "our" gender quandaries surfaces in any number of postmodern science fiction texts. Not surprisingly, it is woven into the fabric of Gibson's sprawl trilogy. In *Neuromancer*, for instance, not only do women function in major plot roles (the villainous 3Jane and the heroic Molly), but the plot itself is controlled by a metaphor of sexual union between two Artificial Intelligences (AIs), Wintermute and Neuromancer. This union is, of course, sexually ambiguous—what, after all, is the gender of an AI?—and Gibson underscores an acceptance of such gender ambiguity in the final paragraphs, where Case, an embodiment of caper fiction's tough guy, becomes involved with "a girl who called herself Michael."[16]

Moreover, Gibson is hardly alone in writing about the altered status between the genders. In Walter Jon Williams' *Angel Station*,[17] the novel's human perspective is split between two characters, Beautiful Maria and Ubu, genetically constructed siblings who share control of their "family" following their father's suicide. These orphans are pitted against—and ultimately defeat—the De Suarez clan, headed by the pseudo-Catholic patriarch Marco. And Williams adds still another gender twist. Maria and Ubu succeed because of their ability to develop and maintain a successful relationship with "Clan Lustre," an alien species organized, like ants or bees, around a female entity known as "Beloved." Here, too, Williams stresses the idea of gender equality, resolving the plot by having "Beloved" give up her idea of dominating humans and come, instead, to live in productive harmony with them.

If all this makes *Angel Station* sound like the perfect holiday gift for the feminist on your list, be warned that Williams' novel is not without offense. Throughout the novel, he injects sexual encounters presumably geared to please the genre's traditionally adolescent male readers. But even here there is an attempt to display a less misogynistic attitude toward the sexual exploitation of women—an attitude captured with a good deal of ambiguity early in the novel when Ubu destroys his father's "android sex toy" (12) named Kitten. The sexual explotation ends, but only through the death of the exploited female and not without a bit of sexual tease. Like Gibson, Williams aims for the "correct" side of gender issues, but he has trouble totally rejecting the format that has been so successful in his genre. Though the resulting ambiguity seems less planned than Gibson's, the literary consequences are similar: the reader is left with a text centered more on an author's gender concerns than scientific extrapolation.

And lest one assume this concern with contemporary gender issues is limited to writers linked to the cyberpunk movement, it's worth considering Dan Simmons's Hugo Award–winning *Hyperion*[18]—a novel that ridicules console cowboys as "cyberpukes."[19] Using a structure of tale-telling meant to echo Chaucer's *Canterbury Tales* (each first-person narrative is headed "The Priest's Tale," "The Soldier's Tale," etc.), Simmons omits a "Wife's Tale" and, instead, attaches a female voice to "The Detective's Tale." Moreover, he subtitles this section "The Long Good-Bye" (326), which, by echoing Raymond Chandler's familiar male detective story titles, serves to underscore Simmons's choice of a woman to fulfill this role. And fulfill it she does. In her physical abilities, her cynicism, and her underlying romanticism, Brawne Lamia reincarnates Chandler's Philip Marlowe—including a Marlowe-like voice (see especially the opening lines of her tale). Ultimately, Lamia's twisting tale of deceit and passion parody, in typical postmodern fashion, Chandler, but it is parody with a definite point: it emphasizes the arbitrary nature of assigned gender roles, especially in genre fiction.

But Lamia is only the most obvious example of Simmons's exploration of gender. In "The Scholar's Tale," Sol Weintraub accepts the traditional female role of care-provider to an infant after his daughter is subjected to a reverse-aging process and his wife dies. The nearer Weintraub's tale approaches the "time-present" of the novel, the more "motherly" become his emotions (see, for example, 305). Clearly, the text is again pointing out the arbitrary nature of Western gender roles—an idea further emphasized by linking Sol's story to the Biblical tale of Abraham and the sacrifice of Isaac (see, for example, 292–93, 296, 308). The Abraham/Isaac story relies heavily on the necessity of having a male child to fulfill the promise that Abraham would be the father of many nations. Yet Simmons shows no hesitation in using a female offspring to mirror Abraham's dilemma; a woman, in his text, is given the same moral and psychological significance as a man.

There are differences, of course, between what Simmons is doing with gender and what Gibson and Williams have done in their works, but the chief difference is one of attitude toward gender, not method in using it. Simmons's metaphor for contemporary life depicts less confusion—is more politically correct, perhaps—than those of Gibson and Williams. But in creating a text that asks readers to see gender issues at least as clearly as it asks them to consider scientific and social extrapolation, Simmons mirrors Vonnegut's move. He shifts attention from "them" to "us." The prevalence of this kind of shift enables contemporary gender issues to surface in many postmodern science fiction texts, but gender issues are a symptom of change, not the cause. Already, the evidence of Simmons's fiction suggests that, as American society moves toward a practical solution to gender inequality, the issue will decrease in attraction for science fiction authors.

Certainly, there are other social issues that are proving more central to the pattern of postmodern science fiction's development. One that serves to illuminate a second move characteristic of postmodern science fiction questions the meaning of human survival. Traditional science fiction, exemplified by John Campbell's "Night,"[20] has asked if humanity will continue to exist in the face of time and technological development. Increasingly, however, postmodern science fiction rejects this question and the dualistic answers it suggests. Instead, it seeks to understand what being human and what surviving mean. By taking up this issue, postmodern science fiction is able to make its second defining move—a move privileging an evolutionary view over a determinate one.

To see this move clearly, once again it's useful to examine a text that hovers near the rim on postmodern science fiction: Philip K. Dick's 1982 novel *The Transmigration of Timothy Archer*.[21] Written near the end of Dick's career, this work tells the story of Episcopal Bishop Timothy Archer, who loses his faith after learning that Christianity and the words of Christ themselves are the product of an earlier desert cult that gained ideal "Christian" consciousness by eating hallucinogenic mushrooms. Initially, the novel hardly feels like science fiction at all: the setting is a realistically drawn Berkeley, California, and the book's major science fiction elements—the magical mushroom, voices from the dead, the lost cult, and soul transmigration—are either debunked or given logical, alternative explanations by the novel's end. However, the fact remains that the impetus for the novel's plot—the discovery of the pre-Christian cult—is a product of science: the science of archaeology. Dick is using the move that rejects extrapolation for issues, shifting the focus from science to the issue of human survival. At this point, however, a second move takes place. For rather than asking if Bishop Archer "survives" the impact of "science"—the first chapter reveals that he doesn't: "he lies like the rest, underground" (11)—the novel redefines "survival" by playfully exploring Archer's "transmigration." As with the move to encompass contemporary social issues, this second move also is made with highly ambiguous signs. By very definition, "transmigration" means passage of the soul from one body to another. Technically, there's no reason this can't mean passage from a living body to a dead one. And by using a first-person narrator other than Timothy Archer, Dick insures that the novel leaves that explanation available. In fact, that's what the narrator, Archer's daughter-in-law Angel, tends to believe—belief hinging on the idea that "there is a difference between the notion of something and that something itself" (238). However, the novel, as a whole, argues against Angel's claim. The plot's two central actions—the bishop and his lover's response to the idea that the bishop's son is speaking from the dead and the bishop's death-causing search in the desert for the mystical mushroom—are both examples of humans acting on notions as if they were realities.

Moreover, when a radio mystic convinces Angel to take Bill Lundborg, the mental patient who sees himself as Archer's ghost, into her home, she realizes, "I had been maneuvered. . . . [j]ust the way Tim could do it—control people. In a sense, Bishop Tim Archer is more alive in [the mystic] than he is in Bill" (252). In short, the notion of Archer's transmigration *is* somehow equal to the thing itself. Nevertheless, the novel resists any definite conclusions, ending with equivocal lines: "Tim would have enjoyed it. Were he alive" (253). But in that equivocation, we see what the novel is finally about: not Timothy Archer's mystical transmigration but the movement in a "real" Angel Archer from definite disbelief to a point of playing with possibilities. She rejects a fixed idea of human survival and frees her thinking to evolve.

Essentially, then, this second move boils down to the creation of a third possibility, an opening up of the closed system of the universe. That this move is at the heart of postmodern science fiction is made clear by Bruce Sterling's Shaper/Mechanist stories, collected in *Crystal Express*, and here again it is tied to the issue of human survival. Superficially, Sterling's vision seems to argue a dark future for those qualities often thought of as defining the term "human." His characters bluntly refer to "posthumanist philosophy" (see "Sunken Gardens"), and the characters themselves have swapped their biological human form for bodies and minds created by technology: "The Shapers . . . had seized control of their own genetics, abandoning mankind in a burst of artificial evolution. Their rivals, the Mechanists, had replaced flesh with advanced prosthetics."[22] In the process, their essential humanity appears left behind. Sterling writes of one of his characters, a woman known as Spider Rose, "Now what was left of her feelings was like what is left of a roach when a hammer strikes it."[23]

However, there is humanity here; Sterling has merely redefined what being human means. For him, humanity is defined not by physical form but by psychological and emotional traits—including greed and a drive to survive. Spider Rose, for instance, with every physical need met, trades with the alien Investors for a pet "able to judge the emotional wants and needs of an alien species and adapt itself to them in a matter of days" (41). Eventually, this pet awakens some semblance of human feelings in this mechanically altered woman; however, when her life is threatened, she strangles the pet to preserve her air and finally eats its decaying flesh to stay alive. As a reward, she does survive—but only as a reincarnation of the pet; through some unexplained process, she has become "eager for the leash" (46). The evolutionary alternative Sterling supplies here allows for humanity to survive, though the irony of the conditions under which it does so raises questions about the value of that survival.

The other Shaper/Mechanist stories reinforce the idea that the ironical stance toward survival is in fact Sterling's individual stamp on this second move. "Twenty Evocations" follows the two-hundred-year life of Nikolai Leng, a Shaper. Shifting loyalties and abandoning loves in pursuit of his own best interest, Leng would seem totally inhuman, if not for his need to explain himself. In the tale's final paragraph, he shouts out his philosophy, " 'Futility is freedom!' "[24] Moreover, despite his death, he lives on through two "Kosmosity archaeologists" who see it as "now our duty to remember" Leng (109). Once again, the human survives, though the value of that survival is much in doubt.

It is that doubt which shifts the focus of these and Sterling's other "posthuman" fictions onto the present. Like many traditional science fiction texts, Sterling's work offers "us" a warning, though the warning is less about where science and technology could take us than about the dehumanizing consequences of philosophical positions and psychological attitudes now. The central issue becomes not technological extrapolation but destructive attitudes in a decadent, consumer/pleasure driven society. In short, his message is less about future science than current socioeconomics.

Gibson's use of this second move is more complex. Like Sterling's stories, Gibson's Sprawl trilogy projects a dark future where technological advances appear to have aided dehumanization, though in Gibson's novels the dehumanization does not occur because humans interact with machines/technology but rather because of the sociological consequences of living in a technological culture. His novels take as their setting not the vacuum of space but the garbage dump of earth: the ghettos and underground created as a result of technology concentrating power in fewer and fewer hands. Vast numbers of humans are essentially redundant, creating meaning in their lives only by linking up to the fantasy world of entertainment (Bobby's mother in *Count Zero* as well as all the constant users of simstim) or by becoming outlaws and mavericks in conflict with the ruling techno-culture. In either case, humans are robbed of the ability to fulfill their need for productive work in a functioning community. Gibson's future would seem to picture humanity surviving but only barely; dissolution looms.

However, Gibson's work offers a view of technology that is more ambiguous than Sterling's, and in that ambiguity he situates his evolutionary move. Increasingly as the trilogy progresses, cyberspace and its Artificial Intelligence "gods" offer a haven in which humans can be humans—though, far more radically than in Sterling's projection, the human form is left behind. By the end of *Mona Lisa Overdrive*,[25] the real world of the factory has become a battleground of death and destruction, and Bobby and Angie Mitchell find life only in the matrix of cyberspace: they become stored data in a technological but sentient matrix. The "meat" of the body is able to be abandoned because science and technology offer a refuge for the total mind, which, for Gibson, is the locus of true humanity. In short, technology, while destructive to human existence as we currently know it, also empowers human beings to evolve.

At the same time, the value of this evolution remains unresolved. In allowing humans to abandon the body, it fulfills the hopes of Lamarckian evolutionists most famously represented by Bernard Shaw in the *Back to Methuselah* cycle.[26] However, there is also something pathetic and tragic about *Mona Lisa Overdrive*'s last picture of Bobby in the real world, a picture seen through the questioning eyes of Angie: "Only Bobby, of all the people in this room, is not here as data. And Bobby is not the wasted thing before her, strapped down in alloy and nylon, its chin filmed with dried vomit, nor the eager familiar face gazing out at her from a monitor on Gentry's workbench. Is Bobby the solid rectangular mass of memory bolted above the stretcher?" (240). With options defined as a "wasted thing" and a "rectangular mass of memory," Angie's question mark is surely the reader's as well; reminding us of the ambiguities of our technological present as well as those of Gibson's future.

Finally, in searching for characteristics of postmodern science fiction, it's important to notice how consistently the texts background these moves with artifacts of popular culture, essentially grounding their realism in a awareness of the physical and sign debris that colors life in the late twentieth century. And just as that situation has led writers from Bobbie Ann Mason to Thomas Pynchon to crowd their fiction with K-marts and sitcom theme songs, so contemporary American science fiction writers have stocked their texts with what Gibson calls "superspecificity"—a response to what he sees as traditional science fiction's "use of generics" (Gibson, "Interview," 135). The result is fiction that makes casual references to "Ono-Sendai Cyberspace 7" decks and "two packs of Yeheyuans" bought with a "Mitsubishi Bank chip" (Gibson, *Neuromancer*, 46, 15).

The effect of this collage of the superficial has been well analyzed in George Slusser's essay "Literary MTV," where he asserts that cyberpunk has rejected the "soul" that is "SF fable" for the surface, "disembodied image." Slusser, however, overstates the case when he asserts, "The dream of such images is total autonomy from reality, and from story."[27] For while the idea of an escape from story agrees with the tendency of twentieth-century art toward abstraction, the idea of removing readers from reality is highly suspect. Rather, by "story," these writers create for their readers a particular and highly individual version of reality—a third move, characteristic of postmodern science fiction and of postmodernism in general. In line with Lyotard's call for "incredulity towards metanarratives,"[28] postmodern science fiction texts assert that only the surface can be known; the "story"—some kind of true version of the facts, of history—either doesn't exist or isn't open to human understanding or description.

In part, this results in what might be called a typical postmodern style emphasizing surface and elements of popular culture, but for science fiction this has particularly important implications. Bruce Sterling and Lewis Shiner direct attention to these implications in their co-written story "Mozart in Mirrorshades,"[29] the final tale in Sterling's cyberpunk anthology, *Mirrorshades*. In this fast-paced fantasy, an alternate time-line Mozart links up with exploiting oil refiners to avoid an early death and trades classical music for rock to get "that car and that recording studio" (238). One of the oil men justifies the murder and mayhem required to smuggle Mozart back to realtime by explaining, " 'I transmitted a couple of his new tunes up the line a month ago. You know what? The kid's number five on the *Billboard* charts! Number five!' " (238).

The story ends without a major point—merely an amusing play with the idea of combining pop and high cultures—but Shiner's second novel, *Deserted Cities of the Heart*,[30] published three years after "Mozart" appeared in *Omni*, realizes the more serious aspects of the combination. The novel is set in Mexico and Central America at a time of chaos. Earthquakes rack the region and clandestine American-financed forces seek to overthrow local governments. In the midst of this situation, Shiner offers an unlikely hero: Eddie, a confused, drug-using, psychiatric patient and rock star. However, the very marginalizing aspects of Eddie's life enable him to fulfill his hero's destiny. His stint in a comfortable sanitarium allows him to study his brother's writing on Mayan culture; his interest in drugs attracts him to the Mayan experiments with hallucinogenic mushrooms; and his money from his music career finances his disappearance into the Mexican rain forest (38–39), where he finds his true destiny as leader of a nonviolent counterassault against the forces of mainstream power and authority. As a part of the popular culture, Eddie is positioned—unlike his more knowledgeable and scientifically trained brother Thomas—to see the decay of the main culture and create the world that will follow it. " 'All those old ideas,' " Eddie explains to his brother, " '[t]hey don't have much time left. . . . You have to . . . you have to make sure you're in the right place when they go' " (312). In this novel, the anarchy of popular culture stands as a "right place."

But it is perhaps Gibson who, in opting to construct the radical fiction of *Neuromancer* on the popular culture cliché of the hard-boiled detective story—what Gibson himself has called "something like a Howard Hawkes film"—has made the most sustained use of popular culture and been the most successful of the contemporary science fiction writers in achieving the "mongrelization" which he sees as "what postmodernism is all about" ("Interview," 137, 132). Here the point is not just that the popular culture figures—Case and Molly; the maverick and his moll—succeed against the establishment. They do that, but their story is actually peripheral to the main event of the novel: the birth of a new creature via the union of Wintermute and Neuromancer, the evolution of man-made Artificial Intelligences to an independent, almost godlike life form. Gibson is making it clear that the caper story, the popular culture product, is the means for readers to glimpse and comprehend this nonpopular culture event. In Gibson's brand of "realism," popular culture is the form that makes our limited understanding of the greater world possible.

In presenting such an idea in fiction, Gibson creates a kind of feedback loop other than the one McHale has analyzed. For if Gibson is correct about popular culture's power to offer readers forms for understanding reality, then his own popular culture genre—science fiction—has an increased validity. Just as the caper story provides reader access to the story of technological/life form evolution, so the science fiction text makes available the story of evolving human life today, a life that more and more is swallowed up in technology incomprehensible to all but elite experts. The "Rue Jules Verne" that appears in a section title for *Neuromancer* takes—has, in a sense, already taken—us to a real place in a real Paris. In short, science fiction is the mainstream—not the mainstream of literature necessarily, but the mainstream of American social development; to return to Shiner's comment near the head of this essay, it depicts the grown-up "now."

The benefits for American science fiction of these kinds of moves are obvious: they serve both to expand the expected and, therefore, "permissible" content of science fiction writing and to alter the perception of what an science fiction writer does. Gibson, for instance, claims, "I don't extrapolate in the way I was taught an SF writer should. . . . That kind of literalism has always seemed silly to me. . . . I had a sense of what the expectations of the SF industry were in terms of product, but I *hated* that product and felt such a genuine sense of disgust that I consciously decided to reverse expectations, not give publishers or readers what they wanted" ("Interview," 140, 141). Similarly, Sterling asserts: "One of my aims is to replace oppositions with ambiguities. I'm not doing everybody's thinking for them. That's a departure from most SF. . . . Ideally, I would like to create a postindustrial literature that would be equally at home in an art gallery or a genetics lab. . . . SF is nearly always a literature of and for people who are powerless. It's mostly an escapist fiction, but *it doesn't have to be*. . . . Real people who are actual litterateurs prefer their literature untroubled by visionary lunacy, whereas to me visionary lunacy is the entire point of SF."[31] Of course, it would be unwise and unfair to claim that Gibson and Sterling speak for every contemporary American science fiction writer, but in their acknowledgement of ambition and willingness to revision an established and financially success-ful genre, they reveal a recognizable spirit.

Nevertheless, a possible threat to Sterling's call for "visionary lunacy" may well arise from postmodern science fiction writers for whom "seri-ousness" is mere imitation of the mainstream. The insidiousness of this danger lies in its apparent high-mindedness. In an essay first published in *Isaac Asimov's Science Fiction Magazine*, Norman Spinrad complains of science fiction writing that fails to fulfill the demands of "tragedy in both senses of the word."[32] Such a stand places almost beneath consideration work such as Harry Harrison's *Bill the Galactic Hero* series and other exemplars of science fiction's BEM branch. But "bad" literature is a part of the science fiction heritage and needs a place in its future—if only to draw toward the stars those eyes incapable or unwilling to plumb the depths of *Moby-Dick*. Moreover, as I've argued, it has already proven its value by supplying a popular culture for postmodern science fiction to exploit. In marking American science fiction's moves toward the postmodern mainstream, the challenge facing both artists and critics is to keep the full genre alive, not just as a publishing market but as an image source for itself and, possibly, future literatures to build upon.

Notes

1. Tom Shippey, ed. *The Oxford Book of Science Fiction Stories* (New York: Oxford University Press, 1992).

2. Lewis Shiner, *Slam* (New York: Doubleday, 1990).

3. Orson Scott Card, *Lost Boys* (New York: Harper-Collins, 1992).

4. David Eddings, *The Losers* (New York: Fawcett Columbine, 1992).

5. William Gibson and Bruce Sterling, *The Difference Engine* (New York: Bantam, 1991; New York: Bantam, 1992).

6. Istvan Csicsery-Ronay, Jr., "Cyberpunk and Neuromanticism," in *Storming the Reality Studio*, ed. Larry McCaffery (Durham, N.C.: Duke University Press, 1991), 186–87; hereafter cited in text.

7. Bruce Sterling, preface to *Mirrorshades: The Cyberpunk Anthology* (New York: Arbor House, 1986; New York: Ace, 1988), xv, xiii.

8. Lewis Shiner, "Inside the Movement: Past, Present, and Future," in *Fiction 2000: Cyberpunk and the Future of Narrative*, ed. George Slusser and Tom Shippey (Athens: University of Georgia Press, 1992), 23.

9. Brian McHale, "POSTcyberMODERNpunkISM," in *Storming the Reality Studio*, ed. Larry McCaffery, 314–15.

10. Kurt Vonnegut, *Player Piano* (New York: Delacorte Press, 1952; New York: Laurel, 1980).

11. Kurt Vonnegut, "Science Fiction," in *Wampeters, Foma, and Granfalloons* (New York: Delta Books, 1974), 1–5.

12. William Gibson, "An Interview with William Gibson," interviewed by Larry

McCaffrey, in *Across the Wounded Galaxies: Interviews with Contemporary American Science Fiction Writers*, ed. Larry McCaffery (Urbana: University of Illinois Press, 1990), 135; hereafter cited in text as "Interview."

13.   William Gibson, "Burning Chrome," in *Burning Chrome* (New York: Arbor House, 1986; New York: Ace, 1987), 170.

14.   Thomas Pynchon. *The Crying of Lot 49* (New York: J.B. Lippincott, 1966; New York: Bantam, 1982), 10.

15.   Bruce Sterling, preface to *Burning Chrome*, by William Gibson (New York: Arbor House, 1986; New York: Ace, 1987), xi.

16.   William Gibson, *Neuromancer* New York: Ace, 1984), 270; hereafter cited in text.

17.   Walter Jon Williams, *Angel Station* (New York: Tor, 1989).

18.   Dan Simmons, *Hyperion* (New York: Doubleday, 1989; New York: Bantam, 1990).

19.   Neil Easterbrook, "The Arch of Our Destruction: Reversal and Erasure in Cyberpunk," *Science-Fiction Studies* 19 (1992): 378.

20.   John W. Campbell, Jr., "Night," in *The Oxford Book of Science Fiction Stories*, ed. Tom Shippey (New York: Oxford University Press, 1992), 95–114.

21.   Philip K. Dick. *The Transmigration of Timothy Archer* (New York: Timescape, 1982; New York: Vintage, 1991).

22.   Bruce Sterling, "Sunken Gardens," in *Crystal Express* (New York: Arkham House, 1989; New York: Ace, 1990), 89.

23.   Bruce Sterling, "Spider Rose," in *Crystal Express* (New York: Arkham House, 1989; New York: Ace, 1990), 29.

24.   Bruce Sterling, "Twenty Evocations," in *Crystal Express* (New York: Arkham House, 1989; New York: Ace, 1990), 109.

25.   William Gibson, *Mona Lisa Overdrive* (New York: Bantam, 1988).

26.   George Bernard Shaw, preface to *Back to Methusaleh: A Metabiological Pentateuch* (New York: Brentano's, 1921), xxiii–xxiv.

27.   George Slusser, "Literary MTV," in *Storming the Reality Studio*, ed. Larry McCaffery, 342.

28.   Jean-François Lyotard, introduction to *The Postmodern Condition*, trans. G. Bennington and B. Massumi (Manchester: Manchester University Press, 1984), xxiv.

29.   Bruce Sterling and Lewis Shiner, "Mozart in Mirrorshades," in *Mirrorshades: The Cyberpunk Anthology*, 223–39.

30.   Lewis Shiner, *Deserted Cities of the Heart* (New York: Doubleday, 1988; New York: Bantam, 1989).

31.   Bruce Sterling, "An Interview with Bruce Sterling," by Larry McCaffery and Brooks Landon, in *Across the Wounded Galaxies: Interviews with Contemporary American Science Fiction Writers*, ed. Larry McCaffery, 219, 222, 223–24, 228.

32.   Norman Spinrad, "Science Fiction Versus Sci-Fi," in *Science Fiction in the Real World* (Carbondale: Southern Illinois University Press, 1990), 22.

INDIVIDUAL FIGURES

♦

Representation and Multiplicity in Four Postmodern American Novels

JOHN JOHNSTON

In addition to the perfect numerical sequence of their publication dates—1973, 1974, 1975 and 1976 respectively—Thomas Pynchon's *Gravity's Rainbow*, Joseph McElroy's *Lookout Cartridge*, William Gaddis's *JR* and Don DeLillo's *Ratner's Star* are linked in many significant ways. Formally, all are large-scaled and excessive encyclopedic narratives, teeming with the kind of information that puts demanding strains on the reader while hardly meeting conventional expectations about what novels should do and what pleasures they should provide. Thematically, they all investigate aspects of contemporary culture and experience that would seem intractable to the humanist or "liberal imagination," insofar as they neither privilege the individual "knowing" subject nor see the workings of contemporary science and technology as necessarily dehumanizing. But most important, all engage us in various kinds of multiplicity, both in the sense that the contemporary world is registered as a multiplicity and inasmuch as they themselves articulate multiplicities in and through their novel orderings and arrangements of heterogeneous kinds of information.

It is this last commonality of aspect that this essay seeks to explore, not so much by way of individual particularities of detail as through basic, underlying similarities. To a certain extent, therefore, I shall be concerned with an important "moment" in the recent history of the American novel, and with the ideas and assumptions that define its context. For to say that these works of fiction constitute a literary "moment" of some significance is to suggest that, taken together, they reinforce and conjugate one another in ways that urge us to recognize a new configuration in (or of) the contemporary cultural milieu. Since this configuration would appear to be related to what Jean-François Lyotard calls "the postmodern condition," it is with postmodernism that I must begin (Lyotard, *passim*).

Much of late has been written about postmodernism, but with little consensus thus far—apart from the general feeling that modernism is now receding into the past—about what it is and how it should be described (for

Reprinted with permission from *Texas Review* 10 (1989): 23–36.

discussions of the problems involved, see in particular the essays of Andreas Huyssen and Fredric Jameson, as well as Hal Foster's collection, *The Anti-Aesthetic: Essays on Postmodern Culture*). Writing about postmodern fiction in 1980, John Barth distinguishes the postmodern writers from those who somehow try to deny the first half of the 20th century. Yet *"it did happen,"* Barth insists, "Freud and Einstein and two world wars and the Russian and sexual revolutions and automobiles and airplanes and telephones and radios and movies and urbanization, and now nuclear weaponry and television and microchip technology and the new feminism and the rest, and there's no going back to Tolstoy and Dickens & Co. except on nostalgia trips" (70). Although Barth provocatively establishes a general context for discussion, he provides no exact or useful definitions; in fact, for our purposes he remains too content to categorize writers like Gabriel García Márquez and Italo Calvino as postmodern simply because they no longer feel constrained to choose between "realism" and modernist modes of writing.

In contrast to Barth's empirical catalogue, Lyotard takes a more strictly theoretical approach toward what he views as an epistemological crisis. That is, Lyotard is mainly concerned with the current critical state of knowledge, and more particularly with the crisis in legitimation following upon our culture's loss of belief in what he calls the "master narratives." These latter provide the basis not only for establishing causal links among events and deciding what is true and just, but also for legitimating the social contract and in fact all governmental processes. But in responding to the widespread feeling that today information no longer fits meaningfully into large narrative models, Lyotard goes so far as to argue that even our capacity to analyze the crisis we are caught in is jeopardized, since the analysis would be founded on the discredited narrative models whose loss *is* the crisis. Consequently, all we can do is trace the crisis back to the two central kinds of 19th century narrative: those of speculation (as in Freud) and those of emancipation (as in Marx).

Let us assume Lyotard's view of postmodernism but modify it to accord with several other considerations. First, I suggest that there is a structural or intrinsic reason for the confusion and disagreement about postmodernism. Basically, the relationship between modernism and postmodernism is neither one of continuity, stable opposition nor paradigm shift (as would be the case in some kind of period break or historical *coupure*). Rather, postmodernism may be conceived as an instance of *Nachträglichkeit*: it comes after modernism in the sense of a belated supplement that reactivates elements of modernism which, in the institutionalization of the latter, have been excluded, repressed or marginalized. (My use of the German term "Nachträglichkeit," meaning deferred action, derives of course from Freud, who employed it repeatedly in connection with his view of psychical temporality and causality. For a useful discussion of the term, see the entry under "Deferred Action" in J. Laplanche and J.-B Pontalis's *The Language of Psychoanalysis*). As both an artistic and critical enterprise, therefore, postmodernism demands a reordering and reassessment of modernism, and especially of the latter's claim "to make it new." The experience of *Nachträglichkeit*, of deferred and retroactive action, entails a very different sense of temporality, and precludes the possibility of "originating" an event or even understanding it in the self-contained moment of its occurrence. If modernist art privileges the ecstatic, visionary moment, or frames the present moment against the mythic time of archetypal recurrence, postmodernist art tends to stall temporality in the endlessness of the present, as in Beckett's fiction, or to open it up to a multiplicity of layered or virtual times, as in Borges' story "The Garden of Forking Paths."

Perhaps another way to formulate this difference in the new literary configuration is to say that postmodern works must create not only their precursors, as Borges said of Kafka, but also the conditions to which they are in some way a response. That is, these conditions are no longer simply "given" as part of some new experience the artist seeks to render "first hand." Rather, what he or she confronts is a preselected set of representations that give rise to problems in and of themselves; in other words, postmodernist works depart from a set of cultural representations which they must assume and critique even as they re-frame or (re)produce them. Of course, every representation does this to some extent: every visual representation re-structures the visual field in relation to prior representations; every written text is a re-writing of prior written texts. But in postmodernist works this operation is explicitly foregrounded or thematized, so that prior representations, rather than "lived experience," become the primary material focus, and the "work" itself consists of this continual process of re-structuration. The necessity of *Nachträglichkeit*—of deferred action—thus applies not so much to the new contents of experience as it does to the form(s) in which it occurs. The postmodernist re-structuration may occur in different ways, but most fundamentally, it seems to me, it always involves the reversal of the Platonic heritage and the reassertion of the logic of the simulacrum.

I am suggesting then that "the postmodern condition" may be described as a situation in which "originals" no longer automatically assume primacy over copies, or a model over its image. In an environment defined more and more by the new information technologies of consumer society, we have become increasingly aware of how difficult it is to separate the meaning and effect of a current "event" from its "reportage" or representation, and of how the contemporary world is saturated with "copies" without originals, and grafts and replications which cannot be reduced to a point of origin or explained by their source. The "reversal" of the Platonic paradigm begins however when we give up the search for the "truth" beneath appearances or the "real" before its distorting appropriation, transmission and/or representation, and attempt to think the relationships between original and copy, model and image, in a new way.

One such way follows from the Nietzschean attempt taken up by the

French "post-structuralist" philosophers to complete the overturning of the Platonic heritage based on relations of identity and similitude. Above all, this means thinking through the logic of the simulacrum (see Deleuze, 1969, 292–307). If a copy by definition is an image endowed with the capacity to reproduce through resemblance the essence of the original, by contrast the simulacrum harbors a difference that makes it an imperfect copy, or a "bad" copy of a copy. This slight (and slighted) "negative" difference is stigmatized by Platonic philosophy, for it poses a threat to the valorization of identity and similitude upon which Platonism is founded. To overturn Platonism therefore one must start from this difference, consider it not a discrepancy or flaw but as what is presupposed by any assertion of identity as the latter's own condition of possibility. And similarly for reproduction or representation, which presupposes repetition as its enabling condition. From this reversal it follows that identity is not an ontological *a priori* as Platonism would have it, but an effect or "simulation" produced by a specific process of selection in the play of repetition and difference. But if identity not only presupposes a prior difference and is itself only a simulation, then the privileged status accorded to the model over the copy or the original over the imitation is no longer warranted. In fact, from the perspective provided by the simulacrum, the "original" or "model" appears to have been constructed out of a need to anchor the process of signification in a prior idea or essence, which is subsequently hypothesized as the origin. By its very nature, then, the simulacrum causes a blurring or slippage of its contextual referents that throws into question the relationship between model and copy; its effects, therefore, cannot be accounted for as merely those of a "bad" copy or distorted representation of something said to already pre-exist it.

A novel by the Australian writer Frank Hardy and the ensuing libel trial it provoked will provide a simple example of this effect. *Power Without Glory* (1950) is a rather straightforward social-realist novel based in part on the life of John Wren, a politically powerful boss of illegal gambling in Australia. In the novel the wife of "John West" is portrayed as an adulteress, and as a result John Wren sued the author for slander. The charge was based on the assertion that even though the novel was a fictitious representation of events, "in the public eye" it clearly stood as a thinly disguised portrayal of Wren's life, except of course for the purportedly malicious and "untrue" portrait of his wife. In the trial both the prosecution and the defense were forced to make assertions that were simultaneously true and false: namely, that the novel was at once "true to life" and blatantly fictional, with the difference in the two positions residing only in assertions as to which was to be taken as which and in what context. At one point in the trial the prosecution even introduced as exhibits the "real" chair and the "real" print of Beethoven described in the novel, in order to make its case that "John West" was a fictional representation of John Wren. What is remarkable is the extent to which both sides became entwined in the coils of such a dubious logic. Clearly only an elaborate and painstaking reconstruction of both the novel's composition and Wren's life could possibly sort out their opposing claims; at the same time, however, there was no perspective available from which one could maintain the "difference": every assertion about the truth or falsity of some aspect of the representation could easily be turned around. Once accused of adultery, Wren's wife could not prove her innocence, especially since she herself was not literally accused, only her fictional double. The trial became a whirl-a-gig of rotating positions: the portrait of West's wife was *either* an aesthetic fiction *or* a "true" portrait of Wren's wife; *and*, Wren's wife was *either* "true" to him *or* a secret adulteress. However, no combination (like the prosecution's "the novel is a false portrait of a true wife") could be sustained against logical contradiction. As a result, there could be no solution in legal terms, since blame or guilt could not be attached.[1]

The case illustrates very clearly the power of the simulacrum to throw into question and make an issue of the difference between an "original" event and its representation, or more simply between a "model" and its reproduceable image. Since the novel's referents could be accepted as neither fictional nor real, one was left with only "differences" that could not be grasped and translated into a legal action. Now it is precisely this kind of "difference"—variously conceptualized by Jacques Derrida, Gilles Deleuze, and Jean Baudrillard as well as by a number of feminist writers—that defines what is at stake today in contempoary "post-structuralist" writing (see Alice Jardine's *Gynesis: Configurations of Woman and Modernity* for an attempt to link the concern with "difference" evident in both post-structuralism and feminism). Baudrillard, for example, argues that we have passed from an order of signification based on production to a free-floating order of the simulacrum that he calls "simulation," in which all referents bend or curve back to their point of origin and the only thing "outside" is an "orbiting nuclear" model that regulates the code of discourse (as in the DNA model) (see Baudrillard, 1983). Properly representational modes, in order to distinguish themselves from everyday reality, can only produce effects of "hyper-reality," since the everyday is more and more governed by the overtly fictional. In fact, for Baudrillard, who literalizes the reversal of Platonism, the "real" is what is now constructed in order to guarantee the authenticity of our representations. For Deleuze, on the other hand, there can be no such neo-Hegelian succession of self-contained semiotic stages; such schemes only serve to perpetuate the fiction of an earlier and less mediated social arrangement. In the infinite play of repetition and difference, what limits play—and thereby produces and controls identities—are apparatuses of power that seek to reduce a variety of "semiotic regimes" to its own binary codes (see Deleuze and Guattari, 1987, 111–148 and 208–231). But whatever their various theoretical differences, these post-structuralist thinkers all take this anti-Platonic "difference" to be primary, both ontologically and politically. Indeed, its current theorization may be said to mark the final overthrow of Platonism initiated by Nietzsche and in that to inaugurate the era of our postmodernity.

In these terms, William Gaddis's first novel *The Recognitions*, published in 1955, can legitimately lay claim to being the first American "postmodern" novel, for it presents a full and explicit articulation of the logic of the simulacrum. In retrospect, *The Recognitions* stands as an immense Janus-faced fictional elaboration: on the one hand, it summarizes the modernist fictional achievement through its use of religious and mythic symbolism, its layering of textual surfaces dense with multiple allusions and many recurrent motifs, its interest in the tragic dilemmas of a central artist figure, and its appropriation and parody of numerous fictional styles; but on the other hand, it anticipates and heralds a new strand of fiction (to be distinguished from the Joycean modernist epic) which combines "Menippean satire" with encyclopedic narrative in multiple ways, as works by Burroughs, Pynchon, Barth, McElroy, Coover, Delillo and others illustrate. In *The Recognitions* the dissolution or unravelling of the modernist paradigm occurs mainly through Gaddis's treatment of the counterfeiter theme, which henceforth becomes a major trope ushering in postmodern fiction. The novel's central character Wyatt Gwyon is an artist turned forger of Renaissance paintings, who, by identifying profoundly with artists like Dierek Bouts, Hubert van Eyke, and Roger van der Weyden, produces a series of paintings that are neither copies nor originals of these Northern Renaissance masters but "simulacra," with an uncanny status very much comparable to that of Pierre Menard's version of *Don Quixote* in Borges' story. Moreover, as we follow Wyatt's career we penetrate further and further into a world of proliferating counterfeits and fakes of every sort and description, to the point where the very distinction between original and imitation, model and copy is harder and harder to maintain. In this undermining of a fundamental assumption of representation, the novel becomes a fictive "theater of repetitions" where identities dissolve in the play of masks and simulations, and the world appears as a proliferating series of things, relations and meanings without central points of convergence and closure. In short, the novel articulates a multiplicity. Yet it is a "chaosmos" rather than a chaos (to borrow James Joyce's coinage), since these heterogeneous series from an internally resonant system (see Deleuze, 1968, 153–165 for a discussion of such a system).

Although the status of representation remains ambiguous in *The Recognitions*, representation becomes an obviously inadequate model for dealing with later, more explicitly postmodernist works. For the latter, the world is no longer simply "out there" waiting to be registered first hand; instead, for the postmodern novelist, experience seems always already framed, multiply mediated, and only available through a set of competing and often contradictory representations. It therefore becomes necessary for the novelist to register this new difficulty, and to make the form of his or her novel an adequate reflection of it. In the remaining part of this essay I would like to indicate summarily how the four American novels mentioned at the outset demonstrate this new problematization and work out different strategies by which to explore it.

Gravity's Rainbow draws mainly on the resources of the "encyclopedic narrative," the modern spy novel, cinematic and drug fantasy, as well as such pop and counterculture media as comic books and tarot cards. The narrator evokes and assumes a wide range of prior representations of World War II—historical, literary, Hollywoodian—in order to give us not yet another version but what might be called their "other" version, not so much because it asserts their own fictionality or lack of "truth" as their complicity with a whole apparatus of power and control—what in the novel is referred to as the "They-system"—which arose out of the new bureaucratic needs and technologies of World War Two and imposed a kind of cybernetic instrumentality on much of the world. Ultimately *Gravity's Rainbow* is concerned with how this system functions discursively, that is, with how it labels and uses any number of representations or "versions" of events. The novel refuses therefore to privilege any single "authoritative" version or to subordinate its varied discourses to a higher or more englobing authorial discourse, which would amount to yielding to precisely those powers and functions that it wants to lay bare. Instead it inscribes an uncertainty and indeterminacy in its narrative structure, and plays with how we might know certain connections between events.[2]

At the novel's outset, for example, it is discovered that a perfect coincidence exists between a map of the protagonist Lt. Tyrone Slothrop's sexual conquests in London and the sites where German V-2 rocket bombs have fallen. That two essentially random distributions correspond point for point constitutes the singularity that will precipitate and bring into view the various agencies by which Western man attempts to define and control reality, whether it be through behavioral conditioning, complex guidance systems, or psychic telepathy with the "other world." As we move closer to the novel's "central" event—the firing of a mysterious German V-2 rocket that seemingly holds the secret of the protagonist's past (and our present) in its instrumentation—the narrative fragments both temporally and spatially, and the protagonist himself disintegrates into different *personae*, thus making, as the narrator adds, many of the present population in the "Zone . . . offshoots of his original scattering." Moreover, by having Slothrop's quest to discover how he has been conditioned and shaped as a subject dissolve into a flight from history and a "becoming imperceptible," Pynchon suggests that Western history itself has become an elaborate trap, a structure of techno-scientific rationality to which the human being is *subiectum*, as Heidegger describes how modern man is subjected to and by the "world picture" (see Martin Heidegger, "The Age of the World Picture" in *The Question Concerning Technology*). But in playing off the novel's own arbitrariness and fictionality against the awesome power and growth of this new technological world order (and into whose wastelands the counter-cultural efforts at resistance simply dissolve), Pynchon also reveals the multiplicity of singularities and oddities, as well as the sheer vitality of life, that this new order must constantly pervert and deny.

Lookout Cartridge also exemplifies, though in very different terms, a novelistic attempt to register an experience that denies the possibility of any simple representation. The novel begins as a kind of mystery story in which the narrator is trying to discover why the film he has made with his best friend was destroyed before it could be processed. However, his search for the answer precipitates so many interconnected events (including the theft of his film diary) that no reconstruction of a coherent sequence of events ever becomes possible. What subsequently appears to be important is not so much the descriptions of the scenes that were shot, or the multiple associations recorded in the diary and the memories triggered in the narrator's consciousness as he ruminates over these things, as what lies between them, in the space they both articulate and prevent from becoming fully visible. In the novel's primary system of metaphors, this space "between" is also defined by the "cartridge" (for gun, camera, recorder) or means by which one system is inserted into another system. Shuttling between various places, especially New York and London, between various groups associated with his daughter, wife, film partner and those in the film, as well as between various times— past memories of the film, conversations that took place in the past or that would later take place, the narrative "present"—the narrator becomes this cartridge between spaces, times, people and different accounts of events. And yet, we finally come to realize, this cartridge is also a "blind spot," for it marks the place of the narrator's insertion into networks of control and determination that are at once familial, social and historical, and that therefore can never become fully visible no matter how many times or places he may come to occupy.

If the novel thus starts from a realist epistemological premise—at a certain time and place the camera recorded these specific images, which thus have a quasi-documentary status—complications also begin immediately: these images in different sequences were about different things in the minds of the two filmmakers, not to mention the associations they would evoke in the minds of different viewers. Cartwright, the narrator, feels that the film was about power: "Power shown being acquired from sources where it had momentum but not clarity"; or, as he puts it later: "power poached on or tuned in on when it lacked direction but had momentum" (McElroy, 77 and 180). The film itself conveys no specific direction to this power, since its episodes are displaced and decontextualized into what the narrator calls a "documentary daydream." Yet a kind of implicit power is amplified by the montage of multiple possible relationships within the scenes: a softball game in Hyde Park, religious mystics dancing around a bonfire in Wales, an

Hawaiian hippy playing his guitar in the London Underground, menacing thugs in a country mansion on the rainy patio of which a deserted TV sits under an umbrella receiving Apollo 15 pictures from the moon; a Corsican montage featuring an international seminar on ecology; the rocks at Stonehenge; bombers taking off from a U.S. Air Force base; a Vietnam deserter in an unplaced room talking with a Marxist revolutionary; a suitcase slowly packed; a bridge; hands laying out TNT; fingers dismantling a kitchen timer; people with black faces and white hair, stray objects, bits of music and voices for "the times we live in." Though lacking a specific political context, the film in the eyes of the narrator was "lurking on the margins of some unstable, implicit ground that might well shiver into revolution." And though he wanted to show "American and England in some dream of action and peace . . . through all the scenes mingling England and America and deliberately unplacing the scenes, there was the cool theme of America itself" (70). America, then, as a place of dislocation, decontextualization, disassociation.

In his search for an answer to the question of what about or in the film poses such a danger that he finds himself at risk, Cartwright—and the reader with him—plunges into an informational labyrinth from which there seems to be no exit. What finally counts, however, is not *why* things happen but *how* they are always intricated with reciprocal influences; indeed, in the complex interactions of sub-systems and interlacing networks of people, powers, and technologies—"in the great multiple field of impinging informations" as Cartwright refers to it—Aristotelian categories of agent, act and object break down into a field of mutually implicative force relations and interference patterns. This is true of the "push" that Cartwright receives in the subway which resonates with other events, as well as of the strange deaths of Jim and Krish, where the victim participates as actively as the killer. And by the end of the novel the destroyed film has become a precipitate of Cartwright's own accumulating power, as he learns to tap into and poach on the various powers whose vested interests in the film force them to reckon with his own position of "betweenness."

Gaddis's portrayal of Wall Street and the manipulations of finance capital in *JR* plunges us into yet another kind of "novelistic space," one constructed entirely out of fragmented conversations among scarcely identified characters. Here the narrative and scenic connections must be supplied by the reader, who thereby acts against the implicit "entropic flux" of the characters' failing attempts to communicate. The central "story" concerns the meteoric growth and collapse of a financial holding company—the JR Family of Companies—headed by a tenaciously greedy 11-year-old, but the reader is mostly occupied with an unfolding multiplicity of *little* stories detailing the failure and wreckage of most of the minor characters. In this subversion of a credible central narrative amidst a total fragmentation of speech, *JR* illustrates Lyotard's contention that today "narrative is being dispersed in clouds of narrative language elements" (Lyotard, xxiv). Furthermore, by deliberately reducing his novel to the medium of recorded speech, Gaddis produces what may be most accurately described as an acoustic collage. It is formed out of the discourses of advertising, big business politics and public relations, the slang of school kids and street people, the ruminations of drunken intellectuals and failed artists, the bitter reproaches of divorcing couples and lovers in turmoil, with all these registered "sounds" fading into and becoming barely distinguishable from the general background noise of our multi-media environment. The elimination of overt narrative filiation also enhances the effect of montage: all is flow—money, finance capital, video images, water, conversation, a radio playing, one scene or character impinging on another. As we are whirled from one node of connection to another—from an old family house in Long Island to a local school, then to the local bank, then to a Wall Street investment firm, and finally to an upper Eastside Manhattan apartment—it becomes clear that no overriding, stabilizing speech will be heard, indeed *could* be heard, no identifiable consciousness could be in control, ever take it all in.

In short, the novel relentlessly demonstrates that it is not production or intelligibility but the ceaseless movement and proliferation of useless objects and information that defines our world; amidst which, every human act becomes an impossible balancing act, a brief and tenuous assertion of order, and breakdown—especially the human kind—occurs where flows are impeded or turned back against themselves. This is most evident when the characters attempt to speak with intelligible purpose and coherent intention, for language in this world is not only jargoned and redundant, but has been reduced to a medium of exchange commensurate with the flux of capital itself, which is to say to a form commensurate with "information theory." In such a state "meaning" is recognizable only as a tic, an idiolect, an idiosyncracy, an archaic effect only incidental to the exchange process—whether communicational or economic. Since the reduction of human reality to the organization of information in communication theory is already a symptom of the furthest abstraction and "deterritorialization" of a sign or language system, Gaddis's fictional strategy enables him to depict the destabilizing and entropic effects of capitalism at *its* furthest point of deterritorialization, simply by reproducing the characters' speech acts in all their fluid incoherence and redundancy.[3]

Whereas *JR* is concerned with information flow and the entropic flux that beset the isolated individual, *Ratner's Star* bathes in the pure and rarefied air of mathematical and scientific concepts. The novel poses the problem of how these concepts relate to the quirks and absurd antics of the scientists and thinkers who invent and manipulate them, as well as to the phylum of singularities from which we derive our notions of space and time, matter and energy. It proceeds by means of replication and implication: the narrative doubles the adventures of Lewis Carroll's Alice in the contemporary and more "realistic" setting of a "think-tank" in the desert, with a Nobel-prize winning boy genius of mathematics as the protagonist. The recurrence of boomerang shapes and holes (black holes, "moholes" and holes in the earth) is motivated by the novel's interest in topography but also links its sections together in odd metaphorical patterns. Similarly, the hermeneutic question that initiates the plot (how to decode a message from outer space) induces a series of what seem to be implicative relationships among the languages of mathematics, logic, science fiction, and babbling, as if one language game, in reaching its limit, is transformed simultaneously into another.

Which all suggests that *Ratner's Star* is not so much concerned with the madness and absurdity concealed behind the apparent rationality of scientific thinking as with an altogether different image of thought: thought conceived as being at least as peculiar as that which it attempts to account for, or interact with. As the novel's plot moves toward an inversion of the quest that propels it—the signal from outer space turns out to have originated on earth—the latter is re-conceived as a "mohole," a void core or multi-dimensional negative energy state theorized by Orang Mohole, Nobel laureate of alternative physics. Almost simultaneously, Maurice Wu, an archeologist and explorer of bat caves, discovers evidence of a civilization as advanced as our own that mysteriously regressed, perhaps as the result of a nuclear catastrophe. And the message itself, decoded by the boy mathematician Billy Twillig, indicates a particular time at which something momentous will happen, perhaps a repetition or a return of *the* event, as if the Big Band theory also applied to civilizations and was about to be re-enacted.

Ratner's Star thus stages an implosion of knowledge, treats scientific and mathematical theory as a kind of pataphysics (as indeed it is), and suggests that our models invented to explain reality have completely displaced that reality. Finally, in this novelistic version of what Baudrillard calls "simulation" and "Moebius-spiralling negativity," thought appears as a special kind of event, anonymous and impersonal, propagating effects that suddenly take on their own force as they resonate through different domains, both human and non-human. These effects, in fact, are exactly what the novel seeks to register, in all their multiplicity and strangeness.

In various ways all of these novels are interested in provoking new images of thought, and exploring some of the new paths along which contemporary thinking is moving. In most readings of *Gravity's Rainbow* paranoia and Pynchon's "vision of modern history" have served as the most common foci of interpretation. But the concepts the novel itself proposes, concepts like "mapping on," interface, and "the zone," as Pynchon's narrator designates the arena of contemporary consciousness, would seem to offer a more fruitful approach. These concepts take for granted the de-centering or "unselving" of the subject that the novel performs and therefore should provide the basis for readings more aligned with the novel's own articulations. Similarly, the mental landscapes and methods of narration in *Lookout Cartridge* call for an approach that departs from the privileged access accorded to cartography and feed-back systems, and the structural—not just thematic—role that they play. In *JR* the multiple networks linking characters, events and items of information proliferate both more quickly and more extensively, since their registration no longer depends upon the operations of a central consciousness. What the novel requires of the reader is an unremitting attentiveness to the disorderings and re-orderings that ceaselessly emerge and interweave out of the flux of contemporary experience; what it provides is a sharpened awareness of the conceptual limits of such popularized notions as entropy and information theory as they are applied to our multimedia environment.

If all four novels explore new ways of thinking in and about the postmodern world, especially as conceived and represented in the generally unfamiliar terms of physics, mathematics, technology and systems theory, it is because this world presents itself specifically as a multiplicity of forces and relations that can no longer be mastered by a centered subject nor even represented by conventional novelistic forms. In this sense these novels clearly participate in the epistemological crisis that marks our era. At the same time, they are not interested in proving by negative example how older styles of thinking prove inadequate to contemporary experience; instead, they adumbrate organizations of our experience more in keeping with the altered notions of temporality and spatiality, order and disorder, that contemporary science now urges upon us. Of course, in recent years the traditional image of modern science itself has undergone what appear to be radical changes, to the extent that some have begun to employ the phrase "postmodern science." (I am thinking here of the new image of science as it emerges in such diverse works as Paul Feyerabend's *Against Method* and *Farewell to Reason*, Stephen Toulmin's *The Return to Cosmology: Postmodern Science and the Theology of Nature*, Ilya Prigogine and Isabelle Stengers's *Order Out of Chaos*, and most recently, James Gleick's *Chaos: Making a New Science*.) If these four novels form part of the same cultural "moment," it is not because they present equivalents in the "literary" sphere, but rather because they challenge received notions about how the elaboration of aesthetic form in a fully contemporary milieu can itself become the occasion for new images of thought.

Notes

1. I owe the discovery of this example to John Frow's *Marxism and Literary History* (Cambridge, Mass.: Harvard University Press, 1986) where it is discussed in relation to theories of textuality.

2. The epistemological validity of Pynchon's historical claims is discussed by Thomas S. Smith in his essay "Performing in the Zone: The Presentation of Historical Crisis in *Gravity's Rainbow*," *Cho*, 12 (1982–83), pp. 245–260.

3. "Deterritorialization" is a concept developed by Deleuze and Guattari in *Anti-Oedipus* and *A Thousand Plateaus* to describe the inevitable dismantling of all traditional codes

in the growth and expansion of capitalism into all aspects of life. Their theory proposes that the primordial flux of desire is produced and coded (given form and meaning) by means of and in relation to a semiotic regime and a territory. In primitive regimes this primary coding is inscribed on the body, in dance, ritual and myth in multiple and non-hierarchical forms, and takes as its ultimate referential territory the body of the earth itself. In barbaric regimes signs undergo a "paranoid" reorganization and "overcoding" through constant (re)interpretation by a priest class, as certain signifiers are centered and become privileged over others, and the ultimate territory becomes the body of the despot or monarch himself. In civilized or capitalist society these archaic and traditional codings are progressively undone or decoded in a process of release and abstraction in which everything of value is such only because of its relation to capital. Thus, in the capitalist regime, there is no longer any corresponding territory except for the "deterritorialized" body of capital itself.

Works Cited

Barth, John "The Literature of Replenishment," *Atlantic Monthly*, Jan. 1980, 65–71.

Baudrillard, Jean. *Simulations*. New York: Semiotext(e), 1983.

Deleuze, Gilles. *Difference et repetition*. Paris: Presses Universitaires de France, 1968.

———. "On Several Regimes of Signes" and "Micropolitics and Segmentarity," in *A Thousand Plateaus*, co-authored with Felix Guattari (Minneapolis: University of Minnesota Press, 1987), pp. 111–148, 208–231.

———. "Platon et le simulacre," in *Loqique du sens*. Paris: Editions de Minuit, 1969.

Foster, Hal. Ed. *The Anti-Aesthetic: Essays on Postmodern Culture*. Port Townsend, Washington: Bay Press, 1983.

Heidegger, Martin. "The Age of the World Picture," in *The Question Concerning Technology*. Trans. William Lovitt. New York: Harper and Row, 1977.

Huyssen, Andreas. "Mapping the Postmodern," *New German Critique* No. 33 (Fall 1984): 5–52.

Jameson, Fredric. "Postmodernism, or the Cultural Logic of Late Capitalism," *New left Review* 146 (July/August 1984): 53–92.

———. "The Politics of Theory: Ideological Positions in the Postmodernism Debate," *New German Critique*. No. 33 (Fall 1984): 53–65.

Jardine, Alice A. *Gynesis: Configurations of Woman and Modernity*. Ithaca and London: Cornell University Press, 1985.

Laplanche, J. and J. B. Pontalis. *The Language of Pyschoanalysis*. Trans. Donald Nicholson Smith. New York: W. W. Norton, 1973.

Lyotard, Jean-Francois. *The Postmodern Condition: A Report on Knowledge*. Trans. Geoff Bennington and Brian Massumi. Minnesota: University of Minnesota Press, 1984.

McElroy, Joseph. *Lookout Cartridge*. New York: Knopf, 1974.

Attenuated Postmodernism:
Pynchon's *Vineland*

David Cowart

Thomas Pynchon, creator of the most significant body of fiction in contemporary America, may have spent some of the last 17 years discovering the limits of the postmodernist aesthetic. *Vineland*, his long-awaited fourth novel, appears 17 years after the publication in 1973 of the monumental *Gravity's Rainbow*, widely recognized now as the most important American novel published since World War II. One naturally asks whether this author's art has developed or stagnated over those 17 years. The bad news: Pynchon has made no effort to surpass *Gravity's Rainbow*. The good news: he has not stood still as a maker of fiction. In *Vineland*, which may represent a turning point for Pynchon, the author keeps his hand in, modifying some of his old tricks and trying out new ones. In a consideration of this novel's traditional and contemporary features, one encounters an evolutionary text, an experiment in literary hybridization. Conceding that the postures of literary exhaustion may themselves be exhausted, the author combines modernist concerns and postmodernist techniques with some of the features of two kinds of realism: social and magic. The following essay, while scrutinizing the vestiges of a style of aesthetic that Pynchon seems to be outgrowing, will glance at the Abish-like question, *how postmodern is it?*, in the course of gauging the traditional elements and fresh invention that compose this hybrid. The argument here, introduced in a brief comparison of Pynchon's career with that of Joyce, will focus on technique and the treatment given history and culture (including myth). The author of *Vineland* views these topics through a postmodern lens: they appear foreshortened, flattened, all surface. Yet the novel's title and its mythic extension of contemporary history hint at a broader view. Though Pynchon tends to deconstruct the myths he invokes, they complicate the rendering of an otherwise comprehensively ahistorical contemporaneity. Through a combination of this eccentric mythography with a moral earnestness expressed as a penchant for political didacticism,

Reprinted from *Critique: Studies in Contemporary Fiction* 32 (Winter 1990): 67–76, with permission of the Helen Dwight Reid Educational Foundation. Published by Heldref Publications, 1319 Eighteenth St., N.W., Washington, D.C. 20036-1802. Copyright © 1990.

Pynchon produces, in *Vineland*, a fiction devoted less to indeterminate post-modernist "play" than to totalizing modernist "purpose."[1]

On the face of it, Pynchon's is the definitive postmodern career. In book after book, he has seemed to be Bloom's "strong poet," creatively misreading his modernist forebears. Indeed, a comparison of his work with that of Joyce, a literary father to generate considerable anxiety, reveals some interesting parallels. With the exception of the late sport *Slow Learner*, Pynchon's 1984 collection of early stories, the fiction-publishing careers of these two writers match up, volume for volume. Joyce's first book-length fiction appeared in 1914, his fourth and last 25 years later, in 1939. Pynchon's first novel and his fourth span a nearly identical period: the 26 years from 1963 to 1989. In the space of exactly a quarter of a century, each of these writers has given his age its gold standard in fiction, the one defining modernism in the novel, the other postmodernism. Yet the two careers move toward an instructive divergence.

The early volumes of Joyce appeared within two years of each other; those of Pynchon, within three. Joyce's first book, *Dubliners* (1914), is a meticulously structured set of linked fictions that anatomize a culture. Pynchon's *V.* (1963), a highly episodic and fragmented novel that at least one early reviewer (Meixner) took to be a congeries of cobbled together pieces of collegiate creative writing courses, is also meticulously structured, also a cultural anatomy. *Dubliners* moves toward a final vision of snowy paralysis, *V.* toward the triumph of the inanimate. *V.* was followed in 1966 by *The Crying of Lot 49*, in which the failure of American promise gradually manifests itself to a protagonist, Oedipa Maas, whose age (28 in 1964, the novel's present), education (Cornell), and places of travel and residence (Mexico and California) seem to make her a female Thomas Pynchon. A kind of oblique spiritual autobiography or conversion narrative, *Lot 49* is Pynchon's portrait of the artist in youth and, as such, corresponds to Joyce's autobiographical novel, *A Portrait of the Artist as a Young Man* (1916).

The seven-year period between *Lot 49* (1966) and *Gravity's Rainbow* (1973) corresponds to the six-year period between *Portrait* (1916) and *Ulysses* (1922). *Gravity's Rainbow* and *Ulysses* are quests, "encyclopedic" fictions that, epic in scope, catalogue whole cultures with broad attention to the literary and historical past. Each is, in its own way, a strange amalgam of family romance and Telemachiad: Stephen Dedalus discovers a father in Leopold Bloom, Tyrone Slothrop in the evil scientist Dr. Lazslo Jamf. Stephen, of course, is Joyce's autobiographical character, and perhaps one recognizes a further element of autobiography in the Pynchon novel too, in asmuch as it concerns a person who, like the author, simply fades from sight after embarking on a quest that makes him the "Zone's newest celebrity" (377) and brings him face to face with the possibility that Western culture "might be in love, in sexual love" (738), with its own death.

As the years went by after *Gravity's Rainbow*, one wondered whether its successor would, unimaginably, sustain the Joycean parallel. What complex, Viconian meditation, its hour come round at last, slouched toward Little, Brown to be born? In what idiom would it be written—would it be dense with Herero and Maltese portmanteau words? Pynchon's fourth novel was announced for early in 1990, but it was actually in the bookstores in late December of 1989. In terms of the paradigm, both dates are significant. The earlier is the 50th anniversary of the publication, in 1939, of *Finnegans Wake*, which appeared 17 years after Joyce's previous novel, *Ulysses*. The year 1990, of course, marks the same 17-year period since the publication of Pynchon's last novel, *Gravity's Rainbow*.

But the parallel falters: *Vineland* is not the postmodern *Finnegans Wake*. At most one can say that Vineland County, California, is as mythic a landscape as "Howth Castle and Environs" and the River Liffey. One can note, too, that Leif Ericson, who gave America its first name and Pynchon his title, is among the innumerable strands in the weave of the *Wake*: "lief eurekason and his undishcovery of americle" (326). But these are frail and exiguous crossties for continuing the parallel rails laid thus far. The breakdown in the parallels suggests that the fate reserved for Pynchon's aesthetic differs radically from that reserved for Joyce's. Modernism, it seems, was fated to end with a bang, postmodernism with a whimper.

Though *Finnegans Wake* announced a new aesthetic in its structure— that of a giant Mobius strip—and in its parodic features (it burlesques the medieval dream vision), it is, first and last, the supreme modernist text. Like its modernist predecessors, it exploits myth, probes consciousness and its mysterious subsurface, and outrages aesthetic sensibility in a prose and structure of consummate "difficulty" (to use Eliot's unpretentious word). The parody, like that of *Ulysses*, is reconstructive rather than deconstructive. If like other modernist works it holds a mirror up to cultural fragmentation (it was published on the eve of the century's climacteric, World War II), it composes the fragments artistically, for the program of modernism, however iconoclastic, was always some kind of cultural reclamation.

But postmodernism has no such pretensions. It was always a holding action, a "literature of exhaustion," self-canceling in its most basic premises. Parody and replication in postmodern literature exist to underscore the death of the author and to allow an extra season or two to exhausted forms. In Jean-François Lyotard's formulation, postmodern literature "puts forward the unpresentable in presentation itself" (81). A literature largely about itself and its own strategies of re-presentation, it perennially enacts the universal semiotic law: there is no "'transcendental signified" behind the arbitrary signifiers—presence is infinitely deferred. The postmodern aesthetic, like signification itself, is a house of cards, and it seems naturally to exhaust itself at a faster rate than other literary movements. Thus the literary apotheosis toward which modernism moves (in a number of texts) is not available to postmodernism, and thus *Vineland* corresponds not to *Finnegans Wake* but to the new literary start Joyce did not live to undertake.

Vineland does not seem to be "self-reflexive" in the approved contemporary manner—a manner that, in all three of his previous novels, Pynchon has shown he can execute brilliantly. But it features at least a few of the quarterings of a postmodern pedigree. It relies heavily on parody, for example, and it favors historical surface to historical depth. It also resists the hierarchization of culture. This refusal to differentiate high culture from low, like the attention to surfaces, is a prominent feature of postmodernist aesthetics. The denial of authority, in all its senses, means the deconstructing of high culture's pretensions to that authority. Thus Pynchon can imagine Pee Wee Herman starring in *The Robert Musil Story* (370). Thus, too, in the multiple parody in *Vineland*—of Ninja fictions, television soap operas, espionage novels, and detective thrillers—Pynchon tends to minimize the "critical distance" that, according to parody theorist Linda Hutcheon, commonly accompanies the specific type of "repetition" that is parodic (6).

Where he does not parody popular culture, he catalogues it. What is remarkable is that, in contrast to his previous practice, he catalogues little else. He systematically denies himself the usual resources of allusion in its full range. In fact, he limits himself to one compound literary allusion and a couple of musical allusions. Only the literary reference—to an Emerson quotation in William James—is presented seriously. Both musical allusions, on the other hand, are comically undercut. When Prairie starts to learn about her mother from Darryl Louise Chastain, she appropriately hears music from *Tosca*, for the tale she will hear concerns the suffering of her Tosca-like mother and the Scarpia-like Brock Vond. But the music is played by a pseudo-Italian band at a Mafia wedding. Similarly, in the novel's elegiac conclusion, an entire Thanatoid village awakens to the strains of Bach's "*Wachet Auf*," evidently with the chorale's powerfully suggestive opening line intended to come to mind: "*Wachet auf, ruft uns die Stimme.*" The music materializes as a "piping, chiming music, synchronized, coming out of wristwatches, timers, and personal computers, engraved long ago, as if for this moment, on sound chips dumped once in an obscure skirmish of the silicon market wars . . . as part of a settlement with the ever-questionable trading company of Tokkata & Fuji" (324–25).

Normally this author peppers his fictions with references that establish historical depth as well as cultural breadth, and readers have marveled at his ability to evoke, in *V.*, turn-of-the-century Alexandria, Florence, or South-West Africa, not to mention, in *Gravity's Rainbow*, the places and feel of much of Europe in 1944 and 1945. These evocations of place and time have generally involved a considerable body of cultural allusion, both high and low. Even in *Lot 49*, where the California setting is not particularly congenial to evocations of high art, one finds painting, literature, music, and film to be important features of the fictional landscape. But through a kind of *askesis* (to "misread" a term of Harold Bloom's), Pynchon here dispenses with the high-culture allusion almost entirely.

Meanwhile the density of reference to the ephemera of popular culture is almost numbing. Pynchon refers often to movies, as in *Gravity's Rainbow*, but here he neglects historic films and art cinema in favor of *Gidget, Dumbo, 20,000 Years in Sing Sing, The Hunchback of Notre Dame, Godzilla, King of the Monsters, Friday the 13th, Return of the Jedi*, and *Ghostbusters. Psycho* and *2001: A Space Odyssey* are the most substantial films mentioned. The author helpfully supplies dates for these films, parodying scholarly practice, and he invents a number of droll film biographies, including *The Frank Gorshin Story*, with Pat Sajak, and *Young Kissinger*, with Woody Allen. Even more insistently jejune are the allusions to the titles, characters, stars, and music of such television programs as *Star Trek, The Brady Bunch, Gilligan's Island, Jeopardy, Wheel of Fortune, I Love Lucy, Green Acres, Smurfs, CHiPs, Superman*, and *Bionic Woman*. This depressing litany—the intellectual horizon of the American mass mind—subsumes less obvious manifestations of popular taste as well: mall culture, "roasts," video and computer games, new wave hairstyles, breakfast cereals, even " 'sensitivity' greeting cards" (38). Pynchon's intent here is not entirely satiric, for no doubt he is genuinely fond of much popular culture. In the introduction to *Slow Learner*, he declares that "rock 'n' roll will never die" (23), and the sentiment is shared by the founders of the People's Republic of Rock and Roll, who name their new state "after the one constant they knew they could count on never to die" (209). Perhaps, too, Pynchon wishes to eschew cultural elitism and demonstrate solidity with the masses. But the virtual absence of historical depth in this body of allusion makes a devastating statement about the shortness of the American cultural memory. This, ultimately, is the point of his constant allusion to the signs and texts of popular culture. Pynchon denies himself much of the cultural and historical dimension of the previous novels and commits himself to imagining the relentlessly ahistorical consciousness of contemporary American society. The implicit judgment of this shallowness, finally, reveals a moral dimension—always in fact an element in Pynchon's work—that distances this author from the moral neutrality or nihilism sometimes alleged to be the postmodern norm.

Unlike the world he describes, Pynchon himself has an acute sense of history that also leavens his brand of postmodernism. His historical consciousness reveals itself in the guise of that universal history called myth. If the myths invoked in *Vineland* coexist uneasily at the edge of a mutually deconstructive exclusivity, they nevertheless provide the story's action with a temporal depth: they render it "historical" in spite of itself. Thus Terrence Rafferty does not err when he observes that "American history plays itself out" in the bed of Brock Vond and Frenesi Gates (109). The play of myth, then, circumvents the nominally ahistorical vision in *Vineland*.

One can sometimes differentiate modernists from postmodernists in their treatment of myth—where modernists exploit myth as universal, instinctual truth, their successors either deconstruct myth as an unreliable "metanarrative" (the breakdown of metanarratives, says Lyotard, is the ground for "the postmodern condition" [xxiv, 34–35, 37]) or examine it as a language that, like all language, speaks its speakers rather than the other way around. Pynchon, as Kathryn Hume demonstrates in *Pynchon's Mythography*, has never divorced himself entirely from the modernist position on myth; and in *Vineland* he has it both ways—privileging at least one myth, deconstructing at least two others. The Faust myth, for example, seems to function in a fairly conventional manner: the federal prosecutor is Mephistopheles; film-making Frenesi is Faust. Yet the myth and the mythical identities prove unstable. The Faust here is also an Eve in the American Eden who betrays her Adam, the hapless Weed Atman. The Mephisto figure, Brock Vond, is also the serpent who tempts them to a fall and a primal murder. These two myths, however, are not at odds, for Faust's passion merely updates that of Adam and Eve. The stories contain the same elements: a diabolical tempter and human souls reaching for forbidden knowledge. But Pynchon complicates matters by introducing, through Sister Rochelle, a *mise en abyme*: a subversive, feminist version of the Eden myth with Frenesi and DL as the primal Eve and Lilith in an Eden in which "the first man . . . was the serpent" (166). This revision of the story seems a minor detail in the novel, and perhaps one at first disregards or discounts it in the desire for a totalizing version of a cherished American literary myth. But its seeming insignificance reveals the deconstructive point: it is one of the aporias around which at least one weave of meaning begins to unravel.

Feminism, by its very nature, is deconstructive—it locates the aporias in the "phallogocentric" discourse of patriarchy. In *Vineland*, the familiar myth undergoes a twofold feminist deconstruction: the patriarchal version of the myth is undercut once by Sister Rochelle's version—and again by the mythic action as Pynchon shapes it. For the mythic individual who makes the moral choice (traditionally an Adam in American fictions: Hawkeye, Huckleberry Finn, Isaac McCaslin) is the American Eve, Frenesi Gates. *Vineland*, then, is a surprisingly "writerly" text: it invites its reader to grapple with closure-resistant, open, multivalent myths that self-de(con)struct under the instruments of analysis.

Yet *Vineland* retains a myth that its author celebrates rather than deconstructs. Pynchon's setting is a representation of the American land; and he refuses to surrender the myth of American promise, which he seems to construe in terms of some continuing, provisional validity of a leftist political alternative to contemporaneous conservatism. The novel's title announces the mythic ground. It evokes more than the California setting and reputation for viniculture. The author situates the imaginary town that gives the novel its name up near the California border with Oregon, and he expects the reader to make the nominal connection with a town on the other side of the continent. The latitude of the real Vineland—Vineland, New Jersey—pretty much coincides with that of the imagined California "Vineland the Good" (322), haven for immigrants like Zoyd Williams and others like him. This implied spanning of the continent at the latitude of its greatest breadth jibes with the novel's symbolic detail to suggest that Pynchon's setting is really the whole vast tract that the Vikings discovered and named Vineland at the end of the first millenium. Thus the title of Pynchon's new novel, published at the end of the second millenium, reminds his American readers that their land has been known to history now for exactly a thousand years.

The novel contains other miniaturized symbols of America. A central example is the People's Republic of Rock and Roll, symbolically the counter-culture America of the sixties, delirious with freedom, under surveillance, doomed, the Richard Nixon monolith at oceanside casting its shadow, an obvious symbol of repression to come. Perhaps, too, Zoyd Williams's house, of which he has been forcibly dispossessed by unconscionable federal power, is another such symbol. At the end, he is flirting with the idea of putting it to the torch—which America's dispossessed may yet do to the house they are unable fully to enter. As in *Lot 49*, Pynchon contemplates the paradoxes of dispossession and preterition in the land of promise. "How had it ever happened here," wonder Oedipa Maas in that earlier novel, "with the chances once so good for diversity?" (181).

Vineland, then, is a meditation on the American social reality, a return to the ground Pynchon seems to think he did not cover adequately in *Lot 49* (he remarks in the introduction to *Slow Learner* that he thinks his second novel merely a long story, not technically accomplished). Though *Vineland* is not *Lot 49* redivivus, one notes points of contact—most obviously the California setting—between the two. In the earlier novel the heroine, Oedipa Maas, meets a member of the Paranoids, an aspiring rock group, and offers to give her DJ husband, Mucho, a tape to plug. Now the reader learns that Mucho "after a divorce remarkable even in that more innocent time for its geniality" (309), has become a successful recording industry executive (like V.'s Rooney Winsome)—and that he has shepherded Miles, Dean, Serge, and Leonard to success.

But where is Oedipa in the new novel? Oedipa realizes at the end of *Lot 49* that the only way she can go on being relevant to her country is "as an alien, unfurrowed, assumed full circle into some paranoia" (182). The heroine of the new novel, Frenesi Gates, is a version of that new, desperate Oedipa—estranged from a man with a Dutch surname and living a furtive, underground existence. Oedipa seems a less flawed person than Frenesi, but both characters are symbols of the American conscience—radicalized in the sixties, coopted in the eighties. The two novels also explore the significance of drug use. In *Lot 49*, Oedipa does not perceive Mucho's involvement with LSD as positive, but it does link him to the marginalized Americans she will come to embrace. In the later novel, the reader learns that Mucho proceeded to addict himself to cocaine before giving up drugs altogether. Mucho's addiction and the horrors, however comic, of the "Room of the Bottled Specimens" (310) are among the book's few concessions that there might be a down side to drug use. But Mucho becomes an entrepreneur as he goes straight—and his entrepreneurism makes him suspect in Pynchon's economy. Here one glimpses the equation that partially accounts for Pynchon's somewhat disturbing refusal to depict drugs in a negative light: taking drugs (as opposed, perhaps, to dealing them) remains a powerful metaphor for the idea of an alternative to the rapacious capitalism and consumerism that afflict American society.

One sees a more meaningful contrast between these books in their handling of history. Oddly, it is the book with ostensibly the more shallow historical draft—*Vineland*, with its one-generation memory—that reveals its author as truly concerned about the way the present evolves out of the past. In *Lot 49*, several hundred years of history are the means to make Oedipa's quest interesting and complicated, but this past is only superficially imagined as accounting for her American present (Oedipa's historical research serves the epistemological theme—the infinite reticulation of "paranoid" interconnectedness—rather than the sociological one that links her story to Frenesi's). In *Vineland*, by contrast, Pynchon again examines the American present, but with specific reference to a recent—and radically different—past. This equipoise between sixties and eighties keeps *Vineland* from being the simple-minded exercise in nostalgia some have taken it for. Far from the sour grapes of some bitter ex-hippie, it is a treatise on the direction history has taken, without our having given it much thought. Moreover, his own implicit political orientation notwithstanding, Pynchon exposes the millenarian canker in the flower children as rigorously as he diagnoses the reactionary carcinoma of the next generation. *Lot 49*, set in 1964, is a story of consciousness being raised—an allegory of sixties America repudiating conformity, racism, and militarism. It looks backward to the Eisenhower fifties and forward to the Summer of Love. *Vineland*, set a generation later in the portentous year of 1984, looks backward to that summer—and forward to some Republican version of the thousand-year Reich. It reveals how the nation has allowed an earlier passion for justice to go dead, to be coopted by a conservative backlash and an attendant dissipation of liberal energy.

In a single generation—from the mid-sixties to the mid-eighties, America veered from a liberal to a conservative bias, from the New Frontier and the Great Society to "Reaganomics," from hordes of student demonstrators to whole undergraduate populations majoring in business, from Yippies to Yuppies. In *Vineland* Pynchon examines these societal extremes and the historical currents they ride or embody. Interestingly contemporaneous with David Lodge's *Nice Work*, a refitting of the nineteenth-century "condition-of-England" novel, *Vineland* would seem in its hybridization also to undertake such an old-fashioned assessment. It is a condition-of-America novel. That condition, as a result of the Reagan revolution and, before that, the "Nixonian Repression" (71) or "Nixonian Reaction" (239), is imagined as darkening, a "prefascist twilight" (371), if not the actual night. "Nixon had machinery for mass detention all in place and set to go," says a Pynchon character. "Reagan's got it for when he invades Nicaragua" (264). The "Reagan program" is to "dismantle the New Deal, reverse the effects of World War II, restore fascism at home and around the world" (265).

Pynchon makes his political sympathies plain enough. But the polemics have little do to with the novel's art, which one sees in the indirection and economy that deliver this and other Pynchon works from the realm of propaganda and didacticism. This author's art—an art far superior, it seems to me, to that of such novelists on the left as Dos Passos or Steinbeck or Vonnegut—commands the aesthetic interest of readers who may find the politics somewhat overwrought. Pynchon contrives, by diving into the wreck of mythic metanarrative, to imbue with extraordinary historical resonance a story that ostensibly depicts the vitiation of the historical sense. He remains the only contemporary writer whose grasp of history's mythic dimensions merits comparison with that of Joyce—and he may yet present us with a fiction on the scale of that writer's last book. One doubts that he spent the seventeen years after *Gravity's Rainbow* on *Vineland* alone. Who knows what post-postmodern extravaganza may follow in its wake?

Note

1. These terms are among those proposed by Ihab Hassan in his tabular differentiation of modernism and postmodernism (91–92). I am indebted to Spiros Papleacos for bringing this book to my attention.

Works Cited

Hassan, Ihab. *The Postmodern Turn: Essays in Postmodern Theory and Culture.* Columbus, Ohio: Ohio State U P, 1987.

Hume, Kathryn. *Pynchon's Mythography.* Carbondale, Illinois: Southern Illinois U P, 1987.

Hutcheon, Linda. *A Theory of Parody: The Teachings of Twentieth-Century Art Forms.* New York: Methuen, 1985.

Joyce, James. *Finnegans Wake.* New York: Viking, 1958.

Lyotard, Jean-Francois. *The Postmodern Condition: A Report on Knowledge.* Trans. Geoff Bennington and Brian Massumi. Minneapolis: U of Minnesota P, 1984.

Meixner, John A. "The All-Purpose Quest." *Kenyon Review* 25 (Autumn 1963), 729–35.

Pynchon, Thomas. *The Crying of Lot 49.* New York: Lippincott, 1966.

———. *Gravity's Rainbow.* New York: Viking, 1973.

———. *Slow Learner.* New York: Little, Brown, 1984.

———. *Vineland.* New York: Little, Brown, 1990.

Rafferty, Terrence. "Long Lost." *The New Yorker,* February 19, 1990, 108–112.

Hebrew/Greek, Ear/Eye, Moral/Aesthetic: Susan Sontag's Bridging the "Archaic Gap"

STACEY OLSTER

In the piece on Elias Canetti that concludes her collection of essays, *Under the Sign of Saturn*, Susan Sontag calls attention to "the archaic gap between Hebrew as opposed to Greek culture, ear culture as opposed to eye culture, and the moral versus the aesthetic" (196).[1] Yet Sontag's concern with this gap appears as a refrain in her essays from the very beginning of her career. Indeed, at the same time that she was jettisoning artistic elitism by propounding happenings that lodged "a protest against the museum conception of art—the idea that the job of the artist is to make things to be preserved and cherished" (*Against*, 268) and prompting readers to consider "other creative sensibilities besides the seriousness (both tragic and comic) of high culture" in her campaign for camp (*Against*, 286), she adamantly refused to sanction artistic utilitarianism, what she called "putting art to use." "A work of art encountered as a work of art is an experience," she maintained, "not a statement or an answer to a question. . . . A work of art is a thing *in* the world, not just a text or commentary *on* the world" (*Against*, 21). That anyone should expect otherwise she traced to "the historic Western confusion about the relation between art and morality, the aesthetic and the ethical" (*Against*, 23). But the frequency with which she has returned to that very confusion—opening her book on photography, for instance, by tracing its own origins to "*some of the problems, aesthetic and moral, posed by the omnipresence of photographed images*"[2]—suggests that the ambivalence she ascribed to Western culture is a chronic condition from which she herself has suffered. What evolves in her writing over the years is the balance she accords the different polarities. Having begun her career by extolling taste as the most decisive thing that "governs every free—as opposed to rote—human response" (*Against*, 276), she, with "more historical flesh on my bones," could remark a decade later that "my understanding of the moral services that works of art perform is less abstract than it was in 1965."[3] With the passing of almost two more decades adding still more flesh to her bones, she would finally write a novel in which she put her own realization to work. *The Volcano Lover*

This essay was written expressly for this volume and is published here for the first time.

reviews 1772 from the perspective of 1992 and replaces the outrageousness of Camp with the outrage of condemnation, based on Sontag's conviction that "taste is context, and the context had changed" (*Saturn*, 98).

Context itself, however, remains a constant for Sontag, whether the subject is the display of a photograph or the designation of an artistic movement. In fact, it is in Sontag's designating her own sensibilities with respect to modernism rather than the seemingly more appropriate postmodernism that context perhaps plays its most important role.[4] Less a phenomenon unique to her own times, modernism is for Sontag a movement whose traits she repeatedly traces back to previous centuries: the intrusion of low culture into high a practice in operation "at least since Baudelaire" ("Interview"), the replacement of events by their representations ("an old doubling of reality now") beginning with the 1839 invention of the camera (*AIDS*, 176), the promotion of the self as an image first evidenced by the romanticizing of the tubercular look in the late eighteenth and early nineteenth century (*Illness*, 29), even the refusal of culture critics who descend from Hegel and Marx to accept art as autonomous form constituting a reaction "little different in spirit from the great conservative critics of modernity who wrote in the 19th century such as Arnold, Ruskin, and Burckhardt" (*Against*, 90).

Yet even less a product of any discrete historical period, modernism is for Sontag a wholly relativistic phenomenon, characterized mainly by its reaction against whatever has become so entrenched in convention as to benumb the senses. Presuming "the history of forms is dialectical," Sontag envisions modernism as part of an evolutionary theory of art: "As types of sensibility become banal, boring, and are overthrown by their opposites, so forms in art are, periodically, exhausted. They become banal, unstimulating, and are replaced by new forms which are at the same time anti-forms" (*Against*, 180). Thus, one encounters the frequency with which she defines these new forms by negation: abstract painting "is the attempt to have, in the ordinary sense, no content," Pop Art has content so blatant that it "ends by being uninterpretable," Camp sensibility is "disengaged, depoliticized— or at least apolitical" (*Against*, 10, 277).

It is in large part the degree to which the anti-style constitutes what Sontag calls a "species of radicalism" and repudiates what has come before it that the artwork it characterizes is judged (*Styles*, 119): "the better the art, the more subversive it is of the traditional aims of art" (*Photography*, 127). At the same time, Sontag remains aware that defining modernity in terms of difference provides no guarantees of artistic direction. She therefore understands that a "radical position isn't necessarily a forward-looking position" (*Styles*, 119)—hence, the notable omission of the word "postmodernism" in her essays: when an anti-style like Camp may recycle more than refute, how can one distinguish pre- from post-? When its origins lie in the late seventeenth and early eighteenth centuries, who is to distinguish old from new (*Against*, 280)? Because she also remains aware that different cultures experience the historical conditions that promote particular kinds of art at different chronological periods, Sontag also recognizes the need to consider modernism in the plural in lieu of modernism as a monolithic singular. While she may see the production and consumption of images as satisfying one of the criteria that distinguish a society as modern, for instance, she understands that the preference for "the image to the thing, the copy to the original" that characterized Feuerbach's view of his society in 1843 may be a state of affairs a country like China, which Sontag visits one hundred and thirty years later, may not even now be approaching (*Photography*, 153).

Much of this theorizing is not unique to Sontag, of course, nor was it when it was originally published. If her 1964 "Against Interpretation" comments about exhausted artistic forms anticipate by three years the underlying premise of John Barth's "Literature of Exhaustion" essay, her 1967 "Aesthetics of Silence" remarks about "mood[s] of ultimacy" and "insupportable burden[s]" of artistic self-consciousness duplicate almost verbatim the phrases that permeate Barth's manifesto of the same year (*Styles*, 6, 14).[5] Sontag's particular contribution to the ongoing debate about modernism—past, present, and post—stems more from her insistence on sensory stimulation returning us to an experience of art defined primarily in terms of sensory pleasure: "For we are what we are able to see (hear, taste, smell, feel) even more powerfully and profoundly than we are what furniture of ideas we have stocked in our heads" (*Against*, 300). Not only would the shock therapy provided by Sontag's desired art counter the "massive sensory anesthesia" that those in the West have been undergoing since the Industrial Revolution (*Against*, 302), but, at best, it also would open up its audience's sensibilities to "meta-artistic activities" (*Styles*, 152). What it would not do, above all else, is assume moral positions, but strive for the kind of "sublime neutrality" (*Against*, 26) Sontag finds emblematized in artifacts as varied as Pop Art, which "blasts through the old imperative about taking a *position* toward one's subject matter" (*Against*, 229), and Artaud's theater, to which spectators go as they would to a dentist (*Saturn*, 36).

In this relationship between aesthetics and ethics, the issue for Sontag is not just one of different intentions or different degrees of efficacy, that "as not all works of art aim at educating and directing conscience, not all works of art which successfully perform a moral function greatly satisfy as art" (*Against*, 128), but one of fundamentally different ways of thinking. As she speculates, "perhaps it's the general tendency of aesthetic consciousness, when developed, to make judgments more complex and more highly qualified, while it's in the very nature of moral consciousness to be simplifying, even simplistic" (*Styles*, 217–18). But holding dual citizenship in the kingdom of conscience as well as the kingdom of consciousness, to give a slight twist to the opening of *Illness as Metaphor* (3), Sontag cannot help but see herself as responsive to both impulses. While certain that any position worth assuming is "a species of radicalism" (*Styles*, 119), she remains uncertain of what particular brand of radicalism she should adopt. Thus, the question she proposes that each artist ask, "What is *my* radicalism, the one dictated by *my* gifts and temperament?" (*Styles*, 119), remains one for which she herself cannot provide any definitive answer. Ambivalent about the nature of her own calling—or, more to the point, callings—Sontag ends up ambivalent about the relationship between aesthetics and ethics that naturally emanates from the multiplicity of those (often conflicting) roles. Two essays, written within six years of each other, illustrate the conundrums of her predicament quite clearly.

Nowhere is the tension of contradictory callings more apparent than in "Trip to Hanoi" (1968), within which Sontag the activist tries to convince Sontag the aesthete that the Vietnamese have an art worth idealizing. Unfortunately, the moralistic country she visits offers this self-described "Western neo-radical" (whatever that means) little in the way of aesthetic stimulation (*Styles*, 228), as indicated by her constant return to the uniformity that keeps impressing upon her how much "[e]verything is on one level here": words all "belong to the same vocabulary"; history is "one scenario, which has been played out over and over again"; the entire ambience is oppressively "monochromatic" (*Styles*, 216, 219, 218). Only by strenuous acts of intellectual calisthenics can Sontag convert aesthetic drab into the sensory dense: what the Vietnamese lack in complexity of art they make up for in the "ingenuity" that marks the art into which they turn daily life (*Styles*, 250, 253). Like the great modernists, from debris they fashion "materials for daily use," the debris coming from captured American planes, the "daily use" being that of self-defense. Like the noninterpretive formalists, they choose "directness and plainness" as "the rule when it comes to expressing something or making a gesture." Like the greatest Camp recyclers, they get the maximum mileage out of every available ounce of intellectual fuel: "As each material object must be made to go a long way, so must each idea" (*Styles*, 255–56). But apparently not far enough, for even Sontag remains unconvinced by her efforts at conversion and ends the essay by returning to the ambiguities of her position as "an American, an unaffiliated radical American, an American writer" (*Styles*, 271).

In contrast, "Fascinating Fascism" (1974), Sontag's essay on Leni Riefenstahl, complements the "Trip to Hanoi" skepticism about pure ethics with its own skepticism about pure aesthetics. Hardly her first critique of aestheticism, the essay extends an awareness of the dangers of retreating into pure aestheticism that Sontag found evidenced in a wide variety of disciplines from the very start of her career: anthropology's "vanquishing [its] subject by translating it into a purely formal code," especially Lévi-Strauss's structuralist codes that reduced mental activities to "fundamentally the same [process] for all minds, archaic and modern" (*Against*, 77, 79); the sci-fi film that turns disaster into spectacle, freeing its viewers to observe the end of the world with impunity (*Against*, 215); the photograph that neutralizes the very distress it conveys (*Photography*, 109); ultimately, the cultural revolution so self-reflexive and meta-artistic that it "has nowhere to go but toward a theology of culture—and a soteriology" (*Saturn*, 47). In addition, the essay on Riefenstahl testifies to Sontag's growing recognition of the greater power photographic formalism has over print: the essay deals not only with Riefenstahl's films, but with books that sell pictures of SS regalia as well. This power, in turn, derives from the greater power Sontag finds possessed by the photographic image itself over the word: it is, then, no coincidence that the criticism of Chinese communism she lodges elsewhere is couched in her criticism of the kind of photography practiced in China, in which "only some things are to be photographed and only in certain ways" by "a single, ideal observer" whose work so contributes to the "Great Monologue" that is Chinese politics (*Photography*, 177, 173). So preeminent a conveyor of images has photography become, in fact, that not only are referents divorced from the reality that generates them (like the "most photographed barn in America" in Don DeLillo's *White Noise*, which nobody can see because it has been photographed so much),[6] but reality is specifically generated for the purposes of engendering referents that will outlive it: as Sontag reminds us, the 1934 National Socialist Party Congress that *Triumph of the Will* chronicles was staged with the production of a film in mind (*Saturn*, 83).

Such preeminence certainly raises questions about Sontag's earlier espousal of film over the novel when detailing "the model arts of our time" to the degree that film's "much cooler mode of moral judgment" contrasts with the "heavy burden" contained within the novel's brand of reportage (*Against*, 298–99). It also brings up short her earlier remarks about "content" being "the lure which engages consciousness in essentially *formal* processes of transformation," enabling us "in good conscience" to "cherish works of art which, considered in terms of 'content,' are morally objectionable" (*Against*, 25). The content of the four films Riefenstahl was commissioned to make for Hitler was Nazi propaganda, pure and simple. As quoted by Sontag, the justification that clears the filmmaker's conscience in later years, not to mention conferring upon her the status of cultural icon, is form: if German in any way, it is " 'perhaps this care for composition, this aspiration to form' " that makes the films that celebrate National Socialism " 'very German,' " Riefenstahl asserts, not the fact that they contributed to a political party bent on genocide (*Saturn*, 85). And though self-serving, of course, there is a way in which what Riefenstahl says is absolutely right, for, as the second part of Sontag's essay corroborates, what made Nazi aesthetics "very German," in the sense of appropriating "the rhetoric of art—art in its late romantic phase" (*Saturn*, 92), was its overwhelming concern with design and beauty, from the clustering of the masses to the cut of the SS uniforms.

Defined by "a characteristic pageantry: the massing of groups of people; the turning of people into things; the multiplication or replication of things; and the grouping of people/things around an all-powerful, hypnotic leader-figure or force" (*Saturn*, 91), fascist aesthetics brings to a head the very powers that Sontag earlier attributed to the photographic image: to make reality a source of spectacle and object of surveillance (*Photography*, 178), to treat living beings as things and vice versa (*Photography*, 98), to frame the world as a set of disconnected snapshots and history as a set of unrelated anecdotes (*Photography*, 22–23), all drained of meaning and reduced to a common denominator, leaving the world a bargain-basement shopping center, "a department store or museum-without-walls in which every subject is depreciated into an article of consumption, promoted into an item for aesthetic appreciation" (*Photography*, 110). Fascist aesthetics also forces the issue of how much questions of taste are functions of shifting historical perspectives. Whereas Sontag once could celebrate time's liberating art from "moral relevance, delivering it over to the Camp sensibility" (*Against*, 285), she now objects when time seems to invite people to look at recycled Nazi art with only "knowing and sniggering detachment, as a form of Pop Art" (*Saturn*, 94). For when historical contexts change, so must the degree of latitude given to taste, and even once around may be too much: "Art that seemed eminently worth defending ten years ago, as a minority or adversary taste, no longer seems defensible today, because the ethical and cultural issues it raises have become serious, even dangerous, in a way they were not then. . . . Taste is context, and the context has changed" (*Saturn*, 98).

If aesthetics and ethics must then be seen as inextricable for Sontag, if, as the epigraph that opens her essay on Godard asserts, " '*whichever one chooses, one will always find the other at the end of the road*' " (*Styles*, 147), how can Sontag reconcile their competing claims for attention? In *The Volcano Lover*, her most recent novel, Sontag provides her own answer. "It was the time when all ethical obligations were first put up for scrutiny," she writes of her late eighteenth-century temporal setting, "the beginning of the time we call modern" (*Volcano*, 115). As depicted in the novel, it also is the time in which many of the aesthetic traits commonly perceived as postmodern are on display. Performing selves are in abundance: fame turns Goethe into a public official, "already one of the immortals," who feels "the echo of eternity in every one of his utterances" (*Volcano*, 157); Viscount Horatio Nelson imagines himself "in history paintings, as a portrait bust, as a statue on a pedestal, or even atop a high column in a public square" (*Volcano*, 193). Spectacles abound, as Vesuvius turns into a tourist attraction and an admiral's funeral occasions "the most glorious [burial] ever staged in England" (*Volcano*, 407). Images proliferate. Camera lucidas deliver images of objects on plane surfaces to artists. The Etruria Ware marketed by Josiah Wedgwood delivers designs from ancient vases, in a full range of sizes and colors, to anyone with enough ready cash to afford them. Walter Benjamin's age of mechanical reproduction commences.

So does Oscar Wilde's age of Camp. "It was the beginning of the age of revolutions, it was the beginning of the age of exaggeration" (*Volcano*,

167), another of Sontag's Dickensian openings asserts, nowhere more clearly evidenced than in Naples, the "kingdom of the immoderate, of excess, of overflow" (*Volcano*, 44), and in no person more emblematized than in Emma Hamilton, who enters the book "a young woman who was beautiful enough to be a Greek statue" (*Volcano*, 144), and by midpoint is exchanging tunics for tassles, indulging in appetites to rival Mae West's, and generating more gossip about her weight than Liz Taylor ever commanded from the tabloids. In this particular Sontag work, however, the hilarity of Camp coexists with the all too real horrors of chronology, which reach their peak during the Neapolitan revolution of 1799 with an extended description of butchery by Ruffo's royalist hordes that far exceeds the "moderate amount of looting, battery, rape, and mayhem" intended and leaves in its wake carnage and cannibalism for which Ruffo himself has been unprepared (*Volcano*, 283).

Such a transference of an actual historical context from background to foreground marks a real departure for Sontag in her fiction. *The Benefactor* merely alludes to the deportation of Jews to concentration camps on one occasion, when its protagonist is forced to hide a woman in the back room of his apartment, and even then names neither the Nazi facilitators nor the fatal consequences of those enforced moves. *Death Kit* periodically interrupts its story with television sound-bytes and clips of dead GIs being transported from rice fields, but never is the war the soldiers are fighting ever identified as Vietnam. And, in the end, both books circumvent even these limited referrals to a real world beyond their covers by surrounding their stories with dreamscape frameworks, in one case, the dreams to which Hippolyte tries to match his life, in the other, the scenario that Diddy constructs between the time he takes an overdose of sleeping pills and the time he actually dies. *The Volcano Lover*, by contrast, offers no dreams to obfuscate history but the nightmare that, for Sontag, constitutes all that is real history.

It is, moreover, a past history the novel presents as exceedingly relevant to the present. Sontag signals her intention on the first page, after recounting her own visit to a Manhattan flea market in the spring of 1992 to check "what's in the world": "What's left. What's discarded. What's no longer cherished. What had to be sacrificed" (*Volcano*, 3). Earlier in her career, such an opening would have served as a paean to the surrealist sensibility Sontag considered "the most pervasive modern option for the aesthete" (*Saturn*, 191), just as the visit it depicts would have invoked the trips to secondhand stores that provided a "mode of aesthetic pilgrimage" for André Breton and his devotees of debris (*Photography*, 78–79), and the collecting of broken cast-offs justified, with reference to Walter Benjamin, as an act of salvage now that modern history had already shattered both the traditions in which whole objects gained meaning along with all future hopes of rejoining them (*Photography*, 76). With Sontag's immediate crosscutting to a London picture auction during the autumn of 1772, however, she subverts all those expectations. Instead of a juxtaposition of images (preferably as unalike as possible) to approximate the perpetual present the surrealists strived for in their art (as exemplified by the form of dream association and achieved through techniques of automatic writing), Sontag begins an extended series of *temporal* juxtapositions that permeates the entire novel (Vesuvias and King Kong, Naples and Newark, European hot winds and PMS, the Cavaliere and the Nationalist Chinese, statues of the Virgin and Terminator movies), and which increasingly draws into the book the catastrophes of historical life: Pompeii and Herculaneum resemble "a more recent double urbanicide" in which "one murdered city is much more famous worldwide than the other. (As one wag put it, Nagasaki had a bad press agent.)" (*Volcano*, 113). Such crosscutting between "then" and "now" aligns Sontag's novel with other fictional works of the recent past concerned with the contextualizing of history, E. L. Doctorow's *Ragtime*, for example, which subverts its opening bromides of what did define the early 1900s—stouter women, summer whites, sexual fainting—and what did not—no Negroes (the novel's term), no immigrants—with mention of the murder of Stanford White, the molestation of Evelyn Nesbit, and a meeting with Emma Goldman, who informed her listener that there were both Negroes and immigrants (and not altogether happy ones) at the turn of the century in America.[7] More important, such temporal juxtapositions enable Sontag to judge the actions of "then" from the perspective of similar consequences that might be on display "now."

For Pompeii and Herculaneum are no ordinary cities overcome by disaster. In *The Volcano Lover*, they are cities whose ruins provide sites for excavations ("The ground holds treasures for collectors" [*Volcano*, 113]), and therefore promote the kind of rationalizing that accepts, even awaits, catastrophe on the basis of the aesthetic production that can result. "Let's take a positive view," suggests the novel's narrator. "The mountain is an emblem of all the forms of wholesale death: the deluge, the great conflagration (*sterminator Vesevo*, as the great poet was to say), but also of survival, of human persistence. In this instance, nature run amok also makes culture, makes artifacts, by murdering, petrifying history. In such disasters there is much to appreciate" (*Volcano*, 112). It is this aesthetic sensibility that characterizes both the Cavaliere William Hamilton, who catalogues the volcano's rocks, and later, in even more extreme form, his cousin William Beckford, who builds a towering abbey to house all his rare possessions, and once so housed, can settle in himself and "cheerfully contemplate the destruction of the world" for having "saved all that is of value in it" (*Volcano*, 337). But in ending the pasage by noting, "The ground is where the dead live, stacked in layers" (*Volcano*, 113), Sontag returns—in very literal form—to the exact kind of mass grave that Diddy has envisioned at the ending of *Death Kit*. The difference is that this time the bodies are not imagined, but itemized, actualized, and, worst of all, aestheticized—as seen in the family members who die of fear and who form "an artless tableau" when dug up from the cellar in which they have sought refuge from the mountain's lava (*Volcano*, 84).

While these unfortunate victims provide the most gruesome examples of humans turned into artifacts, they certainly are not the sole examples of people who succumb to artistic transposition. Emma Hamilton, for instance, models for portrait painters from the age of seventeen, poses in tableaux vivants staged by a London sex-therapist, and enacts so many iconic moments of classical mythology for her husband as to constitute an entire "gallery of living statues" for her Pygmalion-in-reverse older benefactor (*Volcano*, 145). In fact, for all the gruesome quality of the volcano victims uncovering, the transposition they suffer in death may be less grotesque than that undergone in life by the book's main protagonists, all of whom are enshrouded in their own personae while still alive. The Cavaliere becomes an "emblem" when he sits for Sir Joshua Reynolds (*Volcano*, 65). Emma assumes the role of subject when painted by Romney as *The Ambassadress*. And Nelson gets to see his name, initials, and face "multiplying wherever he turned"—on candelabra, vases, medallions, brooches, cameos, and sashes—after he comes back from destroying the French at the Battle of the Nile and is transformed into a merchandizing phenomenon in gratitude (*Volcano*, 198).

The horror here is not merely a question of the aestheticizing's making people look better than they actually do, as occurs in the life-size wax effigies of the book's main trio that the King and Queen of Naples commission, in which an ambassador nearing seventy appears youthful, a woman bursting out of her dress seams looks slim, and a one-armed, one-eyed hero is adorned with medals, stars, and two bright blue agate eyes. Rather, the horror resides more in the stance that being transposed into a work of art encourages those so transformed to take. The unschooled Emma Hamilton truly believes her own publicity: "He tells me I am a grate [*sic*] work of art," she writes early in the book, well before Hamilton even embarks upon his project of restoration (*Volcano*, 128). And she continues to believe in her own greatness right until the very end, when, alone, drunk, and slovenly, she repeats, even augments, the old aesthetic homilies ("Mr. Romney told me that I was a genius, a divinity. . . . My husband thought I was all his vases and statues, all the beauty he admired, come to life. . . . And I was regarded as the greatest beauty of the age" [*Volcano*, 406–407]). This she can do because the source of her aesthetic greatness is only partly to be found in her looks. According to Emma, the major portion derives from an intensity of emotion that remains impervious to the changes that time can wreak on physical charms. This romantic intensity, which grants her life its "great velocity" (*Volcano*, 407), depends upon the quality of single-mindedness. Yet such single-mindedness, in turn, demands a perspective that is exceedingly narrow in scope, so narrow as to ignore anything from the outside world that might interfere with its operations.

Within the world of revolutions and reprisals that Sontag's book sketches, though, maintaining such a removed stance can be hazardous to one's health, and those who refuse to place passion in some kind of political perspective are among the things that get "sacrificed," to return to the novel's opening words. To this end, Sontag relates the tale of an opera diva who "lives only for her art and for love," whose jealousy is aroused by the Neapolitan chief of police in his plan to discover the whereabouts of a political fugitive, who has been hiding at the villa of her lover (*Volcano*, 311). "Were the diva just a bit more sceptical—that is, a little less proud of being passionate—perhaps Scarpia could not so promptly have turned her into a decoy," Sontag speculates (*Volcano*, 314), in which case the fugitive would not have poisoned himself prior to his apprehension, the lover would not have been tortured and executed at dawn, and the diva would not have committed suicide by jumping from the parapet of a castle.

The fate of Emma Hamilton and her lover, of course, proves much less fatal in that it does not entail the loss of life for either one. It remains, nonetheless, just as much a product of political manipulation as that of the fallen diva and her companion. Nelson, whom Britain needs as it prepares to make its entry onto the stage of history as "the greatest imperial power the world has ever known," can remain enshrined in public memory, flaws and all, his reputation "already in a museum and too valuable to be allowed to disappear" (*Volcano*, 348). Emma, who serves no useful purpose, can be left for public scorn, her only comfort her memories of having been "larger than life" all of her life (*Volcano*, 404). The one becomes a museum piece, the other a piece of Camp.

To the extent that Sontag sees the sacrifice of Emma Hamilton as a consequence of being a woman, she extends her a certain amount of sympathy. "Perhaps she is not more emotional than a man," she writes of the passionate diva. "But the combination of emotions with power creates . . . power. The combination of emotions with powerlessness creates . . . powerlessness" (*Volcano*, 314). But, finally, Sontag severely limits even that degree of sympathy. If, in Sontag's analogy, we are all passengers on a boat called history, with better accommodations than those below deck (and there always is somebody below deck), it matters little how much power one does or does not have. "Even if it is not your responsibility, how can it be your responsibility, you are still a participant and a witness" (*Volcano*, 290). Emma Hamilton can look at anything without flinching (*Volcano*, 307)—even the spectacle of Neapolitan revolutionaries being executed, if necessary—but she chooses, along with her husband and lover, to sit out the executions in the interior of an British warship offshore. In that act of omission is her most dreadful act of commission.

By concluding her novel with the voice of Eleonora de Fonseca Pimentel, a Portuguese poet who is sentenced to hang for composing an "Ode to Liberty" during the Neapolitan revolution, Sontag provides an alternative to an art that is completely removed from life. Like most of those patriots executed, who make themselves brave by thinking "they were becoming an image" (*Volcano*, 295), de Fonseca Pimentel is no stranger to the aestheticizing impulse. It is her composing of verse as distinct from his mere collecting of ruins that distinguishes this otherwise minor character from the novel's presiding protagonist, Sir William Hamilton, who goes to his own death without ever having engaged in a creative endeavor of any kind or having "burn[ed] with zeal for anything except his own pleasures and the privileges annexed to his station" (*Volcano*, 418). At the same time, it is the republican conviction that de Fonseca Pimentel brings to her creative endeavors that saves her from being entombed among "the nullity of women" like Emma Hamilton, the most valued object of her husband's curatorship (*Volcano*, 419). And although she refuses to recite her "Ode to Liberty," assessing herself as no more than a "conventionally gifted poet" (*Volcano*, 417), it is for that poem that Sontag preserves her memory. "I wanted to be pure flame," de Fonseca Pimentel states when describing the political activities within which she has submerged her own identity (*Volcano*, 417). She misses her own point, however. It is for her immersion in life rather than her disappearance into pure aesthetics that she continues to burn incandescent.

Notes

1. Susan Sontag, *Under the Sign of Saturn* (1980; reprint, New York: Anchor Books, 1991), hereafter cited parenthetically as *Saturn*. Additional works by Sontag that are quoted in the text are cited parenthetically with reference to the following shortened titles: *Against Interpretation {Against}* (1966; reprint, New York: Anchor Books, 1990); *Illness as Metaphor and AIDS and Its Metaphors {Illness, AIDS}* (1978, 1989; reprint, New York: Anchor Books, 1990); *On Photography {Photography}* (1977; reprint, New York: Anchor Books, 1990); *Styles of Radical Will {Styles}* (1969; reprint, New York: Anchor Books, 1991); *The Volcano Lover {Volcano}* (New York: Farrar, Straus & Giroux, 1992).
2. Sontag's reference to the origins of *On Photography* appears in a note that precedes the Contents and is not designated by any page number.
3. Robert Boyers and Maxine Bernstein, "Women, The Arts, and the Politics of Culture: An Interview with Susan Sontag," *Salmagundi* 31–32 (Fall 1975–Winter 1976): 32–33, 31; hereafter cited as "Interview."
4. For an extended discussion of Sontag's sensibilities as reflecting the paradoxes of the late modernist aesthetic, see Sohnya Sayres, *Susan Sontag: The Elegiac Modernist* (New York: Routledge, 1990), 10–12.
5. See John Barth, "The Literature of Exhaustion," *Atlantic Monthly*, August 1967, 29–34.
6. Don DeLillo, *White Noise* (1985; reprinted, New York: Penguin, 1986), 12–13.
7. E. L. Doctorow, *Ragtime* (New York: Random House, 1975), 3–5.

"Every window is a mother's mouth": Grace Paley's Postmodern Voice

VICTORIA AARONS

"Tell the story again. See what you can do this time."
                    —"A Conversation with My Father"

"She's a character in a book. She's not even a person."

                                        —"Love"

Whose story is it, anyway? One might ask this question, not only of Grace Paley's short stories, but of postmodern fiction in general, with its qualities of indeterminacy, reflexivity, temporal ambiguity and rearrangement, and fragmentation of both character and plot. Like Paley's characters themselves, who battle with her narrators for authorial control of a given story—"I'm trying to tell you something, he said. Listen."[1]—readers of Paley's short fiction feel the need to step into her narratives, to enter the fray, in order to exert some authorial control over the seemingly random ordering of events and characterological display.

But to ask questions of authorial ownership or to impose one's own ordering upon the text is, surely, to try to graft upon this fiction a structure that it consciously subverts. Unlike conventional modes of storytelling, postmodern fiction reveals itself as "a structuring act that becomes its own reality," where fixed notions of authority, (including genre, point of view, and protagonist), intentionally give way to, in Jerome Klinkowitz's terms, "one seamless text of narrative . . . something to be played with rather than played by . . . a void within which one could pose endless structures."[2]

In their undermining of conventional notions of character, subject, and plot, and in their blurring of narrative authority, Paley's short stories might be measured against Philip Stevick's defining criterion of postmodern fiction, "in which the value of the fiction inheres in its inventions, its wit and intricacy of texture, its appeal as a made thing, obedient to no laws but its own."[3] The story, for Paley, *is* the story. That is, the making of fictions forms the central thematic action of her narratives. Her narrators and charac-

This essay was written expressly for this volume and is published here for the first time.

ters—often indistinguishable from each other and from the author herself—in the midst of telling stories of their lives and the lives of families and friends, explicitly refer to the very act in which they are engaged, storytelling. They perceive themselves at once as storytellers and dramatized characters. Part of the fiction is their seeing themselves as fictional. They envision the world through acts of storytelling. "I want to go on with the story. Or perhaps begin it again," one of Paley's character-narrators muses.[4] "What does he want? I should tell him the story of my life?" exclaims another.[5] Of course, this is exactly what Paley's characters do; they tell the stories of their lives. And they do it with conscious self-reflection, self-parody, and with a "critic's eye" for the whole process: "I like your paragraphs better than your sentences," ironically asserts one character to another, the story's narrator,[6] suggesting the degree to which storytelling forms the central thematic action of Paley's short fiction. What this particular character likes is the sound of language, the ongoing flood of words that typically issues forth from Paley's characters.

Telling stories is for Paley's characters a process of self-invention. But self, for Paley, is never isolated from one's place in a community, communities of women, of Jews, of political activists, ordinary people who tell the stories of their lives.[7] Nor is it ever possessed, ever known fully in a moment of self-presence. It is always a reflective telling, a self-referential assessment of the process of storytelling in which the teller never quite controls her own story; characters evaluate themselves as both storytellers and members of a community, and they do the one through the other. There is thus in Paley's fiction a constant building up of interpretive possibilities, as characters become the stories they tell: "She was imagination-minded," the narrator of "A Woman, Young and Old" ironically recalls of her grandmother, "read stories all day and sighed all night, till my grandpa, to get near her at all, had to use that particular medium."[8] It is "that particular medium," stories, storytelling in any form, that becomes the defining act in Paley's fiction, defining in terms not only of the making of character but in the making of fiction.

Such metafictional narratives reveal Paley's playfulness with the literary conventions of the short story as made thing. Yet they do so with a twist that makes Paley's fiction "postmodern." For Paley, stories seem always in the making, both for Paley as author and for the chorus of characters who tell their own tales "within" her narratives. Her framing stories yield, more often than not, to other stories in her texts—characters who take over the telling. Thus we find not so much a layering of stories (the story within the story), but rather one story *giving way* to another, becoming and informing another. No single story seems to be privileged over another, no controlling narrative authority guides the reader's response. Such elasticity defies stasis; it is the *process* of storytelling, not "the story" itself, that defines and controls Paley's fiction. And it does so in ways that suggest that Paley's postmodern stylistic commitments are closely related to her ideological ones concerning the life of the postwar American-Jewish communities about which she writes.

So what's the story? In postmodern fiction, writers ironically pose this question to readers as characters pose it to narrators. The status of the story is always being assessed while in the midst of the telling. And characters make claims, not only for the primacy of their individual stories, but for the ways in which those stories are told. I have argued elsewhere that this playfully ironic and often self-parodic preoccupation with storytelling might be said to be the defining characteristic of Jewish literature and most surely of postwar American-Jewish fiction. One only has to read the stories of the turn-of-the-century Yiddish writer Sholom Aleichem or the novels of Philip Roth to recognize this characteristic.[9] Grace Paley, who might be said to show the indirect influence of the one[10] and to contribute to the unfolding tradition of the other, constantly and humorously reminds us that characters, after all, are fictional inventions, but they are their own invention as much as the author's; they are the story. As one of Paley's characters says to the narrator of the short story "Listening," "you don't have to tell stories to me in which I'm a character" (203). And in another instance, a character, vying for control of the internal narrative, protests, "I see you can't tell a plain story. So don't waste time."[11] These complaints, made with the kind of characteristically ironic insistence that generally defines the discursive relationship among Paley's characters and narrators, call attention to both literary conventions of genre and the construction of character.

"A Conversation with My Father," perhaps the paradigmatic story for Paley's work, is a story, very simply, about storytelling. Of course, "very simply" is always deceptive in Grace Paley's fiction. Her tendency toward economy, toward brief, direct narratives—"to tell . . . stories as simply as possible,"[12] as one of her narrators puts it—is in many ways a dodge. Brevity gives way to numerous ironic complexities and narrative patterning. Paley's stories are anything but simple. On the contrary, they self-consciously call our attention again and again to the intricate texturing of storytelling, to the fictive reinterpretation of history, ironic representations of the past, the making of personal histories, and the ongoing fictive reinvention of the self. For Paley, these generalized issues of identity, historical and individual, are inseparable from the more particular ones of generational conflict among the urban American-Jewish lower middle class in the years of post–World War II economic, ideological, and intellectual mobility.

In this way, "A Conversation with My Father" is a story about the making of fictions and its "double," the making of lives. In it, Paley stages a dialogue between the narrator and her eighty-six-year-old father. It is a story about her attempts to "please him," to make good his request of her, "to write a simple story just once more, . . . the kind de Maupassant wrote, or Chekhov, the kind you used to write. Just recognizable people and then write down what happened to them next" (161). It is a story ultimately about the narrator's inability to tell the kind of story her father wants to hear, just as it is about her inability to accept the inevitability of his dying. In fact, the one resides in the other. Keeping alive the story she constructs, manipulates, and reinvents as the narrative progresses is the means by which she attempts to stave off the predictability of his death. But to say that this story, or any of Paley's stories, is *about* anything is potentially to undercut the very design and conceit of her texts. "What in fact can its subject be when the entire notion of being 'about' something has become a circular question?" asks Jerome Klinkowitz of the postmodern short story (Klinkowitz, 2). The "subject" of a story such as "A Conversation with My Father" is in the telling. It is the process of storytelling and the making of the lives of which it is symptomatic that is both form and theme.

In constructing a story for her father, the narrator in effect constructs herself, makes of herself a character. The invention of stories and the invention of selves are suggestive of an ongoing cultural narrative that is, in fact, through the making of fiction, the making of a life. It is, in other words, interpretive. In "A Conversation with My Father," Paley's narrator invents a story about a woman, "a story that had been happening for a couple of years right across the street" (162), and, as such, immediately suggests the precarious distinction between what is invented and what is real. That is, Paley invites us to remove the frame, to take the quotation marks off the story, in order to see the depth of the relation between narrative and self-invention and the tenuous, fragmenting potential of each. The story she tells is a story whose ending changes in the course of the verbal sparring between the narrator and her father, who, "still interested in details, craft, technique" (164), wants what his daughter will not—in fact, cannot—give him: both well-defined and consistent character and plot, the internally coherent movement from beginning to end.

The narrator refuses to give closure to her story, but rather posits unwritten possibilities for her protagonist's life, possibilities outside of and beyond the confines of the story: "She could be a hundred different things in this world as time goes on" (166). Stories exist, for both Paley and her narrators, as *openings*, as spaces in which to move, or to think about moving, beyond the confines of convention and tradition. And although the narrator would like to comply with her father's request, "*would* like to try to tell such a story," she is quick to qualify her authorial prerogative with the unwavering conviction that "everyone, real or invented, deserves the open destiny of life" (162). Of his daughter's story, Paley's character is forced to draw his own conclusion: " 'Poor woman. Poor girl, to be born in a time of fools, to live among fools. The end. The end. . . . You don't want to recognize it. Tragedy! Plain tragedy! Historical tragedy! No hope. The end. . . . A person must have character. She does not' " (166–67).

Here, as is so often the case in Paley's fiction, the main character of the story, or rather, of the frame story, here the father, steps into the narrator's role and takes over the telling, attempts to make the story his own. In this instance, he demands from his daughter the construction of character, of *a* character that he himself both is and is not. His hold on narrative authority is as tenuous as his hold on his notion of history and of his projection of his daughter's place in it. This ambiguity, created by the flux of narrator(s), character(s), and story(ies) *is* the story for Paley, and the father's insistence on conventional, historical, notions of character and plot parallel his desire to author and authorize her story, her self, which Paley's narrator, the daughter, the "I" of this particular story, rejects.

I am reluctant, here, as elsewhere, to use either conventional category of plot or character to describe the form or movement of Paley's fiction.[13] These terms, I believe, are misleading, both because Paley's short stories intentionally defy any set notion of plot, of beginning, middle, and end, and because this defiance is so clearly thematic as well as formal. Paley's narrator in "A Conversation with My Father" describes it in these terms: "plot, the absolute line between two points which I've always despised. Not for literary reasons, but because it takes all hope away" (161–62). In Paley's fiction, plot, rather, gives way to acts of storytelling. And just as Paley seems to reject notions of plot as limiting, she disavows fixed character reference as limiting of both self-invention and its ironic counterpart, self-delusion. We are offered no clear protagonist, no definitive character with whom we might identify a moral center, a telling authority, save for the telling authority of self-invention, an authority that both "tells," that is, invents narratives and selves, and is "told on," that is, revealed in ways it can't always control.

Typically, Paley's characters and narrators within any given story all participate in the storytelling, an inadvertent rhetoric of collaboration. They are equally omniscient, which is, of course, to say that the notion of omniscience is playfully discarded for what I would like to call a *rhetoric of voices*. With character as only voice, plot becomes rhetoric, a progressive elaboration of voices amid fragments of plot. Paley's stories are moved by voices, by people talking—talking through each other, over each other, around each other. The voices compete with each other, vying for authorial control, each pushing its way into the foreground of the developing narrative, each revealed as partial in its bid for control. Thus we might discard the terms plot and character with reference to Paley's fiction, for terms far less categorically formal and much more descriptive of the linking of narrative form and the theme of contingent, fragmented self-invention in her fiction: rhetoric and voice.

By rhetoric, I am referring to a disjunctive interplay of stories and voices that produce an ironic tension that governs the unfolding of Paley's stories. In "The Immigrant Story," for example, one story, the seeming frame story for the piece, abruptly gives way to a second story, a story that just as abruptly concludes. In fact, these stories seem less to conclude and more to open, to begin again or to allow for the possibility of more beginnings, more revisions.[14] "I want . . . to be a different person," the narrator of the short story "Wants" contends.[15] In telling stories, in retelling, reshaping, and rearranging fictions, Paley's narrators ironically attempt to revise, to reinvent the self. And here, once again, is the relation between storytelling and confirming lives.

"The Immigrant Story," for instance, initially appears to be constructed around a conversation between two people, a conversation from which one speaker, the one presumably not the initial narrator of the overall story, emerges to take over the narrative. His is the story that concludes the story; he gets the final word. "The Immigrant Story" begins as abruptly as it ends. In fact, the story seems to begin in the middle of a conversation, in mid-thought. And the reader gets the uneasy feeling right from the start that he or she is over hearing or, worse yet, eavesdropping on, what would seem to be a private conversation.

"Jack asked me," the story begins, "Isn't it a terrible thing to grow up in the shadow of another person's sorrow? I suppose so, I answered. As you know, I grew up in the summer sunlight of upward mobility. This leached out a lot of that dark ancestral grief" (171). Such an introduction speaks to a history that exists outside the text, a history that defines the relationship between the actors in the piece and a history (a specifically American-Jewish one) that informs the entire narrative interaction that is to follow. It's a history, or rather a response to history, that forms the conflicting ways in which the two characters in the dialogue view the world and their places in it. "I believe I see the world as clearly as you do, I said" (174), affirms the narrator of what we believe to be the frame narrative, the "I" of the story. But there is no concluding bracket to the frame. Her role as peacemaker is challenged by another character. "You fucking enemy, he said. You always see things in a rosy light. You have a rotten rosy tempera-ment" (173). The narrator attempts to wrap up the narrative, to draw a conclusion to their dialogue, and thus to the story: "Rosiness is not a worse windowpane than gloomy gray when viewing the world" (174). Such a closural pronouncement only undercuts itself, however, for the narrative at this point, at the point of seeming closure, opens up, takes on a new course: "Yes yes yes yes yes yes yes, he said. Do you mind? Just listen" (174).

The "new" story, the story that "concludes" the narrative, is now solely Jack's story, or rather his story of his parents, told with rapid detachment, through the lens of Jack's strongly invested but less than definitive vision of their lives and his place within the makings of their world. And just when we seem to be given closure to this, to Jack's legitimating story of his parents' wrenching experience as immigrants and the morally defining characteristics of their life in America, this story too gives way, opens itself up to another story, to Jack's story, told in present tense although about the past, a story that seems to "conclude" with Jack, now both "author" and "character" in his own story: "They are sitting at the edge of their chairs. He's leaning forward reading to her in that old bulb light. . . . Just beyond the table and their heads, there is the darkness of the kitchen, the bedroom, the dining room, the shadowy darkness where as a child I ate my supper, did my homework and went to bed" (175). But this is no more a conclusion than any of the other stories within the overall piece. Indeed, it subverts closure, because it opens the question of Jack's own motives in telling it and in putting himself in "the shadowy darkness," right when we realize he has arrogated narrative authority to himself. The ending is thus abrupt, the final narrative disjunctive, as if it stops in mid-thought, just as it began, between self-knowledge and self-delusion.

Is this the "immigrant's" story, a story that ends with Jack's parents "sitting at the edge of their chairs"? Or is it Jack's story, the story of his childhood, a story that, although closer in proximity to the time of his telling it than his parent's story, shifts into the past tense, "ate my supper, did my homework and went to bed"? Or is it finally Paley's story, a story about a conversation, seemingly anchored to nothing, between Jack and the "I"? No doubt it is, but, in being so, it raises more questions about the relation of narrative, self-disclosure, self-concealment, and stable irony than it answers. If all of this seems mercilessly complicated, it necessarily and intentionally is meant to be so, because, finally, all these stories are really the same story. The lack of traditional quotation marks to designate dialogue suggests exactly that, as does the lack of closure. We are not offered an answer to the question of whose story governs the text, nor to the question of whose point of view controls the narrative.

Thus narrative authority blows its own cover, offering a variety of elastic, fluid, multi-realizable perspectives. In defining the postmodern imagination, Stevick speaks to this particular point: "the author's narrating self does not superimpose a mature manner upon the remembered, experiencing self. Rather, the narrating self is, in its own way, just as naïve" (Stevick, 87). Just as naïve for Paley's fiction means just as potentially self-blinding. There is no "author"; there is only the story, or, more to the point, any number of stories. In Paley's fiction the "death of the author" is simply the death of the belief that self-invention is somehow a centered, or centering process.

Paley's short story "Debts," along these lines, begins with a request to the narrator from a stranger who "said she was in possession of her family archives. She had heard I was a writer. She wondered if I would help her write about her grandfather, a famous innovator and dreamer of the Yiddish theater" (10). But this initial opening to Paley's story is quickly discarded by her narrator, discarded for another story, the story of her friend Lucia. But, again, Lucia's story turns to the story of her "grandmother, also her mother, who in this story is eight or nine" (10). Paley's story "Debts" ends with this last story, the story of the child, Anna, closes with the offhand remark "Hey, Zio, here's your dinner. Mama sent it. I have to go now" (12). Such temporal and perspectival shifts mark the extent to which questions of levels of narration, the staple, and rightly so, of the analysis of fiction, are subverted in Paley as part of the process of making the telling of stories coextensive with the way lives are confirmed, confused, redirected, denied. Someone, we might loosely paraphrase, is always arriving or leaving in Paley's stories.

So we're back to where we began, a return to the question "Whose story is it, anyway?" Is "Debts" the narrator's story? Which narrator? Of course, the story is Paley's, the author. But Paley consciously discards the notion of authorship as ownership. As the title of this particular story suggests, telling stories is the paying of a "debt"; and, as such, the story belongs to someone other than the teller. It is no more her story than it is the author's, once again eclipsing what is fictive and what is real. Characters for Paley and for her narrators take on their own authoritative telling. And in doing so they show themselves trying to invent themselves. The lead narrator in "A Conversation with My Father" cheerfully and willingly relinquishes any authorial control or responsibility: "Actually that's the trouble with stories. People start out fantastic. You think they're extraordinary, but it turns out as the work goes along, they're just average with a good education. Sometimes the other way around, the person's a kind of dumb innocent, but he outwits you and you can't even think of an ending good enough" (163). Once again, the refusal to admit to print a character whose motives, actions, attitudes, and responses are governed, predetermined even, by the author suggests the ironically self-referential and self-mocking stance that Paley takes in and toward her fiction. "Well, you just have to let the story lie around till some agreement can be reached between you and the stubborn hero," the narrator continues (164). This agreement, this ironically collaborative rhetoric,[16] forms the texture, the humorous voice, and the dramatic tension in Paley's fiction and lends itself to the fragmentation—or, better yet, to the fragments—of plot, of stories.[17] There is no final author—just as there is no final story—no definitive source of control and authoritative vision, because knowing how we know and what we know is continually and ironically undercut by Paley.

Ambiguity about knowing might be said largely to define postmodern thinking in fiction. Linda Nicholson, in "Feminism and the Politics of Postmodernism," puts this well, I think:

First, postmodernism can be characterized by the rejection of epistemic arrogance for an endorsement of epistemic humility. Such humility entails a recognition that our ways of viewing the world are mediated by the contexts out of which we operate. This means that not only are our specific beliefs and emotions about the world a product of our historical circumstances but so are the means by which we come to those beliefs and emotions and by which we resolve conflict when dissent is present. This does not entail the position that there are no solutions to epistemic dilemmas, merely that there are no final ones.[18]

For Paley, "epistemic humility" would seem to define her narrative stance and that of her characters, who are forced in the context of her fiction to amend their positions, to rethink their motives, their postures, and to reassess their storytelling impulses. And so more often than not Paley's narrators step out of the narrative flow, or, rather, step aside in order to comment on and revise the direction of the storytelling.

"As is usual in conversations, I said a couple of things out loud and kept a few structured remarks for interior mulling and righteousness," the narrator in the short story "Friends"[19] humorously and self-consciously reflects. And it is a reflection made to an implied listener, an acknowledgment of the reader's participation in the story. It is an ironic acknowledgment that continually breaks the reader's expectations for the ways in which stories are told. The narrator of "The Little Girl," with Paley's keen ear for the diversity of American dialects, pulls up short her story when, just as we are meant to anticipate its seeming conclusion, she undercuts not only the truth of the events she has just described but her mode of presentation as well: "That what I think right now. That is what happened."[20] She first responds with a sense of the contingency of her own narrative, a hedging, allowing for the possibility of revision, and then pulls back, makes a definitive statement. But the final claim sounds like little more than an attempt at self-justification, a matter of convincing herself. Such characteristic ambiguity suggests the kind of humility and naïveté with which Paley's narrators tell their stories; it is a publicly acknowledged recognition of their limitations as characters and as narrators.

It is with considerable humility, for instance, that the narrator in "Listening" can reveal to her friend, whose story she has left out of the telling, her own motives, motives that are less than perfect and incomprehensible to her: "I don't understand it either. . . . How could I allow it. . . . How can you forgive me?" (210–11). Such modes of expression, ways of knowing, create the kind of hyperrealism that distinguishes Paley's fiction, that infuses it with oral qualities of real conversations that take place in ordinary settings, under ordinary circumstances.

The emphasis on talk, on speech, both dialogue and monologue, keeps Paley's storytellers in a kind of time warp of fragmentation and transition. Time is condensed, drawn up, abbreviated in a way characteristic of the postmodern short story: the juxtaposition of continuity and discontinuity, disjunctions forming a sense of the flow of experience. In the midst of seemingly ordinary situations, the remarkable is willed to happen; the quotidian is transformed by the talk that describes it. Paley's characters and settings are demarcated by the seemingly commonplace. Her characters are ordinary; their lives lack real tragic stature. And their stories take place on playgrounds, in kitchens, in taxi-cabs, and in old-age homes. And the stuff of their dialogues is the stuff of everyday living—marriages, children, the stories of acquaintances past and present.

However, in the midst of ordinary experience, Paley captures extraordinary attempts at self-invention. Her characters are capable of great feats of transformation and redefinition. "Reality? A lesson in reality? Am I a cabdriver? No. I drive a cab but I am not a cabdriver."[21] Here, as in other places, one of Paley's characters, through a deft rhetorical maneuver, attempts to redefine himself, reconstructs, reconceptualizes, and transforms himself through language. Here, the character would be his own author, and the linguistic turn, the chiasmic reversal from verb to noun, gives him a kind of authority both denied in "real life" and common to the reality of self-defining subjective life. It is a kind of metaphorical reevaluation that is itself a metaphor for motives of self-invention.

Metaphorical reconstructions seem to be the key here, and in two senses: 1) the specific linguistic transformations that make a life into another one, no matter how tenuously; and 2) the metaphorical dimension of Paley's rendering of the speech act, of storytelling primarily as both a vehicle for and symptom of the desire to form (deform) the self as it emerges in particular situations, often to the surprise of a particular character.

Much of the tension in Paley's fiction comes from the interplay between the metaphorical and the hyper-literal (the postmodern "hyperreal"), the metaphorical that extends and the literal that ends. "During breakfast, language remained on his mind. Because of this, he was silent" ("Enormous Changes at the Last Minute," 130). The metaphor of language "on his mind," like breakfast on the table, allows Paley's character to justify, with a sense of his own cleverness, his silent posture. He might be said to transform what is generally thought of as a metaphorical idea into a literal condition. Often in Paley's short fiction the literal mitigates the metaphorical, creating a story's tension.

In "A Conversation with My Father," in trying to reinterpret and so gain control over her father's old age, the narrator describes his condition in terms that are designed to arrest time and inevitability: "His heart, that bloody motor, is equally old and will not do certain jobs any more. It still floods his head with brainy light. But it won't let his legs carry the weight of his body around the house" (161). The rhetorical inventiveness and word-plays, in this case turning a noun into an adjective "brainy light," are a way of reinterpreting reality for these characters. But the narrator is checked here, her metaphors brought up short by her father's counsel: "Despite my metaphors, this muscle failure is not due to his old heart, he says, but to a potassium shortage" (161).

Despite such insistent reminders of the primacy of real over imaginary conditions, the rhetorical inventiveness allows Paley and her host of ordinary people to reinvent and restructure their real circumstances, if only for the space of a single narrative. They do so through Paley's conviction of language's malleability. "It's what you do with the word," one of Paley's characters triumphantly reveals. "The language and the idea, they work it out together" ("Enormous Changes at the Last Minute," 129). The idea, like the language, is, for Paley, a made thing, an artifact that becomes the measure by which her characters are able to leave the confines of their own limited experience to make themselves a part of a history they themselves invent.

The fictive invention of personal histories is formed within the broader political and historical context that always exists as an undercurrent in Paley's fiction. The personal and the political are never far apart for Paley, if we understand the political to be the wider historical and cultural context to which her characters react and by which they identify a shared sense of oppression, of "historical tragedy" ("A Conversation with My Father," 167). In this way, Paley's writing is pervasively political, explicitly and implicitly so.[22] Yet, the political for Paley is essential to ordinary experience. It puts daily life in its place. While many critics have made much of Paley's political agenda, the political undercurrents in her fiction are finally and ironically subordinated to the individual's response to history. As one of Paley's characters suggests, "I can't spend my life on personal animosities. The way imperialism's leaning so hard on the Third World the way it does" ("Listening," 208). The political can only be understood in personal terms, which is why Paley's literary commitment to political activism, to feminism, and to a general reformism reflects a postmodern impulse in fiction.

The infusion of the personal with the political, a pragmatic understanding of how the world works and of one's limited but no less obligatory capacity to bring about change in it, the absolute conviction that individual expression is the means by which change can occur, all are forces that form and inform Paley's fiction. Her ironic sensibilities, her "conscious lack of mastery," to borrow a phrase from Ihab Hassan (xvi), which is, indeed, her clear mastery, her recognition that endings, in some ways, are always fictions, and that frames are openings for very human expressions of hope and despair, all finally are strategies that give preeminence to voice and that extend the perceived limits of narrative expression. And so Paley's narrator in the short story "The Loudest Voice" can, with absolute conviction, proclaim that "every window is a mother's mouth."[23] Voices, like windows, are openings, beckoning, inviting, and admitting. But, like mother's mouths, Paley's voices are also defining, limiting, organizing of a desire whose fulfillment is finally impossible.

Notes

1.   Grace Paley, "The Immigrant Story," *Enormous Changes at the Last Minute* (1960; New York: Farrar, Straus, Giroux, 1983), 172. Subsequent references are from this edition and are cited parenthetically in the text.

2.   Jerome Klinkowitz, *Structuring the Void: The Struggle for Subject in Contemporary American Fiction* (Durham: Duke University Press, 1992), 2, 4; hereafter cited in text.

3.   Philip Stevick, *Alternative Pleasures: Postrealist Fiction and the Tradition* (Urbana: University of Illinois Press, 1981), 12; hereafter cited in text.

4.   Grace Paley, "The Story Hearer," *Later the Same Day* (1985; New York: Penguin, 1986), 134.

5.   Grace Paley, "Zagrowsky Tells," *Later the Same Day*, 174.

6.   Grace Paley, "Listening," *Later the Same Day*, 205. Subsequent references are from this edition and are cited parenthetically in the text.

7.   In "A Perfect Marginality: Public and Private Telling in the Stories of Grace Paley" (*Studies in Short Fiction* 27 [Winter 1990]: 35–43), I argue that storytelling is the fundamental narrative strategy and thematic concern in Paley's short fiction.

8.   Grace Paley, "A Woman, Young and Old," *The Little Disturbances of Man* (1959; New York: Penguin, 1985), 25.

9.   For a more extensive analysis of issues of identity and community as they relate to Judaism in Grace Paley's short fiction, see my "Talking Lives: Storytelling and Renewal in Grace Paley's Short Fiction" *Studies in American Jewish Literature* 9 (Spring 1990): 20–35. See also Bonnie Lyons, "Grace Paley's Jewish Miniatures," *Studies in American Jewish Literature* 8 (1989): 26–33.

10.   A discussion of Paley's relation to her Jewish literary predecessors is certainly much too complex to go into here. Let me just say, however, that Paley's fiction can be seen as part of an evolving tradition in Jewish fiction, a tradition begun by her Jewish modernist Enlightenment forebears, such as Sholem Aleichem, and that is marked by an ironic humor that thematizes the Jew's place in history. The ironic complexities in the works of these early writers, often satiric in force, give way to the kind of ironic self-assessment we see, not only in Grace Paley's fiction, but also in works by other contemporary American Jewish writers. The tradition of Jewish secular storytelling, begun as a response to the Eastern European Enlightenment, might be said to demonstrate a move from the communal to the individual. But, as I try to make clear, in Grace Paley's works, as elsewhere, individuals see themselves as part of communities, historical communities and communities of their own making.

11.   Grace Paley, "A Conversation with My Father," *Enormous Changes at the Last Minute*, 166. Subsequent references are from this edition and are cited parenthetically in the text.

12.   Grace Paley, "Debts," *Enormous Changes at the Last Minute*, 10. Subsequent references are from this edition and are cited parenthetically in the text.

13.   Although Paley's fiction spans three decades of literary reflection and influence— *The Little Disturbances of Man*, 1959; *Enormous Changes at the Last Minute*, 1974; *Later the Same Day*, 1985—it consistently exemplifies Tom LeClair's sense of the postmodern: "Postmodernism tends to fragment structures and create collages in the text. Character, plot, and setting are the essential elements given order and proportion in realism. Postmodernism diminishes or deforms the significance of these elements and emphasizes patterns of language. . . . how orders and forms in the world . . . can arise out of seeming chaos" (*The Art of Excess: Mastery in Contemporary American Fiction* [Urbana: University of Illinois Press, 1989], 21).

14.   The whole notion of revision, far too complex to cover in this particular piece, might be said to characterize postmodernism. Ihab Hassan, in *The Postmodern Turn*, discusses revision in very interesting ways and, in short, argues that "I see a pattern that many others have also seen: a vast, revisionary will in the Western world, unsettling/resettling codes,

canons, procedures, beliefs" (*The Postmodern Turn: Essays in Postmodern Theory and Culture* [Columbus: Ohio State University Press, 1987], xvi; hereafter cited in text).

15. Grace Paley, "Wants," *Enormous Changes At The Last Minute*, p. 5. Subsequent references are from this edition and are cited parenthetically in the text.

16. To this end, Paley, in an interview with this author, reveals this about the perspectives by which her characters are constructed: "Technically you really can't see a character unless other characters are looking at her or him. . . . It's sort of like in painting. In painting you have light moving in and other shadows; if you have a tree next to a person, the person looks different than if he is standing on a bare plain. And if there are three people in the room they each look different because of the other two. Or they each look more full almost. So . . . characters illuminate each other, densify each other." (" 'The Tune of the Language': An Interview with Grace Paley [*Studies In American Jewish Literature* 12, 1993], 56]).

17. One might argue here that this is a characteristically Jewish kind of humor in its self-mocking, self-parodic, and self-ironic assessment.

18. Linda Nicholson, "Feminism and the Politics of Postmodernism," *boundary 2* 19 (Summer 1992): 68–69.

19. Grace Paley, "Friends," *Later the Same Day*, 80.

20. Grace Paley, "The Little Girl," *Enormous Changes at the Last Minute*, 158.

21. Grace Paley, "Enormous Changes at the Last Minute," in the collection by the same title, 124. Subsequent references are from this edition and are cited parenthetically in the text.

22. Grace Paley in a recent interview with this author discussed the relation of politics to her writing: "My whole feeling is that my interest in writing and my interest in those politics are part of the same thing. . . . I'm interested in how people live. I'm interested in how women live, especially. What keeps me writing are those interests, and they're the same as political interests" ("The Tune of the Language," 55).

23. Grace Paley, "The Loudest Voice," *The Little Disturbances of Man*, 55.

Index

♦